THE PASSION PRINCIPLE

Khadijah,
I see your &
I am waiting for
you to take your
place in the world. Desmond
Now.

Also by Donna LeBlanc
You Can't Quit 'til You Know What's Eating You

THE PASSION PRINCIPLE

Discover Your Passion
Signature and the Secrets
to Deeper Relationships
in Life, Love and Work

Donna LeBlanc, M.Ed.

Author of
You Can't Quit 'til You Know What's Eating You

Health Communications, Inc.
Deerfield Beach, Florida

www.bcibooks.com

The personal stories in this book are true; however, the names and some of the identifying details of the people involved have been changed to safeguard their privacy.

Publisher: Health Communications, Inc.
            3201 S.W. 15th Street
            Deerfield Beach, FL 33442-8190

Cover photograph by Jeff Fasano
Cover design by Lawna Patterson Oldfield
Inside book design by Dawn Von Strolley Grove

TO MOM

CONTENTS

ACKNOWLEDGMENTS

My deepest thanks to Stephanie Gunning, my writer and collaborator for her contribution to this work. Her genius in putting my work into words has truly inspired me and will live in this book forever.

Thank you to my beloved clients for trusting me with the deepest parts of themselves and for allowing their stories to be shared to uplift me and enlighten others. It is my honor to share in a part of their lives.

Thanks also to my best friend, Jackie Griffin, whose love has sustained me through the highs and lows for over thirty years. I am honored to have such a gifted healer as my closest friend. May you be blessed for all those you touch.

My greatest teachers of all have been my family: Mom, Dad, Andrea, Lynette, Diedre, Jarleth and Chuck. Thank you for teaching me some of my most valuable lessons. Dad, Chuck and Diedre, wherever you are in the universe, it is my wish that God's love surrounds you and holds you tenderly in hand.

It is my honor to acknowledge Robert Baker and Ron Baker. You are my teachers, my colleagues, and most importantly, my beloved friends. A special thanks to Robert Baker for his inspired contribution. And thanks to photographer Jeff Fasano.

I give my love and thanks to all those who have touched my life and assisted me on my path, benevolent guardian angels who include Richard Hofstetter, Babette Perry, Sheldon Ginsberg, Catherine Kings, Brian Brennan, Peter Frame, Todd Corollvic, Michele Weeks and so many others.

I am grateful to Peter Vegso at Health Communications for his support through the years. Thanks also to Amy Hughes, Kim Weiss, Brett Witter, Allison Janse and copy editor Marjorie Woodall.

My final acknowledgment is to you, the reader. May this book clear the way, inspire, educate and lift you out of needless limitation so that you can be all you came to be as you share your deepest core passion with the world. You are an original and there will never be another quite like you.

Finally, it is with the loving guidance of the Great Spirit that I have become who I needed to be to bring this work into the world. Thank you. Many blessings.

ꟿNTRODUCTION

You are an original signature presence in the world with special gifts to share, and there will never be another person quite like you. As a spark of the divine flame, when you leave Earth your unique expression of divinity will be gone. There will forever be a hole in the web of humanity that no one else can fill. Yet if you are like most people, by the time you reached maturity you had lost touch with the original source of energy from which your passion flows. You'd forgotten who you were born to be, so you denied your radiance and hid it beneath multiple layers of self-protection, secrecy and disguise.

Most of us go through our adult lives thinking we are making conscious and original decisions. Unfortunately, we're not. Looking back years later, we can clearly see patterns that have taken the place of our originality—our flow—and kept us from being happy, healthy and successful. Our history has determined our future. It's as if we've been entombed under layers of debris, and now everything looks the same. We notice that we keep having the same basic relationship, only with *different* spouses, lovers, friends or bosses. We're aware that contact with our parents, children and siblings could have been better, or we see how we ruined these relationships. We see the money we might have earned or that we threw away and the opportunities we let pass by or sabotaged. We recognize the talents and abilities we could have developed, except we never took the time.

Life doesn't have to be this way. It has the potential at every turn to be fulfilling, surprising, joyous and pleasurable. It is within our power—in fact it is our birthright—to live every day with incredible passion and a true sense of purpose. The secret is to learn how to recognize and break the patterns that keep us stuck and recycling the same stale moments throughout our lives. This is the key to transforming all our relationships, both with others and with ourselves, and having fresh, exuberant experiences and leading lives full of meaning and vibrant possibility. Beneath the patterns lies our passion, and passion can guide us through and beyond the patterns that drag us down.

Passion is a sign that we are connected to the natural love force inside us. Then like waves in the ocean, our presence spreads ripples of love throughout the world.

Young children are naturally passionate about everything. They love life. From top to bottom, their physical senses are wide open. In autumn they're excited about the brightly colored leaves falling from the trees and crunching underfoot. Even the earthy smells delight them. The shape of a single snowflake or a lightning storm can stimulate a child's awe and curiosity. Watching cloud formations or counting shooting stars can fascinate them for hours. Nothing about the world is taken for granted. Every dream seems possible. That's how we are when we're connected to the core essence of who we are. When we are young and passionate, we're on intimate terms with life itself.

It's only once we begin to put on layers of protection, which happens at different stages as we're growing up, that we lose access to the natural passion flowing from our souls. The core essence is so deeply buried under layers of false self that we lose our connection to the radiant being within. Because the false self seeks predictability, life becomes repetitive. Our inner flame gradually begins to dim and is extinguished. As adults, unless we go back and intentionally peel away our defensive layers, we cannot hope to reclaim our full spirit and brightest potential. We are like angels who have fallen to Earth and forgotten that we are divine and radiant beings.

There are four simple questions at the heart of this book: What lights a fire inside you or me? What puts it out? What opens a connection between us? What shuts our connection down? Although it may seem remarkable to you right now, depending on how frustrated or stuck you are feeling, I promise that the answers you'll discover in *The Passion Principle* will give you the ability to improve every kind of interaction you have, even transforming your career and finances. The deep love and intimacy you desire, which formerly may have seemed elusive—or even frightening on occasion—will be available to you now whenever you choose to engage in a relationship.

Once you understand your personal passion signature, you will have a map for how to live your entire life. You will have access to your natural gifts and know how to bring your signature into full bloom in the world. Once you understand your opening and closing formulas, your life is going to improve markedly because you will be able to swiftly override your fear-based patterns and make new and better choices based on love and enthusiasm. By identifying passion signatures in others, and understanding their opening and closing formulas, you'll be able to increase the flow of connection with friends, family and professional colleagues, as well as any strangers you encounter during your daily activities. You'll feel more at ease wherever you go, so the world will become a playground. You'll have more energy and feel lighter and healthier. Everyone will find you more attractive and approachable. You'll freely explore and express your creativity. When you look back on your life a few years from now, you'll also suffer fewer regrets and bad memories.

Several months ago I visited a friend who was terminally ill. We had enjoyed a deep friendship for seven years. But it wasn't until this formerly athletic, vital and genuinely caring forty-two-year-old man was lying in bed in a weakened state that we became truly intimate and shared our humanity on an emotional level. Before that, although we were close, there always seemed to be a few protective walls in place between us. Sadly, a virus attacked his brain, gradually robbing him of movement and sight and destroying his analytical faculties. Fortunately, his loving spirit was intact. The part of him that remained was sweet-natured and vulnerable. In a sense, it was a gift. Once the walls dropped, we were able to connect in a new, more powerful way. As we held hands, he was completely there with me giving me love, and I was able to be completely there with him giving him love.

As long as I had known my friend, he'd dreamed about moving to California. He often spoke about his vision of the beautiful life he and his partner would make there one day. Then only a few short months after they finally made the anticipated move, he was stricken. It seemed tragic and ironic that he had waited so many years. I thought of the many conversations we had had over the years about how we would *truly* start living once we had made money, achieved fame, found love or reached another goal in the future.

One afternoon I climbed into bed beside my friend and put

my arms around him to show him affection and comfort. More than anything else, I hoped he would feel how much he truly mattered. Despite his garbled speech, we talked for a couple of hours. I asked if there was anything he understood now that he wanted to share with me or felt I *should* know. "Stop waiting, Donna," he replied. "You're moving too slowly. Live now."

Later that same day, while my friend was napping, I went down to the ocean near his house. I felt blessed to be able to walk on the beach in the brilliant sunshine, feeling the moist, salty wind on my face and the warmth of the sun penetrating my skin. As I watched birds riding the air overhead, I was overcome with ecstasy for just being alive in *that* moment. Gratitude flooded my heart. I reflected on the incredible love my friend had gifted me with and how our openhearted con- nection—being truly seen, heard and acknowledged—had enabled me to experience my wholeness and truth of being.

Cars were speeding by on a highway behind the beach, while there were only ten other people walking along the shore. Did the people in the cars realize what glorious beauty, oneness and human connection they were missing? Suddenly I stopped, opened my arms wide to the sky and cried out, "What is everyone racing toward?"

It is very easy to get caught up in the sweep of life, to focus on past and current problems and future goals at the expense of the moment. I know that firsthand. For many years, I relied on old patterns of relationship that had been established early in my life to keep me safe. Unseen energy imprints from my parents and family governed my career and relationships. But self-protection was stifling my spirit and purpose. My fear- based choices kept me stuck in yearning and prevented me from actually having the life of my dreams. As I've learned how to recognize and break those patterns, greater happiness, free- dom and love have entered my life than I ever anticipated. I've discovered that every moment of every day and night holds a new opportunity for expanding freedom.

More of us are awakening to the great possibilities of our time. We are realizing and using the power with which we were born to create the lives we want to lead. The source for this emergence is found in our hearts, minds and spirits. Not in one, but in all. What stands in the way is that these parts of self often do not work in union. We cycle and recycle through fragmented aspects of ourselves, until our best intentions also become fractured. Our spark—the creative fire and passion for living that reaches out from deep within us through our talents, gifts, dreams, goals and aspirations—gets put out. Year after year we are left running in circles around the same old stuff, until we cease to be.

Here are some common patterns. Perhaps a few are familiar to you.

Are you a magnet for Mr. or Ms. Wrong? Do you attract women who are needy and clingy—yet simultaneously cold and distant? Do you often pull these women out of financial or emotional disaster situations? Do you attract men who flirt with other women while you're out on a date—and ultimately abandon you?

Are you a world rescuer? Are you a workaholic who feels that no one else can do the job as well as you? Are you the good friend who habitually spends hours on the phone listening to someone else's troubles? Do you knock yourself out to please everyone, but no one seems to notice or appreciate your efforts?

Are you a rager who spews anger everywhere you go, on the job and at home, frightening your employees and children? Are you a gunnysacker who stows anger as if in a big bag slung over your back? Do you keep cramming down your anger, until one day you open up this sack and dump the contents all over whoever has irritated you? Are you a silent fumer who replies, "Nothing," when asked, "What's wrong?" Are you a character annihilator who verbally attacks your family, coworkers, friends and even spouse, saying the meanest, most cutting and belittling things anyone could say?

Do you feel like you're an imposter? The world may perceive you as a good parent, worker, friend or lover, but when you look in the mirror do you see a fraud who doesn't deserve recognition or praise? Do you believe your success is a fluke?

Are you a stagnator? Is your garage so full of junk that you can't pull the car into it? Are your closets stuffed with clothes and things you will never wear or use? When was the last time you tried a new dish or a new experience—was it years ago?

Are you a master of self-sabotage? Whenever a promotion is on the horizon, a relationship is working out, or a potentially lucrative deal or connection is about to be made, do you do something, anything, to keep it from happening? Do you generally orchestrate your own fall from grace?

Are you a master of numbing? Do you use food, drugs, alcohol, work, TV, the Internet, sleeping, or any other compulsive, soothing substance or activity to get through the day? Are you a perennial victim, someone who never "gets a break"? Do bad things always seem to happen to you? Do you feel powerless? Do you just have "bad luck"?

Are you burdened by family baggage? Have you been in therapy talking about your anger toward your parents for years? Do you still resent your father's indifference or your mother's favoritism toward your brother? Are you stuck in the past, forever angry and hurt about what you didn't get from your family?

The good news is that you can learn to defy fear, overcome patterns and embrace passion. You can heal pain you've been carrying from the past and realize the life of your dreams. But you can't begin to transform your patterns until you know how to recognize them.

I read a story in a newspaper several years ago about a man who drove his truck into a national park and got caught in a blizzard. Because he was driving on an upper forest road that had been closed for winter, no one knew where he was. Despite the dire circumstances, the man was determined to maintain a positive attitude and survive. Every day he wrote in his journal about how he had absolute faith that God would save him. As time wore on, the writing became weaker and fainter on the page. Park rangers found his lifeless body when the first spring thaw came. The irony was that the man had half a tank of gas in his truck and a fully charged battery. But from the evidence, it looked as though he'd made no attempt to do anything to promote his own salvation other than believe and wait. It didn't look as if he had honked his horn, or gotten out of the truck and shoveled snow or tried to hike to another access road. It looked as though he never made a fresh and original choice, and as a result, he simply perished in isolation.

The way out of the mess we're in is to deepen our connection to ourselves, others and the world at large. As we go inward and retrieve the lost fragments of our true soul selves that got frozen in the past and integrate them, we are liberated and empowered. By opening up our nervous systems to allow the world and life to filter in as they did when we were little children, our bodies become vessels of energy and spirit. Subsequently, we release old patterns, expand our possibilities and transform our lives. We shift away from repetitive habits that have been limiting our potential for getting what we truly want.

In *The Passion Principle* you will learn that when you are connected to your passion you become a natural force of love in the world. The book is divided into two parts. Part I, The Five Passion Signatures, covers five archetypical energy patterns that have common defenses and relationship styles, as well as evolutionary gifts: the Lover, the Creator, the Warrior, the Visionary and the Prophet. First you'll take a brief quiz to determine your archetype. Then you'll read about the individual passion signatures. You'll learn to recognize their traits in yourself and others, explore their fears and motivations and find out how these show up repeatedly in relationships. You'll discover why each signature's survival mechanisms come to exist and how to heal their wounds. Most important, you'll be guided through an evolutionary process of integrating the unique soul gifts of your passion signature.

Part II, Creating a Passionate Life, covers transformational strategies for many areas of life and different kinds of relationships you may have, including your relationship with yourself, your spouse or romantic partner, your children, parents and siblings, in addition to your friends, boss, coworkers and employees. You'll learn practical skills and information that you can begin applying even as you read the book—tools that work!

Today I am a published author and workshop leader. My therapy clients include successful Fortune 500 executives who fly in from around the country to see me. I make frequent appearances on TV and radio programs, and my ideas are respected. When I stood on the beach in California with gratitude exploding in my heart for having experienced so much life and love with my dying friend, I am proud to say I valued him for everything he gave me, and I valued myself for everything I gave him. Losing my dear friend has been a poignant reminder that no two sets of people relate in exactly the same way. Just as every person is unique, every relationship and every moment is a signature expression of life. When that signature is gone, it can never return. So we must savor it while it is with us, rather than in memory afterward. This means learning to open up and risk sharing our talents, abilities and gifts. It doesn't happen by accident. If we want to experience fulfillment, we must choose to be passionate and let the passion guide us.

Transforming my life has been, and continues to be, an ongoing journey. As you read this book, I invite you to begin a similar journey for yourself.

Part I

THE FIVE PASSION SIGNATURES

CHAPTER 1

WHAT'S YOUR
PASSION SIGNATURE?

People use five signature styles to express passion and seek fulfillment: the Lover, the Creator, the Warrior, the Visionary and the Prophet. These signatures have corresponding survival styles: the Vamp, the Martyr, the Conqueror, the Perfectionist and the Escapist. We'll be exploring these passion signatures individually in the next five chapters. Each has specific evolutionary gifts that are used to open to and reveal the love force within us, and each also has specific survival strategies that are used as closures, for self-protection. Most of us tend to flip back and forth between our more evolved, higher-minded, life-loving selves and our selves that seem to operate mostly through knee-jerk reactions provoked by fear. Unfortunately, responding in a habitual way usually appears to make perfect sense at the time.

On a good day, we're resilient, open-minded and able to cope emotionally with the challenges that life hands us. But on bad days, or in tough circumstances, watch out! Then we're up to our old tricks and games. Since the fearful self seems to sabotage every aspect of our daily lives, romances and career objectives—always in the same ways—we begin to cycle and recycle through similar events. Our higher natures can't win. Despite having incredible dreams, aspirations and potential, we keep stubbing our toes.

Every passion signature has its own way of using its life force, or energy. You cannot see energy, and you may not even believe it exists, but I am certain that you feel its impact around you every day. Emotion is catching. Emotion carries energy. If you've ever had bosses, friends, or loved ones spew anger on you, and suddenly you found yourself feeling resentful and anxious, then you have felt the impact of another person's energy. Similarly, if you've ever been in a room with someone having a great day, you may have walked away whistling a happy tune. Your energy also affects other people.

In relationships, energy is expressed and perceived in different ways. It can be sent and received through the words we use and our tone of voice. It can be sent and received through our body language. Often we reach out to other people using eye contact. This is not just looking at someone. You know the difference between having someone look at you with an invisible veneer over his eyes and no connection, and feeling someone reach out through his eyes to connect. If you pay attention, you'll begin to notice that sometimes the person pulls on you, or pushes into you, through the eyes.

Think of yourself as an old-fashioned switchboard with phone lines coming out of it. Most of the time you're all hooked up. You're plugged into the people you know around you and also those who are far away. Have you ever had a family member who was going to hell in a handbasket and it just wrecked you? That's a sign of an unhealthy hookup. A sign of a healthy hookup is when someone comes to mind and you feel stronger and lighter.

Perhaps the greatest power of relationships is that they can teach us where we need to improve how we use our own energy, as other people mirror for us our healthy and unhealthy qualities. Relationships help us develop awareness of our availability to exchange love and support as an equal. They also help us discover where we are giving ourselves away or leaching off others. As we practice taking good care of ourselves, the reflection we see gradually changes and we begin to sidestep old, unhealthy patterns.

When we are healthy and form healthy connections, our relationship energetics function optimally. We do not push or pull energy. We do not leak energy, like a cracked cup of water, but instead contain it. We are able to assert ourselves and we are able to receive. We are able to respond to our own needs with self-nurturing. As we expand into the promise of our passionate selves, we develop the ability to stand on our own. Like the sun, we radiate energy from our own central source and do not need to hook up with others to gain a sense of self. We are able to love and support others to the best of our ability without allowing them to drain us. We are able to exchange energy in a balanced flow. And if we catch ourselves misusing energy, we can correct the imbalance.

For information on the care and tending of your energy, including exercises about pushing, pulling, leaking and stagnant energy, visit the Web site *www.thepassionprinciple.com/passiontools*.

Understanding your passion signature is a shortcut to a happier,

more successful and fulfilled life. How do you determine your passion signature? Look at both the loving, inspired patterns and the
fear-based patterns in your life. These are your guideposts. . . .

Do you experience any unfulfilling patterns, such as the following, in your life? You want a new job, but end up staying in
the old one because it's safe. You want love, but shrink from it
when it stares you in the face. You are a gym rat who runs for
the hills at the first sign of intimate connection. You are a spiritual seeker who can't pay your rent. You are a therapy junkie
who stumbles endlessly over the same mental garbage. You have
potential and dreams that never seem to come true. Oppositional
patterns such as these are signs that, on some level, fears are running your life. You are locked in place.

So what's in your recycling bin? Let's start with a brief
self-inventory.

What's Your Passion Signature? A Quiz

Please put a checkmark beside any items on the following five
lists that apply to you. There are no right or wrong answers.
Check as many items as fit, including those that are true only
under certain circumstances along with those that seem *very* true
all the time. People embody five common relationship patterns—often several in combination—and this quiz is designed
to help you identify the ones that are most prevalent in your life.

Do You Embody Qualities of the Lover?

_____ Your main focus in life is on your relationships. You
may even have an insatiable sex drive.

_____ You hate to be alone, yet you are frequently abandoned.

_____ When you get in a romantic relationship you drop your
friends and put your beloved at the center of your life.

_____ You can't figure out why people say you are "too

needy" when all you're doing is trying to connect.

_____ At work, you love to talk. You're always leaning over someone's cubicle wall or hanging around the water cooler. At night, you're on the phone with your friends until the wee hours.

_____ Being financially provided for is an aphrodisiac.

_____ You smoke cigarettes, do recreational drugs or drink alcohol in order to nurture yourself when the world isn't giving you what you need.

_____ Others have accused you of flirting with or seducing their mates, when you were just being friendly.

_____ You love receiving gifts because it makes you feel special.

_____ When people tell you their personal stories, you get so excited that you jump in immediately with similar stories of your own. Be honest, you really like having the attention on you.

Do You Embody Qualities of the Creator?

_____ You're the shoulder everyone cries on, the eternal "nice guy."

_____ You often think about food and like to reward yourself with it after giving too much to others. After you put your kids to sleep (or finish your day), you often sit alone in front of the TV eating a pint of Ben & Jerry's ice cream.

_____ You live in a messy house.

_____ If you're single, you're always putting relationships off for fear that if you commit to one now you will be deprived of something else later on. If you're married, you feel crowded by your mate and claustrophobic, so much so that you've even lost your sex drive.

_____ When you make a purchase you think about the money you're losing, rather than the value of what you're acquiring.

_____ You have little time for yourself because you spend so much time taking care of everyone else's needs.

_____ You have trouble with commitment. Whether it is making an appointment or agreeing to meet someone for dinner, you feel tied down, locked in and engulfed.

_____ You're a phenomenal problem solver, communicator and mediator.

_____ You are a bit of a couch potato and have a tendency to carry extra pounds around your midsection.

_____ When you have an opportunity to choose between two good things, you get paralyzed with indecision because you get focused on what you'll be deprived of later if you choose one and not the other.

Do You Embody Qualities of the Warrior?

_____ You are ambitious, self-motivated and generally work hard.

_____ You spend so much time pushing toward your goals that you rarely have enough time to exercise or eat right. You can't remember when you had your last vacation.

_____ You are a sports fanatic and love the adrenaline rush when your team wins. You are an outstanding competitor and like to win at all costs.

_____ In the office, you have no time to socialize because you are determinedly moving toward your goals. You have little tolerance for small talk.

_____ You've been accused of "bulldozing" and "dominating" people, but you're just trying to get to the finish line.

_____ You always conquer your prey, whether that "prey" is a romantic partner or a business deal.

_____ People say you're strong, but inside you feel like a "softie." You wish you could trust someone enough to drop your guard.

_____ You are driven by an internal code of honor. When

you see an injustice, your blood pressure rises. You will fight for the underdog and any worthy cause.

_____ You don't care what people think about you; you always do what you think you should do.

_____ You are a bottom-line, brutally direct person, and your voice can sound like you're barking orders at people.

Do You Embody Qualities of the Visionary?

_____ Your daily regimen often includes a visit to the gym, carefully monitored food intake and precise scheduling. You are an immaculate dresser and have a well-toned physique.

_____ You constantly move toward higher goals, raising the bar for excellence. In fact, you may even have a fear of making mistakes.

_____ You are an optimist. You can put a positive spin on just about anything.

_____ People accuse you of being a "control freak" and "nitpicker," but you're just detail oriented—and with good reason. After all, if you're going to do something, you might as well do it right.

_____ You are known for your social savvy.

_____ You are a masterful lover but, ironically, it may be hard for you to meet Mr. or Ms. Right.

_____ You achieve your financial goals, make regular deposits in your 401(k) and savings plan and regularly balance your checkbook and track pennies.

_____ You are a highly principled, ethical person with tremendous foresight. Everything you do, you try to do perfectly.

_____ People seek you out when they need coaching to achieve a goal, because you are a well-organized planner with effective time-management skills.

_____ It's important that your mate/partner looks good and makes you look good.

Do You Embody Qualities of the Prophet?

_____ You are so sensitive that you often feel like you have no skin.

_____ You are a recluse because the world seems to be a harsh and threatening place.

_____ People keep telling you that you're "spacey" or an "airhead," but you perceive yourself as a dreamer and a philosopher.

_____ You feel as though you're telepathic and can almost read people's minds. You may be a little psychic—or a lot.

_____ If someone yells at you, your mind goes blank, as though you've left your body.

_____ Although you are a megawatt superstar with awesome gifts, you hide in your house so no one will think you're a "freak" or a "weirdo." You may even fear standing out because you could be attacked.

_____ You often forget to eat, and your body may be very skinny and frail.

_____ Sometimes you don't feel like a sexual person.

_____ You like to do jobs where you're on your own and removed from people, such as computer graphics or programming, astronomy or laboratory research.

_____ You have a sense that you don't belong on this planet, as though you are an alien from outer space and different from other people.

Scoring and Interpretation

This quiz reveals your general leanings toward the various mindsets, feelings and typical behavior of the five passion signatures. It is designed to determine the degree to which you embody each of them. Score the quiz as follows:

- If you put any checkmarks in a category, it means you have some of the tendencies of that passion signature (the Lover, the Creator, and so on).
- No checkmarks shows you have no tendencies of that signature.
- Five to ten checkmarks indicate strong tendencies.
- If you couldn't find yourself in any of the statements above, I suggest you give the quiz to someone you love or who knows you well and ask for help.

Please note: Most people are not exclusively one passion signature, so you could easily be a Combo Platter of two or more of them. If you have placed three or more checkmarks in more than one category, it means you have strong combination tendencies. You will want to pay special attention to the traits of every passion signature that is even a little bit true for you, as each reveals a different aspect of your character.

Are you the Lover? If you possess many qualities of the Lover, you thrive on one-on-one relationships. You are a superhero of nurturing who delights in exploring other people and their lives. You feel uneasy when you're alone. Ironically, your life in the past may have been marked by abandonment. An issue you need to work on is standing on your own two feet. If you're unattached right now, finding new love is probably a major theme in your life. You just don't feel as though you were cut out to be single. You are at your best when you're in an intimate, loving relationship. (See Chapter 2.)

Are you the Creator? If you embody a number of Creator

traits, you are one of the best problem solvers, communicators and negotiators on the planet. You have a world-class ability to get inside other people's skin and bring them together. Because you can see all sides of an issue and help people arrive at a common understanding, you give the word "peacekeeper" new meaning. But you frequently take care of others at your own expense, perhaps to the point of martyrdom. So you also have a tendency to withdraw. People can easily overwhelm you, and your fear of getting trapped makes you a bit of an isolator. You have bursts of creativity that lead you in several directions at once, but you probably lack follow-through. Your energy is scattered. Once you cultivate focus and discipline, you'll be empowered to share your talents with the world generously. (See Chapter 3.)

Are you the Warrior? If you have several Warrior characteristics, you thrive in a leadership role. This can mean leading a family, leading a struggling business to financial security or leading troops onto a battlefield. You are probably a bit rough around the edges, and your mouth sometimes gets you in trouble. Underneath, you have a good heart, pure intentions and loads of integrity. You do what you must to take care of your clan (as you define it), even if you must ignore your own needs. At times you may feel deeply misunderstood by the world, and in the past you've probably been betrayed—or feel that you were. You would benefit from overcoming your tendency to try to dominate people. Life does not always have to be a battleground. (See Chapter 4.)

Are you the Visionary? If you exemplify many qualities of the Visionary, you are motivated by excellence and beauty. An optimist and a born leader, you aspire to bring out the best in others and want to make the world a better place. Whether you're planning a business deal or a family vacation, your attention to detail is fantastic. You set high goals and thrive in a clean, well-ordered environment. But you're also a bit like a rat caught in a maze because you are such a perfectionist. You live so much for a future outcome that you probably don't enjoy today as much as you could. You manufacture how you feel and have difficulty being authentic if your reality is less than positive. You are challenged to let down your emotional guard and ask for help. Once you figure out how to drop your mask and let others be imperfect, your relationships will improve. If you learn to live for the process rather than the goal, you'll have more energy to spare for the real experience of living, and your efforts will begin to bear fruit. (See Chapter 5.)

Are you the Prophet? If you possess many qualities of the Prophet, you are a powerful being. You feel as though you have great spiritual teachings or new scientific knowledge to share with the world. But you live in obscurity due to your fear of coming out and getting annihilated. You have psychic abilities, although you might not have identified them yet or developed them. You've had several out-of-the-box experiences and probably have difficulty translating what you know of the nonmaterial world into language ordinary folks can understand. You have a sense of being alien. You would do well to find someone you trust and establish a grounded relationship with this individual. You also need to get more in touch with your body. Taking these steps will ground you. (See Chapter 6.)

No matter which passion signature or signatures you identified with, make a personal commitment to observe your thoughts, feelings and behavior as you go about the day. Read through the chapters in Parts I and II and explore the concepts you find there. Then come back and review the self-inventory. Soon the patterns articulated in the quiz will become much clearer—even obvious—to you.

CHAPTER 2

THE LOVER/VAMP

If you are the Lover, your passion is connection, the intimacy of giving and receiving. Whether you are sharing your gifts and talents with the world at large, or you are having a one-on-one relationship with a lover, a friend, a family member or a coworker, you enjoy fusing your essential being with everything in life. That's what gives your life meaning. Connecting with other people makes you feel grounded, secure, needed, valued, supported, happy, good about yourself, comforted and loving.

You shine in relationships, and you thrive on them. Since love is the main focus of your life, when you're not in a romantic relationship, you're probably looking for one. But you can also honor the choice to be solo, if that gives you room to develop your gifts and talents. When you do decide to have relationships, of the five passion signatures, you are the most comfortable about getting close. At your best, you are enormously nurturing to your friends, family, lovers and mates. You were born to participate in a loving, committed and fulfilling relationship, which can serve as the backdrop to your entire life. You can teach others how to love and "do" intimacy. Many people crave loving connection, but fear what comes to you so naturally. When the Lover is in bloom, you light up the world. Your enthusiasm, creativity, charisma and openness make you irresistible. Your glow ignites the glow in others and helps them grow into their full potential. That's why Lovers are wonderful people to know and love.

But as the day is followed by the night, the Lover's glow casts a shadow. At their worst, Lovers are energy vampires, overconnecters who fuse with a grip that can be intensely smothering. As the Vamp, they can be desperately needy, self-centered and depleting. In anger, they can whip up a storm and strike out with lethal words, wanting to hurt those who have hurt them. Vamps can burn out the people in their lives with drama after drama.

Vamps can be very charismatic and sexy. When they turn their attention in your direction, they can charm the pants off you. As long as the experience lasts, you'll feel as though you are the most brilliant, fascinating creature in the universe. The trouble is, it may not last long. As soon as they've got you hooked, they are likely to move on to greener pastures because Vamps are attracted to the unavailable. Deep inside, they feel unworthy; therefore they don't want to be members of any team that would have them. Lovers have a special talent for intimacy, but until they learn how to be self-nurturing and to give without expecting something in return, they often use moments of connection to feed off the energy of others. They seduce you so that you'll validate them in the mistaken belief that this gives them an identity. Sadly, they often don't know how beloved and wonderful they are. At best, they are empathetic, generous and loving. But wounded Lovers, Vamps, are endlessly searching for praise, so like junkies they're always looking for the next hit. Vamps don't allow themselves to feel the love you're giving them.

If these words seem a bit harsh, just remember that the Vamp is only the unhealed aspect of the Lover. Every signature has light and dark qualities. We all have our share. That's part of the human experience. To deny our extremes doesn't serve anyone. Since almost all of us had a Combo Platter of passion signatures dished up for us, including the Lover/Vamp, remember that any finger I'm pointing in this book is aimed at me too.

The Lover's passion for connection develops from emotional wounds incurred during infancy. At this age the mother is the source of everything to the child. Babies literally feed off the energy of their mothers in this stage of development. Research has shown that underprivileged infants raised in orphanages without the constant touch and love that a mother would give them fail to thrive. Children need a mother's attention to develop a sense of self, and a sense of self-worth, just like they need mother's milk. She is life, safety and love. If the mother is able to meet her baby's needs, the baby moves on to the next stage of development. But if the baby's needs for nurturing are not met easily and lovingly—perhaps because the mother is nervous, ambivalent, scared to breast-feed or working too much to breast-feed—the baby gets "frozen" between the ages of birth to two years. Emotionally, Vamps in adulthood are much like babies, waiting to receive energy, love and permission to live, love and contribute to the world. They don't truly believe they matter or have worth (or else wouldn't we shower them with love?), and they fear abandonment, the loss of a caretaker. To persuade others to meet their needs and end their sense of yearning, they've learned to be sneaky and seductive.

Throughout their lives, Vamps seek fusion in their relationships—much like a baby fuses with the energy of its mother—to compensate for an early lack of nurturing and to protect them from similar pain. The ironic twist is that the addiction is to *yearning after*—not to actually having what they say they want. Confronted, they initially deny this. However, once Vamps are old enough to have lived through several patterns repeatedly they begin to see that it is the truth. Underneath, the baby that got stuck somewhere a long time ago imprinted the feeling that, "I am not good enough to receive the love I crave. I yearn for it. But if it shows up I must push it away and go after the person, job or situation that remains elusive." That's the Vamp's love map.

If you are the Lover, the part of you that is frozen in babyhood doesn't realize that *you* are the source of your own love and nurturing, and everything else you need and want. This tiny fragment of your whole being is eternally searching for sources outside you from which to draw love. When the Vamp part of you is triggered and running your life, you will use your energy to attach to others and pull on their energy. You feel endlessly needy. Nothing is ever enough. Your sense of self comes from your object of affection. Your singular fixation on this person feels engulfing because it is like the obsession of a small child for its mother. Think of how infants behave when separated from their mothers for any length of time. Even if people love you, they probably won't stick around for this forever because it's unpleasant. As adults, nobody can provide energy endlessly to another or give another a sense of self for very long. Therefore, it is up to you, the Lover, to help the frozen baby fragment to grow up. As an integrated person—one who has done the necessary work—you can fulfill your own needs very well and have tremendous, *delicious* gifts for relationships. You know instinctively how to do intimacy and how to fuse appropriately with another in love.

As a part of standing on your own and supporting yourself, you must also develop your talents, gifts and abilities, and begin to share those with the world. The Lover has many talents. You are in greatest harmony when you are in any relationship that involves a genuine exchange of energy, emotion, ideas, time and attention. But relationships do not always involve sex.

By the way, we all have aspects of the Lover in us, although some more than others. There's no shame in it. Infancy is a vulnerable stage of life when we are still so wide open to the world that we are extremely sensitive to wounding. If you are a Lover, it may interest you to know that as soon as you become aware of your less-than-desirable Vamp tendencies, they are perhaps the easiest patterns to resolve. Connection lights your fire and inspires you, whereas Vamp energy seeks a host to feed off of and hinders true connection. So embrace the passion! Your gifts as the Lover will enable you to have exactly what you desire most—romance, friendship, community—as soon as you integrate them with the wholeness at your core.

Go to *www.thepassionprinciple.com/passiontools* to receive a free handout on the Lover and other passion signatures.

The Story of a Lover/Vamp

"It seems like my wife's always rejecting me. When I come home after a long day of work, she's usually feeding the kids or helping them with their homework. While she's busy in the kitchen, I approach her just to try to give her a hug and kiss. I love her, and I need her to take care of me, too. But she never gives me what I need. She pulls back. These days, we sleep with our backs toward each other in the bed."

Fred was an upper-level manager at a Fortune 500 company. During the day, he was an indefatigable problem solver. Everyone relied on him, and he felt important. Like a nursing mare, he carried his employees as though they were foals attached to his teats and sucking on him for dear life. But although he was a tower of strength on the job, when he went home he transformed from the king of the hill into a big baby. Each night, without realizing it, he expected his wife, Brenda, to recharge him. He was pulling on her energy to fill his own sense of emptiness. He was Vamping her.

To Brenda, who owned a successful restaurant and came home exhausted, it felt as though her six-foot-three husband was constantly tugging on her sleeves whether they were in bed or getting the kids ready for school. His eyes, his tone of voice and his touch always seemed to say, "I need something from you. Feed me. I am hungry," much as an anxious child would demand attention from a mother. He never stopped and asked, "How was your day? Was it a tough one for you? How are you doing?" Their interactions were always about him and his need for a hug. As a result, she dreaded his approach and had grown colder toward him over the years.

"I get home from a long day of work, I've got four needy kids hanging from my legs, and here comes Fred doing the same thing. I don't have four kids. I have five! He makes me want to crawl out of my skin."

In our counseling sessions, the couple explored the distance that had developed between them. Fred was going to Brenda as the source of his renewal after expending energy during the day. But, like him, Brenda was tired from the stress of running a successful restaurant and taking care of the children. Having anyone else drawing on her resources was simply too much. Her husband's behavior felt draining to her, parasitic, so her natural reaction was to pull away. But the more she pulled away, the more abandoned Fred felt and the more he sought her attention—creating a vicious cycle. They were stuck in an agonizing rut.

Transforming Fred's piece of the couple's relationship dynamic began by helping him understand his passion signature as the Lover. On the job, he sought popularity among his staff and was also highly motivated by his boss's approval. So he expended his energy pleasing people and working extra hard to be a star performer. But he wasn't satisfied with his accomplishments unless he was receiving accolades, and thus the pattern was depleting him. He needed to relocate his source of approval within himself.

When Fred got home, he wasn't giving his wife room to breathe. Instead of allowing her to meet him halfway, when she was ready, he made untimely overtures and found himself confronting an emotional brick wall. His Vamp behavior was inadvertently hitting upon one of his wife's *closing formulas*. Instead of reinforcing their intimacy, he was shutting down their connection. As they disconnected, it stirred up his innate fear of abandonment. Then Fred collapsed, felt resentful and pouted. He needed to stand on his own feet. But he also needed reassurance from his wife that she was still there. That was an *opening formula* she would ultimately learn to maintain their connection.

I suggested to Fred that he pay attention to what he was thinking and feeling during the day, especially when he was around his wife, and simply observe whether or not he had expectations of being taken care of, or any sense of anxiety or resentment about not getting what he wanted. Remember, the Vamp aspect of self is like a baby. It doesn't know that if it waits half an hour, it may get exactly what it needs, or that it can take care of itself. It's waiting for Mommy and feels as though she may never come back, even if she's just stepped into the next room for a minute or two. Another interesting thing about the Vamp is that this fragment of a person's personality is preverbal. Infants don't have language skills, so they feel wordlessly hungry. Crying babies often wail as though the world is ending. When their Vamp is activated, people typically forget to ask for help or to negotiate time frames with those they view as their caretakers. By activated, I mean that the nervous system has been triggered to go into survival mode.

The next evening, Fred had a flash of insight. "Aha! I'm standing around sulking, feeling resentful and impatient. But Brenda is busy! We are both fried. Right now, she needs my help with the kids, rather than another child making demands on her. I can't just unplug yet." Pictures from childhood arose in his mind. He recalled how his father had never lifted a finger at home, not to cook meals, not even to pick up a dish or help his mother in any way. Fred didn't want that kind of marriage. He had always dreamed of marriage as a partnership of equals, yet he wasn't holding up his end of the deal. He immediately saw that it was within his power to change the way things were going.

When Fred turned to Brenda and asked, "Is there anything you need?" she first was stunned and then relieved. Over the next few weeks, as he took up the slack around the house, she began letting down her guard, and the couple got closer again. Because her husband gave her a chance to renew her own energy at the end of the day, she had more energy to share after the kids were in bed. The romance in their marriage rekindled.

How to Recognize the Lover/Vamp

As adults, wounded Lovers, the Vamps, are usually slender and may look undernourished. Both males and females tend to hunch forward slightly, so they seem to have caved-in chests. Since their sense of self comes from outside validation, they can be very flirtatious—even seductive. A female Vamp generally dresses to show off her body, in order to attract attention and validation. Her clothing selection may expose her navel, and she may be stroking her own belly casually with one hand, frequently stretching her arms overhead, flipping her hairdo around or thrusting her pelvis forward. Her body language oozes sensuality. Imagine a kittenlike chanteuse languidly draped across the top of a piano. That's her! At her best, she has skills of appreciation that make others feel as radiant and delightful as she is. At her worst, she's overly flirtatious, and other women do not, and perhaps cannot, trust her around their men. After all, those unavailable men she's flirting with are likely to be their boyfriends.

If you confront her, a female Vamp will deny this behavior or say, "We're just friends." Her denial can make you want to pull the hair out of your head. One man said of his Vamp girlfriend, "She's always pushing for a commitment from me, but there is no way. She is too flirtatious with my friends. The other night at the bar she jumped in guys' laps, touched their arms, stood too close and held deep and engaging eye contact. Hell! One of my friends asked me which man she was with. I told her later. She denied what she'd done and said I was being jealous. We fought all the way home in the car."

A male Vamp tends to be gangly with spindly arms. He's not muscular or bulked up, but has a quality of softness to him. The stranger at the bar who instantly undresses you—and more—with his eyes is a Vamp. Like the female, he is also a seducer and loves attention. The male Vamp may draw people's focus to him through humor. At his best, he's magnetic and the life of the party. At his worst, he is a raging narcissist. One woman said of her new, younger husband, "It's maddening. I cannot sit and watch a TV program without him pulling for attention. He talks over the program, interrupts and has even walked into the room and changed the channel without even noticing I was there. It's all about him—and it drives me crazy."

At his worst, the male Vamp is like the vampire Lestat from Anne Rice's famous novels. He's as charming, suave and persuasive as Count Dracula, and he feeds on female sexual energy. He may seduce hundreds of women and never get involved in a relationship. Before a woman is interested, he generously meets her every need; he's supremely attentive and is an amazing listener. But as soon as he gets a woman's love, he casts her aside. "She's not good enough for this reason and that reason," he would say as he picks each one of them apart. Each is not the woman he's seeking; however, that doesn't stop him from going to bed with her. The ethics don't matter to him, because he's a Vamp and that's how his unhealed aspect tells him he must feel. He's empty and yearning.

Another version of the male Lover/Vamp has less assertion in his nature. He is a thoroughly devoted man who loves to be in a committed relationship and would never dream of cheating on his woman. His wife or girlfriend is his power source, so he's always there for her and always feeding off her energy. His entire sense of self relies on this attachment. In the case of one Vamp like this, the man was so passive that his wife had to post a note on the front door reminding him to turn off the TV, sound system, computer and lights whenever he left home. He was a sweet man, but very limp and frail.

Healed male Lovers, who are self-aware men working on

their relationship styles, retain their charm and generosity, yet refrain from using these gifts to manipulate others to validate or fulfill their needs. Relationships are a priority, so they are available. They understand how to connect without siphoning off the life force of their partners. They can give energy generously and receive energy freely. In their presence, you feel nurtured and supported because they give from their hearts. When an integrated Lover has hugged you, you feel his generosity of spirit as you feel his heart pouring love into your heart.

If you've ever seen two people intimately hunched over a table staring into each other's eyes with their faces two inches apart, chances are you were watching two Vamps in conversation. Vamps engage others with constant eye contact, using hungry, alluring gazes to draw people in, and their eyes typically communicate a sense of urgent need. You feel as though you could drown in their eyes. Vamps stand right in front of you when they speak, and they lean in closely toward you. They may even put a hand on your shoulder and turn your body to ensure you're looking directly in their eyes. Vamps will suck the life out of you in this position. You will feel a pull through their eyes and perhaps even through your solar plexus or sexual center. Lovers, on the other hand, can energize you in this position, because you feel intimately connected and seen by someone genuinely interested in you who recognizes your value. They are able to give as well as receive energy.

At a party once, when I was trying to get to the restroom, a wounded Lover friend of mine was hanging on my arm in such a way that I couldn't leave. I had to stop her and say, "You've got to back up and let go. I'll be right back." Of course, she meant no harm. She was just swept up in her desire for connection. Another time, I had a Lover/Vamp houseguest who kept following me from room to room as I was moving about my home looking for a book. As my main passion signature is the Creator/Martyr, a type that can easily feel engulfed, his behavior was driving me nuts. Because I understood what was going on, I said, "Hey, do me a favor. Hang out in the living room. I'll be back in a jiffy." Then he was content to wait. The Lover and Creator types most often hang out together as friends and intimates. As a Creator, I have noticed that Lovers make great, nurturing friends and loved ones, especially when both parties involved are aware of each other's opening and closing formulas.

When speaking, the Vamp often uses a whispery voice or hushed tones. This has the effect of making people move closer into the Vamp's space, so they can hear clearly. The wounded Lover may also talk incessantly, for instance, being the student in a class who asks question after question and then feels proud that his or her "dialogue" impressed the teacher—even if no one else in the room gets to ask a question. A Vamp acquaintance of mine came back from a workshop one time and excitedly reported, "It was as though no one else was there but me!" The Vamp doesn't always listen to the answer, even when given the information that's been requested. It just isn't taken in. Vamps have a hard time feeling grateful for what they've got, as they're seeking *more* to overcome the fear that they might lack something later.

Whether attention is positive or negative, loving or angry, the Vamp is interested in it. Vamps swiftly lose interest if no one is around to support them and validate their activities. It's the whole mirror-mirror-on-the-wall scenario. If someone isn't there to reflect the Vamp, does the Vamp exist? And who's the fairest one of all? "Please let it be me," begs the Vamp when that shadow aspect of the Lover has been activated. Parents whose inner Vamps have run amok perceive a child's accomplishments as their own and feed off their children's energy. A mom might flirt with her daughter's boyfriends or enroll in the classes she takes. A dad might buddy up to his son's friends. Everybody else thinks these parents are great, but their kids hate being around them.

The Vamp fuses with you in a way that feels violating. One twenty-eight-year-old client said, "I love my friend, but if I show that I prefer anything, she wants it. If I like a man, she wants him. She also wants to know where I bought my new clothes, so she can get the same ones. As much as I complain about this, she never gets it. She says she's not doing anything."

I suggested, "Give your friend time, and share the information about the passion signatures and their wounds with her. Otherwise, she'll keep seeing the world through an infant's eyes. But when she gets it, she'll really get it. I have found that Vamps often learn this material more rapidly than the other signature types. And when they are healed, they make great friends! I surround myself with Lovers for their nurturing and sensitivity."

If your passion signature is the Lover, it is vital that you acknowledge and take responsibility for the qualities of the Vamp that you demonstrate when you're feeling insecure. It's not that the world is "jealous" of you or "wants to suppress" your beauty, self-expression or humor; we love those traits, which you possess in abundance. We only want to share the space that's available. Earth is not the All-Me, All-the-Time television network. Rather, it's the You-and-Me station, and you're a talented programmer.

As the Lover, you know the secrets of deep connection better than anyone. Thus, the world is relying on you to model for us the finer points of intimacy and relationship. Some of the most amazing actors today are Lovers. Their success comes from their ability to fuse so completely with their characters that they become them. It's as though they are channeling

another being into the world. Remember, you are here to contribute what you most value! Thus, your incredible gifts
include your generosity, humor, affection, appreciation, empathy, loyalty and nurturing. Sharing a hug with an integrated
Lover is as satisfying and restorative as a massage. You feel
nurtured and supported whether this person is your lover,
spouse, friend or employee.

Vamp Relationship Traps

Lovers need to watch out for four patterns that can keep
them stuck in a cycle of emotional hunger, and that can repeatedly cause them to pursue unfulfilling relationships with emotionally wounded people or sabotage potentially fulfilling
relationships with healthy people. If you're a Lover, awareness
is the key to transforming these destructive Vamp patterns.

- *Unavailable? How Attractive!* You spend much of your life
  yearning. In fact, you are addicted to wanting more. The
  world—and everyone in it—is the object of your desire.
  So you rarely enjoy what you have, and instead are constantly prowling for what you don't have. If you're in a
  department store and notice a shopper admiring a pair of
  pants you passed over, you may suddenly find yourself
  wanting those pants fervently. Likewise, meeting an
  unavailable man or woman can trigger your Vamp tendencies. It's an obstacle you feel you *must* overcome. The
  more disinterested this person is in you, the more you pine
  and obsess about attracting his or her attention.

  Take a moment and look deeper at the people who have
  shown up in your life. How many times have you been
  attracted to the unavailable person, someone who is a "challenge," while the available people you know seem ordinary
  and uninteresting to you? Do you have a pattern of

becoming bored with people once they are available or committed to you? Do you lose interest in someone after you've had sex with him or her? Do you reject people who pursue you, because they are "too clingy," "boring" or. . . ? Do you continually want what you cannot have, and then, once you have it, don't want it anymore? Beware of such traps.

• *It's Your Job to Take Care of Me!* You finally meet a man or woman who seems to be perfect in every way. You feel loved and adored by this person. So you blow off your friends and clear your schedule. You wait excitedly for phone calls and dates with your new love. You want to spend every minute possible with him or her, and you do—for a little while. Then your love interest gets busy . . . and you don't understand why he or she needs time alone or, worse, with someone else. You take it personally, feeling rejected, angry and hurt that your mate isn't always there when you need him or her. So you try harder . . . and harder . . . and harder to get attention, doing and being whatever you imagine you have to in order to curry favor. "Perhaps I don't deserve the attention?" you wonder. "Maybe I'm not good enough."

Although your significant other may tell you that you are being clingy or needy, you don't get it. Isn't your mate supposed to be there all the time? Isn't it your partner's job to take care of you if you're in a relationship? Your lover says there's another facet of life that needs tending (e.g., a job, studying, family activities). You pout, whine and rant about how he or she isn't giving you what you want and need—with the underlying communication being, "It's your job to TAKE CARE OF ME!" Sadly, the complaining and hanging on you're doing actually pushes your lover away. You may also see yourself turning into somebody you don't like very much.

• *Alone Again. Abandonment.* This is the Big Kahuna of
destructive patterns for the Lover. It's your ultimate night-
mare. Oddly, your own insecure behavior and thought
loops can transform your fear of abandonment into a reality. Simply being alone can trigger such strong anxiety
that you feel abandoned even if you're not. So you begin
pulling energy and demanding attention from the people
in your life. You call your friends and talk their ears off
about your troubles, until they begin avoiding you. Or you
decide to abandon others before they get the chance to
abandon you. Until you learn to be your own companion,
your overwhelming desire for instantaneous gratification
will drive a wedge into every one of your relationships.

You may also fill in "the gaps" in your schedule, the
times when you're alone, with compulsive behaviors and
addictions, such as cigarettes, alcohol, shopping sprees,
masturbation, one-night stands or television-viewing
marathons. These behaviors are harmful to your body,
mind, spirit and pocketbook, and they can only serve to
numb your feelings temporarily. Until you face your
painful feelings and survive them, they'll rule you. You'll
never know that you are safe to be alone, and you'll never
be at peace when you are separated from the people you
love.

A charismatic and well-educated Vamp woman has a
habit of rapidly becoming "best friends" with one acquaintance after another. She uses people like an addict uses
narcotics; always looking for the next hit of excitement.
Like a cat toying with a mouse, she is fascinated with her
friends for a few weeks or months, phoning daily to chat
and arrange subsequent encounters—so much so, in fact,
that these objects of her affection are overwhelmed. But
then, suddenly, she gets bored and drops them altogether.

Now they cannot get her on the phone; it's as if she doesn't
know them.

• *Energy, Energy, Energy.* "I have a right to their energy 24–7,"
you say to yourself. The deepest part of you doesn't know
that you are self-sustaining. It thinks your life force is
dependant upon drawing it from others. You have not
learned self-renewal yet. So as one man said to me after he
realized his married girlfriend wasn't going to leave her
husband and five kids, "I am going to die. I am lost. I have
been depressed with the covers pulled over my head for
days. She doesn't want to be in a relationship with me anymore. I really don't think I can survive this." You are the
Leaning Tower of Pisa. Your love interests are completely
burned out.

What can you do if you notice someone becoming stuck in
one of these four patterns? Try an opening formula from the
next section. Following that information, I'll suggest several
activities designed to assist Lovers in their own healing and
transformation.

Lover Opening and Closing Formulas

It is important to understand and have compassion for the
fears underlying the behavior of the people in our lives. When
we care for others by helping them to remain open and connected to us in a healthy way, it is of mutual advantage. We are
stronger together than we are alone, because our passion signatures are complementary. Rising to meet the challenges of
another's passion signature fosters special abilities in us, and
our relationships give us the opportunity to share these gifts. If
you have a Lover in your life, a person with whom you want to
maintain a good relationship, such as a spouse, a child, a friend

or a boss, there are several ways you can support and reassure the Lover.

Occasionally, most people get busy or feel the need to be alone to regroup their thoughts. Be aware, as you are heading toward your study, turning off the ringer on your telephone or leaving on vacation, that the Lover's abandonment issues may get triggered by your departure or absence. Since you know that your presence is intensely significant to this person, take a moment to reassure the Lover that you're coming back. Be specific about the time frame if you can. You might even offer to check in, if it's appropriate. You don't have to change your plans or give up your personal freedom in order to be kind to the Lover. Adopting this simple strategy truly helps the Lover stay calm.

Ironically, being too available can be a Lover/Vamp closing formula. You have to strike a delicate balance with these sensitive creatures. Lovers are hot-wired for yearning. They are stimulated by desire and anticipation. What will it be like, they fantasize, when they get your love and attention? This doesn't mean we can't have long-term relationships with Lovers, it just means we have to move in for fusion and back away so they can chase us a little. If we show up as constantly adoring and available it may neutralize their excitement and is a closing formula. When you love a Lover keep in mind that to keep the fires burning, there needs to be a dance of seduction.

Verbal appreciation in the form of positive feedback and sincere praise are opening formulas and always highly nurturing to the Lover. You could never reach the limit of the Lover's tolerance for hearing genuine remarks that demonstrate your love and approval. Using words to communicate appreciation is a skill that's often mistaken—by the uninitiated—for empty flattery. But if you would like to see the Lover open up and radiate with happiness, this is an ability you will benefit from cultivating. In return, the Lover showers love on you.

At home, in the office or among friends, the Lover wants to please you, feels gratified by pleasing you and is designed by nature to be pleasing. In my own office, when I've expressed my enormous gratitude to the Lover for her stellar work helping me with marketing, I've seen her face light up and her eyes open wide with joy. She is a healed Vamp and receptive to energy. She doesn't deflect my compliments as a Vamp would. Vamps won't accept compliments, because they are trapped in a cycle of yearning and feeding. As we've worked together longer, the better quality of my associate's work has been due to her feeling appreciated. She has told me, "I love working here."

On days when I've seen my associate tired and contracting, I'll walk up to her and offer her a hug or pat her on the back. Even the simple question, "Are you feeling okay?" begins to open her back up. She responds to being cared for. Everything the Lover does is done for the purpose of connection, even work. Lovers will open up if they feel valued.

Of course, it is not appropriate to manipulate Lovers through their desire for love, affection and acknowledgment. If this is a temptation to you or something you have done in the past, there's one thing it tells me: you're a bit of a Vamp yourself. It is a sure sign that you are Vamping when you manipulate people's affection.

If you avoid eye contact and turn your body away from Lover/Vamps, it's a closing formula because they are eager to share intimacy with you and they don't feel received. A few different things might happen depending upon how conscious they are of their own motivations. First, it could hurt their feelings. Second, they may pull harder to get your attention. And third, they might lose interest in you altogether because they're not getting any feedback or feeling received. Lovers are

naturally emotionally intimate people; they want to nurture
you by sharing connection and making you feel good.

When you're having a conversation, look directly in the
Lover's eyes and touch him or her casually on the arm, another
opening formula for the Lover. These are signals that you care,
which can both establish and reinforce your connection. The
Lover thrives on receiving and giving affection.

Transforming Your Destructive Patterns

If you're a Lover, you can transform destructive Vamp tendencies and let your gift of love shine brightly. The following
tips will help.

- *Ask for Help.* Whenever you feel like you need to be res-
  cued, stop for a moment and take a deep breath. Then ask
  yourself what it is that you really need. Is it comfort,
  advice, reassurance or an extra hand? Consider whether
  or not you can fulfill this need on your own. If you cannot,
  the situation doesn't have to become a melodrama. When
  you require help, simply reach out and ask for it. Be clear
  and direct. And give people permission to say no if they're
  too busy or unable to respond. Remember, this is not a lit-
  mus test of love. Allow room for others to help, rather than
  sustain you.
- *Time Alone.* Make a list of all the things you love to do or
  that you've wanted to do and never tried. Pick one item
  from your list, and spend time during the next week pursuing that activity on your own. It may feel strange at first,
  because you're not used to taking care of your own needs,
  but stay with it. You may have fun—or not. That's okay. If
  you discover you don't enjoy this activity, pick a different
  one. The purpose is to develop self-reliance, learn to satisfy
  your own desires and be joyful. Meditation is extremely

valuable for the Lover. It can help you learn how to renew you own energy and develop on your own. Through meditation, you will learn to tap the depth of your being.

- *Create a Project and Follow Through on It.* You are a capable and creative person with so much to contribute to the world. Nonetheless, it's easy to give up on a project when no one is around to reinforce you with praise and admiration as you take the individual steps that move you toward its completion. As you work on the project you select, encourage yourself with internal messages of acknowledgment. In your mind or aloud, say things like, "Good job!" and "You're doing great." There's nothing wrong with fantasizing about public accolades and ultimate recognition of your brilliant qualities and accomplishments. Images such as these are fun and make powerful motivators. Yet they're pale imitations of the satisfaction and confidence that come from real follow-through. Besides positive self-talk, you might also seek a mentor who can help you understand the steps you need to take to succeed, or look for role models whose endeavors you can examine, and then follow their footsteps.

- *Practice Listening.* One of the most amazing gifts we can give others is to hear them. As a Lover, your passion is for connection and intimacy. So you're going to enjoy the rewards that accompany the ability to listen very much. Rather than indulging the impulse to jump in with a self-referential comment after a friend or loved one finishes a sentence or thought, keep the focus of the conversation on that person. If it's useful, you might think of this as giving someone else a turn to shine. Ask a question that leads to more information or clarifies your understanding. Then ask another one. If you notice yourself turning the conversation toward you, just acknowledge it and then ask the speaker to continue.

This technique deepens communication.

Observe how well people respond to being heard. You may be amazed at how much they want to share. In addition, you'll discover that, after they've had their turn, most people will give you a similar opportunity to share your thoughts and feelings.

• *Learn to Stop Pulling Energy.* Probably the number one pattern causing you to be deprived of the connection you crave is pulling on other people like a needy baby. This doesn't allow a healthy exchange of energy. One woman said of a man who acted like this, "It felt like my date was devouring me with his eyes. It was just too much. I couldn't talk to him anymore. I refused to go on any more dates because he seemed like a hungry predator." In my own life, a woman I had only just met ran me off because almost immediately she grasped my hands and told me, "Don't you feel how close we are? We are sisters! Can't you feel it? I feel so close to you." I was overwhelmed and dumbfounded by her instant expression of intimacy. It made me wonder what could be the matter with me that I didn't feel the same mysterious connection she believed was so evident. From then on, I avoided her.

If this might be your pattern, ask your friends to tell you honestly whether or not they sometimes feel drained by you. And don't deny the answer that you get. Ask if your gaze is too intense, if you talk too much and if you seem to have too many ongoing dramas. Although it may be tough to hear the truth, be grateful that you now have the awareness to transform your behavior. Especially, you must learn discernment about eye contact with the opposite sex—your girlfriends, boyfriends (if you are a woman) or married coworkers. Sometimes your comfort with deep eye contact that's not intended to be seductive can be misinterpreted. Practice softening your eyes, taking a breather in conversations and letting the focus of attention be on others, and stop running the dramas. Instead, try sending out your energy and allowing connections to happen naturally.

CHAPTER 3

ꝗHE CREATOR/MARTYR

ꝗ f you are the Creator, your passion signature is creativity. You are driven to make a positive contribution to the world. Creating harmony gives you peace and fulfillment and enables you to relax. You are an easygoing, likable, people-oriented person. Of all the passion signatures, the Creator perhaps is the best at friendship, negotiation and communication, as you would love for everyone to feel happy and fulfilled in equal measure. At any age, you are a mature soul whose counsel is sought by others. Your masterful problem solving and reasoning abilities make you adept at helping others think through difficulties and come up with the best solutions People's lives and dreams truly interest you. When you're feeling good, you are very supportive and joyfully celebrate the accomplishments of others. You are empathetic to people's feelings and insightful about their needs. You also possess the rare ability to listen and draw others out of their shells. It's easy for you to put yourself in someone else's shoes and to embrace many points of view at once and synthesize them into one solution. Such qualities make you beloved by those around you. When it comes to your gifts and talents, you are the quintessential late bloomer, but at your best, you are industrious, reliable, persevering and adaptable. Your gifts make you a terrific problem solver, negotiator, mediator, counselor and mate.

On the flip side, your wounded aspect is the Martyr. Here you may be wishy-washy, unable to make decisions because you don't trust yourself. Opportunities often tend to show up in pairs. When this happens to you, you ask everyone in your life how they would handle the situation, or which opportunity they would choose. If you choose A, you feel deprived of B. If you choose B, you feel deprived of A. Your indecisiveness can cause you to lock in place, make no choice and ultimately deprive yourself of getting more out of life.

As the quintessential people-pleaser and rescuer of the world, you can martyr yourself. You tend to put everyone's needs ahead of your own until you become depleted of energy. Then you withdraw, give the world the silent treatment and emit fumes of resentment. At your worst, you are passive-aggressive, dropping bitter comments that are intended to sting, or you use your physical presence to dominate those around you because you feel claustrophobic. When you provoke someone to attack you, your subsequent anger gives you permission to shut down and stop giving. As the Martyr, you may be a belly-stuffer, a person who eats too much, to renew your energy and for emotional comfort.

Creators go the extra mile in support of others. When they

stand behind you, rest assured that they're committed, loyal and dependable. It's like having a fan club. Your happiness and success are tremendously important to them, but so, alas, are the happiness and success of many others. As Creators' lives are occupied by numerous responsibilities and relationships, it may be necessary to share them with a wide community of friends or business associates. It's hard to feel secure in relationship to Creators when they're in the Martyr mode and go into isolation. If you approach them too quickly to show love and affection, they are likely to run in the other direction in order to avoid feeling engulfed by your needs and expectations.

Creators' biggest challenges are to set boundaries, so their needs are balanced with the needs of others, and to nurture themselves. Once they learn the ways to be self-loving, contain their energy and draw boundaries, they enjoy vibrant, harmonious relationships and have rich, creative lives that make the world a much better place for everyone. Through commitment, they ultimately learn about their depth of being and how to share generously without losing themselves. Generally, they are incredible humanitarians who know how to draw together communities of people for a creative purpose.

The passion of the Creator to express the self emerges from wounding that occurs in early childhood, between the ages of two to six or so. During this developmental stage, children are learning how to do everything from walking and feeding themselves to tying their shoes and reading. In the process, they're discovering their individual identity. Children naturally explore the world through creative play. For this child, however, what should be play is perceived as work. At this age, Mom and Dad are the queen and king of the world, and children are bonded to them for survival. The Creator often feels overwhelmed by the needs of the mother, especially at a time when the focus should be on the child's development.

Mom may get locked in a war of wills with this child. A male child in particular finds himself fighting her for control. At an early age, by trying to keep the peace when chaos rules the home, a female child becomes the family's little counselor. It often seems to Creator children that they must give up their needs in order to take care of the mother, father or other parental figures. Then they spend their lives fighting the engulfment of their "mother" or other parental figure in everyone they meet. In extreme cases adult Martyrs live with their mothers while blaming them for their missed lives. Adult Martyrs also hurt themselves to get even with others.

When a youngster's parents do not support the child's emerging individuality and accomplishments, or act as though the child is merely an extension of themselves, the child gets locked into a strange pattern of reversal. Even as the child wants to create, the child also wants *not* to create because the child fears that the creations will be stolen. One Creator I know had a mother who talked endlessly with the boys she brought home as a teenager. By the time she was twenty, she decided she didn't want a man in her life, as she was so angry with her mother for taking over whenever she brought a boy home.

Here's why reversal happens. To stabilize the connection with the parent, the child tries hard to be obedient and do the "right thing." But the child begins to lose interest in creative activities as the parent habitually takes over when the child expresses his or her individuality. The child feels angry and senses the futility in making an effort, and the creative impulse becomes tainted by the fear of deprivation and loss. This child seems to mature quickly, as the child adopts an adult point of view. Joyful self-expression is too burdened by responsibility. The child fears the parent will steal his or her sense of self.

In adulthood, Martyrs fear loss of self. They would do

almost anything to avoid the pain of engulfment, so they hide from situations where they perceive that risk. They are also so wide open energetically that they soak up other people's energy like sponges and are easily overwhelmed. One Creator stated, "I cannot sit in the middle of a room of people because I start feeling overwhelmed and pick up everybody's energy."

Exposure, simply being seen and heard, can make them feel vulnerable, as it stirs up strong fear of humiliation. There is a strong sense of shame about the self who lives under the surface. As a result, they limit self-expression and sabotage their creativity. They have bursts of creativity and then either start thinking about what they might lose by coming out with it or the privacy they will be deprived of once they are exposed. So they lose steam in the middle of projects. Unfortunately they can live with delusions of grandeur about the talents that live within them. Oddly, to the Martyr, holding their talents back seems like the higher road.

Since Martyrs also live with a near-constant sense of deprivation, they can be miserly and withholding or have strange habits with money. They may feel poor even though they have a million dollars in the bank. Or they may save for years and then blow their million dollars quickly. Or they may never be able to "make money" or "build capital" because they resist commitment to the things in life that would bring money to them. They don't look at the value of things; they look at their cost. This tendency causes Martyrs to undervalue others and disregard their needs. Furthermore, it often makes them suspicious of other people's intentions. They may feel as though they will lose, be tricked, miss out on something or be deprived if they make an expenditure or commitment. A corporate attorney and real estate tycoon with three homes in different countries, for instance, told me he couldn't afford to pay for a nanny to give his wife a break from child rearing. He complained incessantly about her monthly spending; nonetheless, they traveled the world regularly, jetting off to one destination after another. Martyrs can have strange spending habits, and if they acquire money, they may find creative ways of getting rid of it out of a sense of unworthiness. A high-powered corporate attorney complained to his wife about the price of lettuce. A stock market trader complained that he could not afford the price of the couple's counseling he and his wife sorely needed—right after he had emptied his disposable income account to pay for an elaborate $200,000 yacht.

If you are the Creator, the part of you that is stuck in early childhood needs your compassion and support to claim your rightful place in the world. You are a magnificent and highly resourceful being; however, the wounded fragment of your per-sonality that is the Martyr believes you are here to save the world. You feel you *must* take care of others in order to receive love. When the Martyr gets activated, or triggered, you tend to disperse your energy through giving yourself over to others and then resenting them later. Like a sponge, you are porous, so your body soaks up all the negative energy from those around you. People feel better around you because you let them dump their problems on you. Even your body is often soft and fleshy. Although you often look heavy and substantial, you're actually porous and vulnerable to the energy of everybody around you. You may wish you weren't so sensitive. After you have soaked up everyone else's runoff, you feel too tired to follow through on your own endeavors. One Martyr said, "I can take care of everybody else's problems; I just can't take care of my own.

You have powerful bursts of brilliant, creative energy, and then halfway through a project you lose steam. You lack the dis-cipline to follow through. There are two lions at the gate of your self-expression. One is that you are so creative in so many differ-ent directions that you have trouble focusing. If you are a writer, for example, you can look at an issue from so many different angles that it seems to become an octopus with too many arms. Overwhelmed, you do nothing. On the other hand, you were trained to withhold self-expression for fear of having your gifts stolen. As a result, you lose interest.

Being creative stirs up your resistance. On one hand, you hunger to express your inner voice. On the other hand, you rarely take credit for your creations and so can find creativity painful. Adult needs so overwhelmed your childhood needs that now you often can't figure out what you need, and when you do, you have trouble asking for it.

Hang in there, Creator! Your day has come. Your joy is at hand. I promise. As a person with a major Martyr aspect, I've also had to learn about the conflicting impulses that govern our passion signature. Once you decide to be your own best friend, and begin giving as well and as much to yourself as you give to others, you will begin to unlock the old gates of protection that now only serve as barricades between you and the success, love and happiness you long for and so richly deserve. As your passion is creativity, self-expression is the key to integrating your gifts with the wholeness of your being.

The birthright of the Creator is that you are creative in many different directions and it is in your nature to share this with others. You are an inspiration to others. Equal to the amount of confusion you have been lost in for most of your life is the number of choices you can access. You have the power to be very creative and passionate about your endeavors. In fact, you are among the most creative people on Earth. To tap your inner wellspring, however, you must practice consistency and follow through. To build your passion you must commit to yourself and your creativity. Since you tend to be the proverbial "ball dropper," you will have to get used to picking the "ball" back up time and time again. You must overcome fears of being trapped, overwhelmed, humiliated, punished and deprived. You must also unload any stubbornness and resistance you feel—and you have a bit of both!

Go to *www.thepassionprinciple.com/passiontools* to receive a free handout on the Creator and other passion signatures.

The Story of a Creator/Martyr

Jack, a thirty-two-year-old man, could not keep a job. He had a history of getting fired for criticizing his bosses. When he came to me for counseling, he'd just been let go from yet another high-paying position in a corporation. His parents, both successful professionals, had provided him a good education and were now supporting him. "I'm about to get another job, so I don't really need this," he told me.

"Before we begin I would like to get on the same page," I said. "I see you. You're brilliant at pulling the wool over everyone's eyes. You're over thirty. You have a good education and an expensive apartment in Los Angeles, and your folks are paying your rent. Obviously you're smarter than me, because you don't have to go to work and yet have everything you could need or want. You are a master of working the system. So I won't treat you like you are broken when you're clearly brilliant." That got his attention. A sheepish grin crept over his face, as if some part of him was relieved to have been busted. He opened up.

When I asked how he felt about work, he recalled a few childhood experiences. As an eight-year-old, Jack had started trading baseball cards with his friends. This specialty expanded into all sorts of collecting. He had taught his little brother to do the same. By twelve, he was running their two-man operation and had become a serious collector. He gave his small business a name and made his brother its treasurer. He had fun buying and selling cards at swap meets until his father got involved. His dad was excited about the businessman he saw in his son, and he thought it would be a great way to connect and spend time together.

When his dad saw the money Jack was making, he decided his son should treat collecting as a "real" business. In an effort to help, Jack's dad showered him with advice, monitored the progress of the business and showed disappointment when Jack made decisions other than what his dad wanted. Jack soon lost interest.

As a teenager, Jack became interested in comic books. He started another business, but his father got involved in that one, too, and so he gave it up. Throughout his childhood, he'd often heard his father comment and rage about how hard he had to work to support his family. As a self-employed industrial engineer, his dad had suffered many setbacks and financial hardships while raising the family. As a result, Jack feared becoming strapped down with responsibility. "I've got to be honest with you," he told me. "My dad still gives me advice all the time, and I hate it. But when I'm not working, I need his money—so I don't feel as though I can refuse to listen."

Jack was a classic Creator/Martyr. He had a good creative mind and the skills that were necessary to succeed in business, yet he repeatedly sabotaged his career and was filled with self-doubt. On some level, he didn't want to branch off into any creative ventures for fear that his father would engulf him, and he might fail. He didn't want to grow up and take responsibility for his life because he might end up carrying a heavy burden like his father. Yet he'd done little to set his father free of the burden of supporting him.

As the Martyr, Jack pulled his father in, and then he resented his father's involvement in his career. He believed he had to perform to make his dad happy. Therefore the angry kid inside ran a good game. He saw himself as the victim of the unjust world. He communicated his trials and tribulations to his father with such drama that both parents thought he was somehow incapable of more. He asked his father for advice on everything from fixing his car to whether or not he should take his next job. Deep inside, he felt entitled to financial support because he was mad about having his creativity and past successes stolen from him. He also got away with being rude and provoking his bosses, since he had his parents' money as a security net.

When we're on a positive path through life, the conscious mind tries to move us forward. But until we address our emotional blocks, they'll always detour us to the same old destination. Jack was smart enough to see that he was repeating a pattern related to an underlying fear of engulfment. As soon as he saw this, he phoned his father and made two requests: to stop sending money and to stop coaching him. He thanked him for his support and informed him that he'd decided to learn to handle the day-to-day ups and downs of a career on his own. He also expressed willingness to move if he could not afford his lifestyle. Last time we spoke, Jack reported that he'd found a new job and was being groomed for management. He bought his own home, and his relationship with his father was transforming into a friendship.

How to Recognize the Creator/Martyr

As adults, Creators may carry extra weight around the middle. They tend to put on body fat in an unconscious attempt to block the energy that easily pours into them from others. They can be physically soft and mushy. The role food plays in their lives is a complicated issue for people who share this passion signature. It has as many tentacles of meaning as an octopus. Martyrs are emotional eaters who use food to fill up the emptiness they feel inside and to recharge their batteries when they get drained. They may believe that a meal is a "reward" for something they've done. The trip to the snack bar to consume secret hamburgers may be the only pleasures in a series of responsibilities they endure without complaint. It enables them to comply on the surface while a rebellious inner voice says, "I deserve this after everything I have done." Or Martyrs may snack excessively as a punishment in moments of self-disgust. Going on a diet triggers immense anxiety and deprivation.

The fear of deprivation can be so all consuming that Martyrs feel driven to eat everything a diet plan says to stay away from. So Martyrs start a new diet on Monday after gorging the night before on Mexican food. This cycle happens over and over. In addition, the loss of physical body fat can cause them another feeling of deprivation. Martyrs feel uncomfortable when they "lose" weight. They feel less physically safe in the world as their layers of protection melt away. Martyrs hate themselves for being fat, yet are unaware of the profound need for the excess food and fat in their lives. In my years as a practitioner, I have noticed that these issues are a significant reason diets so often fail.

In addition, being heavy is like walking around with a security blanket. Because Martyrs want to keep the world at a comfortable distance, anyone who's attracted to them poses a subtle threat—that person might want to get closer. Extra weight can be a barrier to sexual intimacy. It's also a buffer from the world. One television producer I know got the show he always wanted and immediately found himself running to the kitchen and packing on the pounds to quell his anxiety.

Furthermore, since Martyrs tend to withhold thoughts and feelings and are in conflict about self-expression, a large body gives them a weapon with which to get their point across. It's much harder to push someone around when they have substance. Although they may remain silent about their needs, you can still "hear" them. It may also give them an excuse for why they aren't going after what they say they want. Instead it's, "When I lose my weight I will . . ." or "I don't have love because of my weight."

Their fear of engulfment often extends to claustrophobia. For instance, an overweight Martyr joined me one afternoon in the sauna at our health spa. Her anxiety about having enough space was evident in how she stretched her body across as much of the bench space as possible, to the point of crowding other people. Similarly, when I first arrived in New York from Texas, riding in crowded elevators made me feel smothered. One time, an elevator car got crowded, and I physically blocked another passenger from getting on. To this day, I have been known to take the stairs in a pinch.

Yet another reason Martyrs tend to put on pounds is that they are fatigued from doing too much for others. Rather than exercise, they typically make excuses to rest, because they are not in touch with their bodies. They often have deep self-hatred and a self-destructive streak. This means that if they feel too good, they feel bad about it. Since Martyrs tend to push themselves too hard and undernurture themselves, they are very susceptible to this pattern. Food takes the place of letting significant others into their intimate lives in a permanent way. Friends are great, but having a long-term spouse or lover is a challenge. Martyrs always think, "Yeah, I'll do this now, but it isn't forever." Thus they are the classic couch potatoes, sitting alone at home, snacking and watching TV. If they have a family around them they comply and meet everyone else's needs until they explode over an upset that gives them permission to storm off to the bedroom with a headache to be alone.

The female Martyr is the nice woman who can't say no to requests from friends, family, coworkers or the PTA. She may be the overweight friend who spends hours listening to her girlfriends lament about their boyfriends or husbands and then inhales a pint of ice cream when she needs to feel better herself. Hers is the shoulder that everyone cries on. She probably doesn't pay much attention to her appearance, choosing clothing to disguise her shape rather than emphasize her best features. She also may have an eating disorder. I wrote my first book, *You Can't Quit 'til You Know What's Eating You,* to help this woman.

At her best, the Creator is the ultimate welcoming presence, a woman who gathers an extended family around a holiday dinner table and sees that everyone feels valued and included. She is the wise elder and nurturing mother of every community in which she participates. People feel safe and happy around her. She has healthy boundaries, knows how to replenish her own energy, doesn't allow others to drain her and spends time developing her own gifts, talents and abilities. At her worst, she's cynical and bitter and gossips at others' expense. She's sad and lonely, and her home is a chaotic mess. If you violate her in any way, she'll stop taking your calls and cut you out of her life. She is passive-aggressive and provokes her world to attack her.

The male Martyr is the friendly, teddy-bear–like man who lives and works in a disordered space. He's the yes-man who lacks follow-through. He's the nicest guy in the world. He's reasonable, logical and great to talk to, a fantastic problem solver, and he will do anything for you. But confront him about anything and he withdraws into silence. Trying to resolve a conflict with this fellow can be mind-bending. He does nice, generous, loving things and then suddenly flips into resentment or withdrawal. He asks for advice with a problem and then rejects every possible solution that's offered. Also, as a rule, he's late. But if you get annoyed waiting for him and dare mention it, he'll accuse you of wanting to control him.

The male Creator, at his best, is a supportive father figure and mentor, a man who is a skillful communicator and a world-class negotiator. He disciplines himself to take care of his physical body and takes the time to take care of his own needs. At his worst, as the Martyr, he is a doormat, pushover and wet noodle with a five o'clock shadow. His dreams are unlikely to be realized because he's been hiding his light for years under a bushel of details and projects and responsibilities that reduce his wattage.

The man or woman who can't make a lasting commitment to a project of his or her own is usually a Martyr. The trouble is that Martyrs see so many sides to anything they pursue that it is difficult to focus and let go. They want every stone to be unturned. They get distracted, delay action, don't have the energy for follow-through and fear loss of freedom if they commit and fear being engulfed by the consequences. That's why if those of us who embody this passion signature don't face this head-on we are probably the most likely of any to die with our gifts inside us. One Martyr said, "I think of these great ideas, but before I take action another thought will come into my head that cuts that one off with, 'What about this?' I feel like I'm standing in the middle of a room and can't move, so I sit at the television night after night and eat TV dinners and chocolate." This type can thrive in collaboration, once they get past the fear of commitment.

Papers may pile up at home because Martyrs put off reviewing them and tossing them out on a regular basis. If they have three tasks, they won't do any. Soon the mountain of paperwork seems vast and insurmountable. So the Martyr ignores the papers. The Martyr's kitchen can be a pigsty unless conscious action is regularly taken. Stacks of plates and cups pile high in the sink and on the counters and stove. Cabinet drawers and doors are only half-shut, and fresh food that belongs in the refrigerator has been left out to spoil. Martyrs don't see the details of their environment in the same way other people do. They have the ability to narrow their vision and block out anything they don't want to see. But then the whole mess is too overwhelming to clean up. They promise themselves that they will do it later. Martyrs see an open space on the counter as a place to put things down. Other types want to look at a clean counter of open space to feel peace of mind.

On the job, the boss doesn't have to hire an extra person because the Martyr does the work of two people. The Martyr, the endurer, suffers in silence. Unfortunately, despite knocking themselves out to please, people rarely notice or appreciate them. Eventually, they get tired of feeling "taken for granted" and retaliate by withdrawing. Workaholics who believe that no one else can do their job as well are Combo Platters with a strong Martyr aspect. They will always give in and say yes. They long to be indispensable. After all, if others need them so badly, they don't have to take the risks of exposure and loss that come when you step onto center stage with your own projects.

Public speaking is often terrifying to Martyrs. Revealing who they are and what they care about can trigger intense shame and acts of self-sabotage. If they take a step forward, they usually find a way to take a step back. When I began leading workshops on recovering from eating disorders years ago, I felt totally undeserving of the spotlight. So I'd return to my hotel room, where I smoked and ate nervously from the mini-bar. "Who am I," I thought self-loathingly, "to be in this position?" I was terrified that I'd be exposed and humiliated as a fraud. The accolades I received brought up tremendous feelings of shame.

During several years offstage, I purposefully focused attention on transforming my wounded patterns using the methods described in this book. Today, I am able to share my passion and purpose in seminars and on TV without engaging in self-destruction.

If you are a Creator, please recognize that the world desperately needs you to come out of hiding. People are hungry for the nourishment that you provide by opening up to your passion. We long for you to feel happy because you are so creative when you're fulfilled. The lie you're living is that your fulfillment diminishes us and our fulfillment deprives you. The truth is that everyone can be fulfilled. Harmony is possible. It's not a pipe dream. Once you embrace your value, you'll give yourself permission to contribute. Your life's transformation has to begin at the source—within you.

Martyr Relationship Traps

From my experience, there are four main patterns that Creator/Martyrs need to become aware of and address on an ongoing basis if they want to stop being dragged down the same worn-out paths in their relationships and careers. These are the grooves and ruts keeping them stuck in isolation and feeling miserable.

- *Too Overwhelming. Too Much.* Turn off all those leaking faucets. You are not the energetic power plant for everybody within a hundred-mile radius. You've made so many promises, taken on so many responsibilities, and gotten so many people hooked up to your energy that the pressure on you is immense. While you may sometimes act as though you've got the stamina of a mule, you are not a beast of burden! Drop the pride you get from enduring. If you don't change your mode of operation, the next straw you agree to carry may be the straw that breaks your back. When that happens, you're going to have an emotional meltdown. Probably you'll slam the door on the people in your life, go on an eating binge or do something passive-aggressive to provoke an attack and catalyze others to disconnect from you. When you help others too much you build strong muscles, but their muscles remain weak. You are preventing them from learning their lessons, whether through pleasure or pain.

In your romantic life, your fears of engulfment can absolutely neutralize your sex drive. If you're single, you may blame your lack of availability or willingness to date on your workload and convince yourself that the "timing is off." Later, when you've completed some project or passed some scheduling milestone, *then* you'll be ready for a relationship. But the truth is that you're afraid of being smothered. And actually, you are smothering yourself. You long for intimacy, but it brings up scary feelings. You'd rather isolate yourself. Potential mates may give up on you. You can be the quintessential flirt as long as no commitment is involved. The "C" word makes you want to escape. Or perhaps you're already married, but now that intimacy is expected, you want none of it. You'd prefer to watch pornography on the Internet or cable TV than to make love. When your spouse makes advances, you feel numb. It's as though your marriage has neutered you. You might have an affair, but once you're divorced you remember how much your mate meant to you. You live with the losses you create by acting upon your fear of the loss of freedom.

Through *commitment* you will learn the truth of your identity and what you actually have to offer to the world. Commitment will give you the freedom to achieve your potential by giving you a foundation to stand upon. First you must commit to small things, such as showing up for appointments rather than breaking them. Then you must expand to ever-larger commitments. This will enable you to grow and learn more about your gifts and talents.

- *Needy? How Attractive.* Let's face it. You don't always feel so great about yourself. In fact, too often you feel downright unworthy of attention, admiration and support. So what do you do to compensate? You surround yourself with needy people. Then, my friend, you come off looking mighty good. Their dependence on you makes you feel like a superstar problem solver, loyal compadre and accomplisher of stuff. In addition, people's "deficiencies" are a good excuse for you not to take care of your own business. After all, if you were to succeed, they might envy you or feel bad about themselves in comparison (you imagine). Also, they just need you so much, it wouldn't be fair to be self-centered by reserving time for yourself (you decide).

You possess the incredible ability to see and bring out the good in people. But you don't serve others well if you always step forward and take over the problem solving in their lives. People will only become more capable and expand past their former limitations when they learn how to do things for themselves. So take a look at the people in your life and see whether or not you're invested in their dependency. If you encourage them to learn and do, how do they react? Do they make efforts to grow, or do they refuse to try and threaten to withdraw their love from you? Do they give you as much encouragement to evolve and take risks as you give them? Are you holding yourself back? If you feel an attraction to someone whom you perceive as "broken" or "hurt," it's a clue to pay attention to the dynamic of your interactions. Ultimately, no one is going to thank you for treating them as less than your equal.

- *I Can't Commit Now. Someone/Something Better Might Come Along.* Here's the bottom line. You are often motivated by your fear of deprivation. You have fantasies about your greatness and how good things could be in the future *if only* someone/something gives you the opportunity to shine. But you hate your life and want to escape it. You finally meet a great guy or gal, someone open and available to you who doesn't make you feel as though you're being drained. At first you're excited, and then, suddenly, you find yourself feeling trapped. You want to spend less time together and hang out with your friends more. You start noticing this significant other's flaws and mundane characteristics. "Sure, he or she is *okay*, but I don't think I am cut out for a relationship." If you choose this person, what about later? What would you be sacrificing by tying yourself to such an ordinary mate? Thus, you pull back and disconnect. You'd rather wait for someone better to come along.

Or maybe you've recently started a new diet or exercise regimen and don't want to explore the field of dating prospects until you've transformed your body. Once you've lost the ten pounds or are sporting an abdominal six-pack, *then* the ideal partner will come along and be attracted. The "schmuck" who likes you today is only someone with whom you're marking time until a better person shows up and notices you. Of course, your core problem is your negative self-image. As you don't feel worthy of love as you are, you don't want to connect with anyone who accepts and loves you with your supposed imperfections. Frankly, until you commit to your life and give yourself permission to be happy, you won't ever have your dream relationship. You'd rather go on depriving yourself than risk the loss of your freedom.

I once sabotaged an enormous television opportunity with this line of thinking. "If I commit to this program, what if a better one comes along?" Unfortunately, it's easy to miss out on everything by committing to nothing. Opportunities seem to show up in twos for the Creator. In my own life, I have laughed many times over this propensity. On the same night, I will be invited to two great events. I used to torment myself over what to do, often ending up staying home. Now I make a choice and stick to it. So get in the habit of making a choice and learning from that choice. Talk to someone to help you weigh the pros and cons.

- *Stop Giving Your Energy Away.* Let yourself be shallow for once. When your good friend has been pouring his troubles in your ears for two hours, it's a sign that something is wrong. Now is when you should avoid asking those deep or probing questions. You have got to stop expending your valuable life force in the vain attempt to save other people. Otherwise, you'll be depleted. A fabulous exercise for the Martyr evolving into the Creator is to practice the I Don't Know exercise. The next time a friend or family member comes to you with one more in an endless stream of problems, say, "I don't know the answer to that," or "I don't know how to help you. You might want to get some coaching." Let the ball they tossed you drop right between you. Notice how light you feel as you get off the phone early and have an extra hour to spend on your own interests.

Creator Opening and Closing Formulas

Everyone has blind spots. Therefore, we must rely on others to help us be aware of when we are repeating unhealthy patterns. If you have a Creator in your life who seems to be falling into one of the Martyr relationship traps, consider supporting that individual with one of the following opening formulas.

When you have a relationship of any kind with a Creator, remember that this individual is highly sensitive to your emotions and energy—perhaps more so than to his or her own. In childhood Creators were programmed to be vigilant about other people's needs because their own voices and identities were stolen, and their personal needs were frequently overridden, given up or never identified. To maintain a flowing, open connection between you, it's very important to maintain awareness that the Creator is a separate individual from you and to communicate clearly your self-reliance. If Creators sense you pulling on them, or imagine you might, they begin to feel engulfed. Be sure to ask Creators what they need in any given situation, and give them a turn to share themselves while you listen, ask questions about them and help them explore their areas of need.

No matter how much you desire to show love and affection, do not forget to give the Creator space. Depending on what your spouse, child, sibling, or friend has been doing, and with whom they've been interacting up to now, the Creator may need some distance and time to stabilize his or her energy and feel whole again. Creators are sort of like domestic cats. They care about you and enjoy your presence, but they feel safer if they're allowed to come to you when they're ready. If you approach too quickly or forcefully, you risk shutting them down. If you see the Creator's body language closing like a flower, sit across the room or go into another room. Be patient. Soon the Creator will come and purr in your lap like a kitten.

The language of freedom is magical for the Creator. This person naturally feels a bit more content living alone than everyone else. Their homes become their safe places, their atmospheric skins, which allow them time and space to restore their energy. For this reason, even if they are married, they need a room to call their own. It is someplace they can go and pull away from the world to be restored.

Because of their history of engulfment, they unconsciously feel hemmed in by any kind of commitment, whether it is an agreement to meet for breakfast on Sunday or an intimate relationship. This is true even when it's an imagined commitment, but most particularly after intimacy and connection. This is the classic wake-up-the-next-morning-and-run person. So expect it. Pull your energy back. Tell them they are free to go and do what they need to do to take care of themselves. Encourage them to take a walk, go to the gym or spend an evening with friends.

Do not use zippy one-liners like, "You need your space, again!" to make fun of them or make them feel guilty in any way when they pull back; otherwise, you will close them down. Creators will feel ashamed of their "irrational" need for distance and become compliant. The guilt prevents them from taking the time they need to rebalance, so they continue feeling smothered even if you are ten feet away from them. Compliance from a Creator is the kiss of death for your relationship. Do not take the need to pull back personally. It's not about you. Creators will come back to you when they feel truly free of any pulling. Then they can discover their own need for you.

By the way, this can be tricky when Martyrs and Vamps are having a relationship. The Lover and Creator pairing is one of the most common. One of the classic ways the Vamp complains about distance is through one-liners like, "You never want to have sex anymore," "You never have enough time for me," "You always want to be alone," or "I know how to love—and you don't." All of these guarantee that you'll be sleeping alone or back-to-back for one more night. The Vamp wants to live in fusion. That's not healthy. The Martyr wants to live in separation. That's not healthy. Both types need to come out of this polarity and explore interdependence.

In the workplace, the freedom and space opening formula could take the form of setting an appointment to do business when a matter is not urgent, asking the Creator to step over and see you in your office when he or she has a moment, respecting a closed door as a sign that the Creator is managing his or her affairs or requires privacy, and conducting business during regular business hours instead of at night or on the weekend.

Another opening formula for Creators is to assign a more structured person to work on the project with them to make sure that deadlines are met. Also, don't give them too many things to do at once or they will get overwhelmed and do nothing. Don't sit them in the room with a bunch of Vamps, or they'll end up speaking with them about their problems and won't get anything done. The Creator is a born negotiator, a communicator, a problem solver. Put Creators in any role like that, which also has little paperwork, and you'll have them right where they can serve you best. If someone is a Combo Platter Creator-Visionary, that person will also be amazing at detail work.

The Creator can easily get lost in a frenzy of thoughts that provoke a flood of overwhelming emotions. At such times, communication is blocked and connection difficult to maintain. To help a Creator end the cycle of internal stimulation, regain equilibrium and feel at peace, ask what the Creator needs *right now*. If you know your Creator well, you might gently make a suggestion to take a break, a walk in the park or a bath. If you ask Creators what they need, they may not be able to answer the question immediately. Wait for the response. It's as though these people are lost in the woods, and your question is a trail of bread crumbs leading back to the present. Helping Creators define a specific need—for example, for rest, a hug, space or assistance—and communicating it aloud serves to anchor them. Expressing a need, feeling or concern may feel threatening, so please be a compassionate listener. Give your full attention to the person in front of you, and simply acknowledge what you're told. A good follow-up question to, "What do you need right now?" is "How can I help?"

Creators are so used to get-togethers where people place them in the role of the listeners that if they don't get a turn by the end of the conversation, they truly resent it. If you're giving a Creator a turn, and you shift conversation back to yourself in the middle of listening, that's an even worse violation. Creators may not tell you; they'll just shut down. Ask Creators a deepening question about the topic, like, "How did that make you feel?" "Is there more you wanted to say?" or "If I were in your shoes, I would feel . . . How did it make you feel?" Keep the focus with them until they seem done. Ask if they want your opinion about the topic or if it is okay for you to express yourself now. Leave breathing room around what they are saying. Think about giving Creators a turn. It will be up to you to monitor this closing formula, because the Creator/Martyr won't have a clue about how to take and keep the focus. Creators are uncomfortable talking about themselves. So be aware. If you've been talking for half an hour, and there seems to be no turn in the tide, you are probably speaking with someone operating in the Martyr mode. The Creator who has learned about his or her needs is more adept and makes sure to take a turn and be heard.

Creators flourish when they are seen and heard. Acknowledging their abilities, accomplishments and contributions replenishes their energy and makes them feel valued. Genuine praise and expressions of gratitude fill up their hearts and open them up. By contrast, teasing Creators, especially in public, is a closing formula as it triggers intense embarrassment. When Creators discover that it's safe to reveal their authentic selves to you—because you've honored, rather than humiliated, them—their confidence and self-esteem grows. Then they feel comfortable sharing their wonderful talents and skills.

Healed Creators make great spouses or business partners because they are reliable, committed, rational, have integrity and are truly interested in your point of view. When you're having a disagreement, they don't fight to win; they fight for real harmony. They're good communicators because they listen well instinctively, so you feel fulfilled, heard and safe. It's wonderful to help Creators remain open so they freely do all of this.

Transforming Your Destructive Patterns

If you're a Creator, you have the potential to become a master in the area of human relationships. The tips below describe a few of the skills you'll require.

- *Learn What Your Needs Are.* Part of this is learning to say no. With time you will learn how to establish healthy boundaries—expressed directly, using words—with the people with whom you live and work. Don't make them guess what your needs are. Be explicit and be calm. You may not know your own needs because things often exhaust or overtax you on an invisible level. You have a tendency to pick up other people's negativity and problems energetically. So use your feelings as your guide. If you're too tired to talk on the phone, say, "This isn't a good time for me, as I'm tired." If you're too busy to help, say, "I'm not available for that, as I'm busy right now." If someone presses you to change your answer, there's no need to waffle about your decision or apologize, just say, "Thanks for calling (or asking). But in this case, I must say no." This doesn't mean you're inflexible. When you have energy, time or interest, you are free to say yes. Besides having more energy and feeling less overwhelmed, when you set clear boundaries you'll find most people honor them, and your self-esteem will increase.

You have a lost child within you. Save that child, nurture her or him, and you will blossom into being who you are in your soul. If you notice that you continue worrying about people's needs and problems, or feel guilty for not stepping in and "fixing" things for them, sit silently for a moment and purposefully imagine those people being turned over to God or a higher power. This will reassure you that they're being cared for, and they're not alone.

- *Develop Discipline.* You are extremely creative and have bursts of productive energy; however, that energy may fall flat unless you regularly take stock and are honest about your behavior. If you want to succeed in anything, you cannot follow every impulse and distraction or else you'll fritter your life away. The tool you need to stay on top of the tasks you plan to accomplish is discipline. Breaking projects into baby steps can make them feel more manageable. But you must not evade taking those tiny steps.

Understanding your tendency for reversal—one step forward, one obstinate step backward—it's vital to plan healthy strategies ahead of time to nurture yourself and also to cultivate a reliable support system. It's important to take care of your physical body and maintain your home environment. When your body is healthy, you'll have more energy. When your home is uncluttered, you'll think more clearly and get more done. Remember, your home is your second skin. When it's messy, you feel chaotic and stagnant inside.

Whatever it is, always encourage yourself for picking up the ball you dropped. Never berate yourself for dropping it. With time, you will notice you get better at this. Years ago I lived 24–7 in a messy house and my bills were never paid on time. Now I have small episodes like this, but I have adapted to feeling so much better when things are organized that I hire three different assistants periodically through the year to help me organize my closets and my house and with my ongoing to-do list.

For exercise, walk a mile and build from there. You'll gain confidence as you stick to a regular program of activity. At home, your salvation may be to hire a professional organizer or housekeeper. Face it: Cleaning is not your strongest suit. You probably need help. Throughout your career, you'll also benefit from forming creative partnerships with disciplined collaborators who do not steal your thunder. Discipline is the antidote to the sense of hopelessness you sometimes feel. Get someone else involved in your creative endeavors who will require deadlines and collaboration. I advised one television producer who had had an ingenious movie script mulling around in his head for twenty years to join a screenwriting class. Within three months he had half of it completed.

- *Be Sweet to Yourself.* As a Creator/Martyr, you are likely to feel threatened by your own lightness of being. That's because your nervous system doesn't equate happiness and pleasure with the sadness and guilt that "should" be felt by an unworthy, self-hating being such as you. You may have already noticed that occasions of euphoria, expansion or accomplishment in your life are often followed by an emotional constriction or behavioral backlash. There is a strong possibility that if you do something good for yourself, or something wonderful happens, you may later hurt yourself to take the goodness away and tip the scales back toward sadness.

In order to develop a greater capacity for happiness and pleasure, it's essential that you practice being good to yourself. Ultimately, this will make it possible to receive — and truly feel — love and support. You can retrain your nervous system so that it doesn't automatically shut down or retaliate by triggering you, for example, to overeat. Here are a few possible ways you might experiment with this concept:

— Try replacing mean and self-critical thoughts with sweet words of encouragement and approval. If you catch yourself thinking, "I suck at this," or "I'm a hopeless case," follow it up with, "That's okay. I'm doing my best."

— To handle moments in which you feel undeserving, plan healthy ways to be gentle and self-nurturing, such as taking a walk or a bubble bath, calling a friend for support, or buying yourself a bunch of flowers.

—Begin a gratitude journal where you keep track of the good things that happen in your life every day and the positive things you've done for yourself and others. As it's easy to focus on deprivation and the things that are pressuring you, this journal is a way to pat yourself on the back and remind you that your life is rich and rewarding. Some of the best things seem ordinary until we pay attention: the sunshine, trees, a freshly laundered towel and so on. Here you celebrate what you have, not what you lack. And what if your to-do list had fifteen items on it and you only did twelve? Your journal is a place to give yourself credit and approval for what went well and got completed. If you are kicking an overeating habit, praise yourself when you throw away the rest of the chips. Never reprimand yourself for having eaten them in the first place.

• *Exercise*. This is a major healing formula for the Creator. Since you tend to pick up energy from the world around you and store it in your midsection where it becomes stagnant, you need to be wrung out like a dishrag. Yoga is an excellent activity for the Creator because it keeps your body twisting and releasing what gets stuck in the abdomen. Give yourself a goal of exercising three times a week—and stick to it. But always be encouraging, no matter what you do. Don't go crazy trying to lose weight, especially since yours is the passion signature best known for combining exercise and ice cream. One man stated, "I exercise a lot, but I just can't kick my ice-cream-at-bedtime habit." Totally healthful eating makes you feel too deprived, so do your best. In Paul Pearsall's book *Super Immunity,* he states that research has shown it is not a perfect diet that makes you live the longest, it's how you feel about your life. So support yourself no matter what you do.

Do something a little bit vigorous that makes you sweat. This is more likely to help you slim down and also to release toxic buildup in the body. Walking in nature is great because the sun, wind, water and trees are great balancers of the human body and energy field. Do anything that moves your energy, and you won't succumb as easily to overeating. Imagine you are pulling energy from above, filling up your energy field and any holes that may be in your field. Practice surrounding yourself with a bubble of protective energy.

CHAPTER 4

THE WARRIOR/CONQUEROR

If your passion signature is the Warrior, you are a born leader, a chief or a queen. You live with a deep sense of purpose or dedication to a cause—whatever cause you choose to set before yourself, from getting a fledgling company off the ground to fighting for the underdog. You lead with humility. Courage is your nature, and your courage inspires others to access their own. You are intensely goal-oriented and have a strong mind. Above all else, you are motivated to seek the good for all, beginning with your family and other loved ones and extending to your colleagues, community and country. In a battle, you're the protector that people want at their backs, because you are known to walk your talk, stay the course and do the right thing. Those around you honor you for your service and good judgment. You are also a magnetic personality and have a powerful sex drive. At your best you are humble yet confident in your abilities. In time you become the wise and trusted elder of your tribe, a brilliant role model and a mentor.

Your ultimate challenge as a wounded Warrior is to overcome your compulsion to win at any cost. As the Conqueror, you can be aggressive and intimidating, even when you don't intend to be. When you're feeling hurt, threatened or angry, or you're lusting after an outcome, you may succumb to the urge to direct your considerable powers purely toward domination. Like the proverbial bull in a china shop, in this mode you muscle your way through every obstacle while leaving a stream of destruction in your wake. Secretly you enjoy the fact that no one can stand up to your brute force. Accomplishment only feeds your appetite for victory, making you hungry for more and greater conquests.

Warriors are probably the most misunderstood of any passion signature. People have strong reactions—either favorable or unfavorable—to Warriors. On the inside, they are sensitive people who are deeply affected by the events around them. But on the outside, they often come across as domineering. They have a keen sense of right and wrong and manage their lives according to an unwavering code of ethics—and they expect you to follow suit. Because they have an exaggerated sense of responsibility, they believe it's their job to run the show, carry the ball and save the world. They willingly shoulder the burden for family, friends and business associates, even when it means delaying gratification of their own needs. Injustice outrages Warriors, so they are apt to charge into the fray like a White Knight on behalf of the underdog or to challenge anyone whom they perceive as getting a free meal ticket at another's expense.

If you have a relationship with a Conqueror in any zone of life, you've probably noticed that this person has a hot temper. Forget winning arguments with Conquerors! They make a point to know the rules about everything and tend to see the world through black-and-white goggles. There are no gray areas in the Conqueror's field of vision. This type of rigid adherence to principle can cut a huge blade through intimacy. When they direct their booming voices, penetrating eyes and blunt remarks in your direction, it can feel as though you're being blown across the room by a blast of water from a fire hose.

At their worst, Conquerors tell you how to think and undermine your sense of self and self-esteem. They project an arrogant know-it-all quality, and can be controlling and verbally abusive as mates. In the book *Why Does He Do That?* author Lundy Bancroft illustrates the extreme negative of this passion signature. Conquerors are likely to tell you that you don't know what you are talking about, that you are naive, just don't get it or should shut up and think their way. There is a right way and a wrong way. Of course, Conquerors know the right way and you are an idiot. Since they don't care what you think or feel about them, they can be true tyrants when out of balance, especially when they drink alcohol. Conquerors can be so overbearing that at times you may feel as though your being doesn't have any value at all to them. They boast that they don't "need" anybody. They will escalate any disagreement with their point of view into a shouting match. Oddly, they are mostly blind to the impact they have on others. They believe they're only being honest and direct and assume you'll appreciate them not beating around the bush.

What are the origins of this passion signature? During the maturation process, around puberty and adolescence, the teenage Warrior decides that the world is not a safe place. At that time an overpowering force in the home makes being

sensitive or delicate too risky. Combative skills are developed
in response to threat because the core essence of the Warrior
feels as vulnerable, and as needing of protection, as a soft
bunny rabbit. Under the surface, there's actually a Lover waiting to be discovered (see Chapter 2).

Danger in the home may come from a parent who is often
angry, a heavy drinker or childlike and inappropriately needy.
It may come from an opposite-sex parent who enrolls the teen
as a surrogate spouse. This could take the form of engulfment,
flirtation or seduction, such as from a stressed-out single mom
who casts her son in the role of "man of the house," a dad who
has his daughter accompany him to social events that his wife
refuses to attend, or a parent who responds sexually to a son's
or daughter's puberty and adolescence with alluring eyes or
inappropriate hugs and kisses. To please the parent, the teen
does his or her best to measure up, but inside feels fraudulent.
It also happens when parents belittle a sensitive boy, or when
girls are told they're not as good as boys. In both instances, the
home is a rough environment, so the teen toughens up, adopting a blusteringly macho personality.

One sure sign of parental energy violation is if the way the
parent looks at the child with affection gives the kid the creeps.
One man's divorced mother had him giving her backrubs in
her nightgown when he was a boy. One woman's father used
to ask her if she'd been out rubbing up against boys. She
recalls that she always cringed when he approached her and
gave her wet kisses or patted her bottom as she passed him.

Female Conquerors are a unique breed of woman because
they make a decision to abandon their femininity around
puberty for survival. If no one is watching out for a teenage
girl, she has to protect herself from the sexual advances of boys
at school, men in the communities where she lives and sometimes her male relatives. She literally feels as though wolves are

surrounding her. I am a Warrior as well as a Creator type. At the start of high school, I weighed 115 pounds and had blonde hair down to my waist. Grabbing started. By age twenty-one, I'd put on weight, wore heavy-framed glasses, hardened my voice and used the "F" word liberally. One day I told my dad I was buying a motorcycle. He said, "No, Donna, don't! You've lost your femininity enough." He could see the change, yet he did not know that he was partly the cause of it. Another Warrior/Conqueror woman told me, "More than anything as a teen, I wanted to be considered cool and tough by my peers. I hated 'girly' girls. But I didn't understand what I was giving up." Another place some women lose their precious femininity is in a male-dominated workforce. One woman said, "Once I gained fifty pounds, dropped my voice and became aggressive, the men stopped treating me with such disregard. I learned how to fight like a man."

In adulthood Warrior/Conquerors feel passionate about putting their considerable power into the service of what is right and good. Emotionally they are frozen at puberty, an age when most of us feel a degree of confusion about identity and long to define our place in the world. Their greatest fear is that someone will discover their weakness and then make them appear or feel "wrong." They bridge the gap between their low self-esteem and feelings of "not good enough" and their intended goals by using brute strength and intense willpower.

Whether male or female, Warrior/Conquerors are career-, success- and achievement-driven. Only once they have conquered the world will they live the good life, accept the accolades they deserve and let themselves enjoy love and leisure. As a result, they are ambitious doers and accomplishers, control freaks and power mongers. They spend their lives driving toward a future that never comes. Unfortunately, they are the people most likely to die of heart attacks, strokes, bleeding ulcers and the like, due to a lifetime of not listening to their bodies and pushing through stress. They rarely let people help them or be their equals. Instead, they tell themselves that they are superior to those around them, as well as superior to the situations in which they find themselves. Ironically, their feelings of "not good enough" drive them to prove themselves either by being the smartest person in the room or the strongest or the richest or the most accomplished. This false sense of pride can get them killed, as they will stand up and fight anyone they think is disrespecting them. Don't tangle with these people on the highway, in a bar or on a dark street at night. One newspaper headline quoted a Conqueror who said, "I had to shoot him. He disrespected me."

Some Conquerors feel that they are evil on the inside. This inner sense of shame for childhood abuse causes them to do self-destructive things in the name of pride. One Conqueror got in a beer-drinking brawl at a football game because he thought some guy pushed him. He lost his eye with a knuckle punch because he just couldn't let the insult go. It saddens me when I see the number of Conquerors who die young over foolish pride, ignoring the needs of their bodies or driving themselves for their cause.

If you are a Warrior/Conqueror, it's to your advantage to let down your guard and cultivate humility. What you stand to win is everything for which your soul hungers: success, love, admiration and a leading role in a community of capable participants. As you continue to evolve throughout your life, you'll lose the need for an external enemy and discover the fierceness at your core. You'll be known as the chief or the queen.

In your passion, you are the great and humble leader you were born to be—someone who has no need to raise a sword.

Go to *www.thepassionprinciple.com/passiontools* to receive a free handout on the Warrior and other passion signatures.

The Story of a Warrior/Conqueror

"Big companies are all the same—they're old-boy networks. But it's all right. Those backbiting imbeciles can screw me today, but I'll screw them tomorrow. I've started a new business that I'm running inside our company with some of my staff."

Karen, an Italian American woman originally from the Bronx, was simmering and spoke in a bitter, sarcastic tone through clenched teeth. She'd come to see me for help in addressing her anger. She had a chip on her shoulder about being a woman in a male-dominated corporation. As the head of a division within a multifaceted organization, she'd done such a superb job of training the two hundred employees she managed that they had become self-reliant and were interchangeable. The people under her supervision respected her talents and authority, but her bosses had passed her over for promotion and higher earnings more than once. And it had just happened again. Somehow she kept being lined up against smooth-talking junior male colleagues who, although they were less effective in business matters, were so much better at schmoozing the company president than she was that they were leaping beyond her.

Together we explored Karen's role in the pattern she was experiencing. When I asked, "What's in your recycling bin?" she told me about her family of origin and her marriage. She was the only girl among four male siblings, and her dad openly favored her brothers and ridiculed her. Her mom was extremely submissive. Karen rejected that way of being. In adulthood, she purposefully married a man who wouldn't try to push her around. But she didn't admire him. They had four kids, so there were many household duties to be managed; however, according to Karen, he was a passive and inept mate.

"Donna, you can't count on him for anything. He says he's going to pick up the kids, but he doesn't. He says he's going to pay the bills, but he doesn't. He says he's going to take out the trash, but he doesn't. My mom and dad think he's the greatest guy in the world. In fact, everyone loves and supports my husband. But he's a loser. I'm tired of protecting him and making him look good to the world."

I asked, "Are you aware of your tone of voice and the sarcasm it communicates? It sounds to me as though you're saying that this guy is the stupidest, slimiest idiot on the planet, with no value whatsoever—nor the ability to contribute."

She said, "Really?" She had no clue of how she was coming across. I said, "I see how intelligent you are and how frustrating it must be for you, but I also see how delicate you are inside. All this roughness, gruffness and sarcasm has been put on top of that sensitivity because you were raised in an environment where you felt dominated by men and had to compete against your brothers. But you're a buttercup."

Karen got quieter and her sarcasm dropped away. "You're right," she said. "I don't feel strong and tough like I come across. I feel that nobody's hearing me. I have something to prove, and I feel like I have to fight for everything I get." Out of her historical anger at her father and brothers, she'd created a life for herself where men let her down and became her enemies, and she could never win her boss's approval. In the workplace, if she perceived someone as intelligent, cooperative and straight shooting, she was respectful and supportive. But her biting sarcasm toward those she perceived as jerks, idiots and brownnosers turned many colleagues against her.

I spoke with her about cutting out the open disregard for managers, peers, she didn't respect. As a typical Conqueror she was stabbed in the back by all the "imbeciles" for whom she had little regard as she carried her company to the goal. Ironically, in three previous companies her enemies kept their jobs long after they betrayed her, and she was fired. All too often companies are not about the bottom line. They are about turf, clicks, games and power struggles. Conquerors fall short in this arena because they are not game players. They think their hard work will carry them. Sadly, this is rarely the case.

Although Karen was like an ox, dragging the company plow across the fields to success, to climb the corporate ladder she needed to develop social abilities she lacked. Her personality had little color, and she didn't try to play the game. She felt her abilities should have spoken for her. Unfortunately for her employers, who managed her without insight into her passion, all the gifts, talents and abilities that she could have directed toward making the company grow were being funneled into her new business instead.

Karen chose a course of action with my guidance. At home she would give her husband a chance to contribute to the family's well-being. She agreed she'd lay off the sarcasm and treat him as she would an equal. In the workplace she would also monitor her biting comments. She would adjust her body language to appear less forceful and threatening, for instance sitting back in her chair, unfolding her arms and not staring intently into people's eyes. I suggested she speak in softer tones—but definitely using a real rather than a pretend voice. We explored ways she could demonstrate respect. As a result, she soon noticed much less friction in her workplace.

The Warrior/Conqueror is an interesting passion signature in a specific regard. Something in their minds tells them they don't need help because they can figure out and lick any problem on their own. They have tremendous pride and believe they have to be strong. Asking for help is a sign of weakness. This happened with Karen, even as she made modest progress forward in therapy. She decided she was "fine" and "knew what she needed to do." I wished her well, and we parted company. Their tremendously sharp minds can make Warriors feel superior to other mortals. A few years later Karen got in touch, and I learned that she had divorced her husband and remarried someone with a little more pep and had quit the corporate world entirely to pursue a private venture. She was relatively happy, she said, although she could see she still had Conqueror tendencies. I invited her to come back and do more work with me if and when she felt ready.

How to Recognize the Warrior/Conqueror

Warrior/Conquerors may look like ancient Roman gladiators. They often have strong upper bodies with barrel chests and intense eyes that seem to pierce holes through objects and people. And they've been known to tip their chins down a bit when holding eye contact, so it can seem as if you're looking at a ram in springtime about to charge. They're actually trying to push energy out of the forehead and eyes—using mental force—to influence you or pin you down. As Conquerors, their speaking tones may be loud, low, sharp, authoritative, intimidating or caustic. Whatever the case, they address others as a superior would, projecting their voices to penetrate the listener. Their choice of words is always direct and to the point. Conquerors can sound like a commander general barking orders, even when asking a beloved spouse for a cup of tea.

Warrior/Conquerors have strong intellects and are not afraid to draw conclusions. They think like they speak: at the bottom line. It's difficult for them to understand why others don't see things as clearly as they do or share their opinions. In fact, they can't believe you'd make a mistake over something so simple. And they let you know. One Conqueror said, "God, it is so hard to work with such idiots!" They think they are right, rarely change their minds and don't suffer fools gladly. If they are conversing with someone who is pussyfooting around a topic, blowing smoke up their skirt, rambling on or with whom they disagree, their irritation is evident. They may tap their fingers or flick a pen on a conference table to discharge their annoyance or shift their focus to another task. The word "multitasking" was probably invented to describe Conquerorlike behavior.

The female Conqueror presents herself as a hard-driving, masculine woman. In the workplace, she's the no-nonsense corporate executive some people would call a castrating bitch because when she tells you to jump, you are compelled to answer, "How high?" When she's unhappy with your work, she can eviscerate you with a single glance and comment. Although her words may not be a literal accusation or putdown, her tone of voice and body language are. Underneath her comments, you read her saying, "You idiot! How can you be so stupid?" She also can be a screamer and rageaholic.

Once a client of mine, an apple-polishing corporate vice president, was losing sleep at night because he couldn't figure out how to handle his Conqueror boss. Although he was willing to do what she wanted to earn her approval, she refused to clear space in her calendar to meet him and explain what that would be. She never admitted being wrong or mistaken about anything, even when she herself caused a problem. She was abrupt and aggressive and had a thundering voice. He believed she despised him. After I explained his boss's passion signature and pointed out a few opening formulas, he learned how to manage the conversations better, and she eased up on him.

In her personal life, the female Warrior/Conqueror is less accepted than she is in the workplace. Her headstrong qualities, inner drive, conviction and bluntness often keep men at a distance. The Conqueror was overwhelmed by male energy growing up, so she's afraid to be gentle and receptive. She doesn't want to let a man assume any control over her life.

Thus, she may marry a man who is passive, and later come to resent him for not carrying his part of the load. It frustrates her no end that she "has to do it all." But that doesn't stop her, because it's the right thing to do. So she raises the kids, holds a job, pays the bills and manages the house. To the world she resembles a Sherman tank. Inside she feels like a buttercup — and also deeply misunderstood.

At her best the female Warrior is a woman who radiates power, a queen. She's like a giant redwood tree that stands when everybody else has fallen. Oprah Winfrey possesses many qualities of the Warrior who has integrated her gifts. She is feminine and gentle; however, she always exudes confidence and inner strength. She speaks with authority. She supports hundreds of employees through her many businesses. On television she has generously shared her pain and struggles growing up and is a living role model of success for women and men alike. She participates in social causes across the nation and around the world, gives generously to others and conducts herself with humility. She has become an exemplary role model for women across America and even the world. She is the icon of our day.

The Warrior is recognizable by the way she walks and talks and presents herself in groups. Those who know her consider her commentary on a topic important. People naturally look to her for her opinions, approval and insights. The Warrior is the powerful church lady who serves as the matriarch for her family and community. Although she's too hard when she's the Conqueror, she's generous, compassionate and humble after she's done her inner work. Senator Hillary Clinton is a Warrior. She went through hell as the First Lady and put aside her needs for the cause — the presidency and her husband — without acting victimized. You may not agree with her choices; still you have to admire her loyalty and grit. It's characteristic for the female of this passion signature just to put one foot in front of the other, driving forward with endurance. You don't know where her inner wellspring comes from, but you can see she's tapped into her source.

Being a male Warrior/Conqueror is more acceptable in our culture than being a female of this passion signature, since power is considered an admirable trait for men. It's even an aphrodisiac to some women. The male Conqueror is the beer-drinking guy who spends hours watching sports on TV with his buddies. He may have been a football player or wrestler in high school. He's the quintessential road rager who is likely to blow away the passengers in his car with his expletives aimed at other drivers. He thinks people are absolute idiots on the road and blows a gasket when he confronts traffic jams or slow drivers or when someone cuts him off. He does a lot of things to dominate others and show his superiority. On the golf course, for instance, he may tell his partner how to swing, what club would be better to use and so on. He's impatient.

At work the Conqueror is willing to carry a heavy load for long distances. But he's brutish and pisses people off in the process. As one man put it, "I worked for a ten-million-dollar company heading fast toward bankruptcy. My job was to get things done. I worked days, nights and weekends. Whatever the company needed, I gave. Then one day, out of nowhere, they cut me. After I got fired, my best friend told me that I'd made some real enemies behind the scenes. He said, 'You don't play the game. You go for the goal. But if you run over your own guy on the way to the goal, he'll stick out his foot and trip you up the next time you run by.' I found out that I built enemies in staff meetings. I was too aggressive, and my co-workers felt I embarrassed them in front of the boss. They didn't want me around anymore, even though I saved the company."

Conquerors can be the ultimate tyrannical bosses. They lose

sight of how harshly they come across, and how difficult this makes it to communicate with them. Confronting a Conqueror can be a scary proposition, because they don't like to lose or be wrong, and cannot say they're sorry. Their pride is at stake. Until they face the emotional wounds from adolescence, it can be very unpleasant to work for them. You won't get their respect unless they determine that you deserve it within their system. They aren't gracious or subtle and have no social acumen. Instead, they are brutally headstrong. Once they set their eyes on a goal, they keep pushing everyone toward that future. It's not until much later in life that they realize they were always trudging toward a future that never came. After being in their presence, you feel as though you've been clobbered with a club or energetically zapped. That's why betrayal seems to follow the Conqueror like the plague. They put the knife in your hand to stab them in the back when you get the chance.

Conquerors see the world in terms of right and wrong, black and white. That, in combination with their anger and desire to win, can lead them to carry a principle to an extreme that's personally harmful. My cousin's mother-in-law died, and the funeral home accidentally buried her in the wrong casket. Irate and grieving, her husband decided to sue them and hired a lawyer. He was ready to go to court over a very small amount of money. He already had a lawsuit going against their neighbors and another with the phone company.

"Are the years of litigation *really* worth it?" I asked.

He replied, "It's not about the money. It's the principle of the thing."

At their best, male Warriors are wonderful providers who support both their children and employees in being able to surpass them. They stand firmly behind their wives and life partners, honoring their opinions and accomplishments as much as their own. Like the chief of a tribe, they also share their strength with everyone they know. A beloved friend of mine who recently died was a massage therapist. I laugh when I think of him toting a massage table, a backpack filled with sundries and a huge bag of sheets and towels around the streets of Manhattan. I called him my Clydesdale. On one occasion, after traveling overseas with a tour group, we arrived at the airport early in the morning. I was exhausted and thought I would drop. I was struggling with my luggage. He turned around and slung my bags over one shoulder, hauling his own on the other. I stood there aghast, unable to believe his reserves of strength. Through the years, I've found him to be an example of the best traits of the Warrior. He inspired others with his strength, his lion's heart and his ability to withstand adversity.

Warriors have a sense of camaraderie with one another. If they're not warring, they can rest in each other's presence because gut instinct informs them they're alike: no-nonsense, no lies, blunt-speaking and trustworthy. They recognize the rules of integrity. If push comes to shove, they watch each other's backs. Warriors are a tribe.

Conqueror Relationship Traps

If you are a Warrior/Conqueror, it can be hard to accept responsibility for relationship struggles. This type says, "I feel 'fine,' I'm sure I'm 'right' and I wish others would just stop being 'so sensitive.'" But experience shows that these types of thoughts are indications of not being grounded in one's expansive and integrated being. People of this passion signature are most likely to fall into three traps that limit their relationships. Do any of these seem like familiar patterns to you?

- *Et Tu, Brute? Betrayal.* You don't mean to conquer everyone and everything in your path; it's just that you get as focused on your goal as a caveman would be hunting a woolly mammoth. With spear in hand, you run full force toward the beast and stab it through the heart. Only then do you realize that, as you raced across the tundra with the rest of the hunters, some were trampled. Back at camp, a few hunters glare at you angrily, their pride deeply wounded. Dismissively you think, "Well, if they aren't strong enough to ensnare the mammoth, they should stay out of the way!" Nothing matters to you except that you are bringing home food for the entire tribe. Weeks go by. When a lion pounces on you, the other hunters do nothing. You are eaten alive.

In counseling, one Conqueror told me, "In my marriage, I never worried about the intimacy between my wife and me; instead, I worried about winning arguments at all costs. Now I can see that I pushed her away." Our conversation had started because he couldn't figure out why his wife didn't want to get close to him anymore.

Betrayal may come from loved ones, close friends or coworkers. Yet you remain unaware of, or don't care to understand, how you make enemies. You don't pick up on the fact that you come across as dominating, arrogant, controlling and conceited. Nor do you see how you overpower those around you. Nonetheless, your behavior causes others to feel oppressed, jealous, angry and aggressive. People turn against you because you ask for it.

- *You Are My Conquest.* Do you prefer beginning a relationship to staying in one? Do you regularly toss your romantic partners aside as though they're wishbones off a turkey? If so, you probably view people as sexual conquests. Like a climber who thrills on the adventure of scaling a mountain, seduction is a peak experience for you. Getting someone into bed gives you an incredible high. It means you've won the day and proven your worth. You've arrived at your destination—the summit. But your elation is temporary, and it is soon followed by a sense of deflation. Even as you celebrate your victory and potency, the excitement of new love begins to fade, and you lose interest. You feel motivated to move on and go after a new challenge.

Business deals are like sexual conquests to you. A commercial real estate mogul worth more than five hundred million dollars said, "I don't have time to take off, as I've got to build my business. Hell, my wife shouldn't complain. She lives the high life."

I asked him to stop a minute and listen to what he was saying. "You already have more money than you can spend. You're fifty-two and never see your three sons. What business is there to build? You drink every day to relieve stress, your marriage is a shambles and you have ulcers. At this rate, you'll only be alive a few more years anyway."

He paused, took a breath and replied, "You're right." But he only showed up for one more session, claiming that he didn't need the help.

Although you show loads of bravado, since you don't truly value yourself you do not realize how attractive you are. There's an internal split between your ability to love and your sexuality. You thrive on the validation of multiple love interests. But once a potential mate or romantic interest connects with you, or is yearning for your attention, you perceive that individual as "weak" or a "loser." Something must be wrong with this person if he or she loves you. You don't let anyone get to your heart because you see needing someone as a weakness. You have an idealized mate, someone "much better," whom you project meeting in the future. You spend your life charging toward a future that never comes.

- *No Time, Too Busy. I'll Try to Fit You In.* You are the classic type-A workaholic who not only works seventy-hour weeks but also donates free time to several charitable, religious or political organizations. After all, it's good for business to sit on more than one board of directors, right? You've always got a new deal cooking on the back burner. "Just this next project," you promise your spouse, "and then we'll get away." When you finally do go on a vacation, you bring along your paperwork and make sure your colleagues can reach you by telephone. Your family only tolerates this because, frankly, they don't know how to restrain you. They can't compete.

Everyone knows you have a tendency to overcommit and overdo. You may be the only one who doesn't see how problematic it is.

My dad was a Conqueror. When he got home from work, he took the stress of his day out on anybody who got in his way, including the family cats. We kids laid low when he came home and tolerated him until morning, when he went out chasing success again. On what he didn't realize was the last night of his life, while he waited to go to the hospital where he was scheduled to have open-heart surgery, he told me, "Donna, I wish I had slowed down, been there more, spent time with you kids. I don't think I did anything for you."

Unless you lighten your schedule, you'll miss out, like my dad did, on having healthy relationships with the people you love and befriend.

Warrior Opening and Closing Strategies

If you care about a Warrior/Conqueror, it's helpful to keep sight of the fact that this is a tenderhearted person who only has a hard outer shell. The Warrior longs for the day someone will be wise enough to see the truth and brave enough to pass through the barrier. Inside there's a Lover who is hungry for gentle nurturing. The Warrior longs to lay down the sword and rest in the arms of someone trustworthy. Approaching Warriors with consistent tenderness makes it safe for them to drop their guards and let their softer sides emerge so they can receive, as well as give, love.

Conquerors have trouble allowing others to contribute to their well-being. They are more comfortable generating ideas, pursuing activities and giving to others than they are resting, listening and receiving affection and support. Once when another friend was kindly offering my Warrior friend Pat some much-needed advice, she went into her Conqueror mode. She wanted to shut him down and destroy him, as she suddenly felt dumb and inadequate. He was only talking to her. If you see this happening when you're conversing with a Warrior, for instance hearing the voice get louder and condescending and seeing the eyes get fierce and the chin drop, understand that the person in front of you is wrestling with resistance to being controlled and self-doubt. A Conqueror's terrible fear of not being good enough makes that person resistant to letting you think you know more.

Phrases that are opening formulas honor the Warrior/ Conqueror's intelligence and ability, such as, "You're so smart about/so good at . . ." or "What if . . .?" Rather than *telling* the Warrior/Conqueror what to do, posing a suggestion as a question keeps his or her mind open. Phrases that are closing formulas include, "You need help," "You look like you're having a problem" and "You're wrong about . . ." Avoid competing over who is *right*.

Particularly if a Conqueror is in an aggressive mood, act passive. Stand back at a distance, and don't look him or her in the eye continuously. (Consider how you'd handle a wild dog.) Soften your voice. Do not engage in arguments or make sudden movements. Remain calm and steady. I had a disagreement once with my Warrior/Conqueror acting coach. She basically told me, "It's my way or the highway!" Even though she hadn't changed my mind, I brought her a lollypop and said, "I thought about your point of view, and I can *understand* it." She became my most loyal advocate. Her bark was worse than her bite.

When the Warrior/Conqueror is venting rage, don't resist it. Never tell a Conqueror—or for that matter anyone in your life—to calm down. That is an accidental anger escalator. Also never tell the Conqueror that he or she is "making too big a deal of it" or ignore him or her. These will escalate the Conqueror to do more to get your attention. Instead, say, "I can see how you feel that way." Try light humor or tell him or her that the anger is sexy. Your admiration can "accidentally" diffuse the Warrior.

Of course, if you fear a Warrior may get violent, remove yourself from this person's presence until he or she cools down.

When you sense the Warrior/Conqueror slipping into an aggressive mode, for instance using harsh words or an abrasive tone of voice, you might just lean back on one heel and lightly say, "Easy." Or find another calm signal to remind the Warrior/Conqueror compassionately that you feel him or her, and the force of his or her passion is threatening to overwhelm your connection. If you communicate judgment, the Warrior/Conqueror may interpret it as betrayal and close down.

Affirming a female Warrior/Conqueror's femininity can shift her from being puffed up like a thorny blowfish to being soft and girlish in an instant. Like letting the air out of a balloon, a compliment helps her shrink to her real "size." She loves being seen and accepted just as she is. With your help, she feels safe and confident and can move back into flow with you. She respects the man who isn't scared away by her intimidation tactics, but actually *likes* them. Keep in mind that she originally put on the blustering voice and pushy energy because she felt threatened by male energy during puberty. But inside she is still the delicate girl she once was, and she will love you even more than she already does for helping her find this authentic self she left behind. Think of her as a butterfly hiding out in a walnut shell.

One CEO sat with me and lacerated her husband and her inadequate management staff. I said, "Beth, it must be difficult to be so intelligent and yet feel you have to be so tough in these environments because no one else will carry the ball if you don't. I can see that underneath you are quite sensitive, and you have a tender heart. I know you want someone to see through all this and lift the burden from your shoulders." Her eyes softened and became tearful. I continued, "You've got to show these people your softness and stop attacking them for what you see as their weaknesses. Right now they are afraid of you. They are afraid to make a mistake, so they become even weaker and more needy in your presence." She committed to try this. Her world responded to her new openness with all the support she ever needed.

Affirming a male Warrior's masculinity also helps him relax and feel confident. He's a rooster crowing at daybreak. More than anything, contributing to the good of the whole motivates this type of person. But he may need feedback to remember. If you honor the Warrior for his contribution to your life or cause and tell him that you respect his passion, he'll view you as an ally. Although he may not be the guy you are going to sit down and have a long chat with after dinner, you can trust him with your life. He will watch your back and be loyal to the end. Make sure you keep your word, because his word is as good as gold. Betrayal is the worst thing you can do to a Warrior/Conqueror.

Warriors value honesty, forthright communication and loyalty. If you sense an air about them of, "What can I do for you?
I'm in a hurry," get to your point. Warriors can't stand to be
told long stories. And don't take their sense of urgency and
tone of voice personally—it's not about you. When you need
their attention, an opening formula is to make it clear what you
want and show them how it could be a win-win solution.
Warriors love the winning feeling. So state your piece, and
then let them mull it over.

Another excellent formula to open the Warrior is humor—
clean humor, nothing caustic or debasing. When Warriors are
entertained, they belly laugh with gusto. Humor moves them
out of their heads and into their hearts, and they'll love you for
this gift. Since Warriors intimidate a lot of people, they respect
those who can hold their own in their presence. Use sensitivity
and tenderness with them, and they'll melt like butter on a
warm summer day. They hate weakness and neediness and will
get aggressive toward you to knock that out of you. If they perceive inner strength and outer availability, that's a real turn-on.
They don't like people who don't follow through. You may
think they are angry with you when they are just trying to
make a point. Their passion may sound like they are yelling at
you. Ask them if they are angry, and let them know it sounds
like they are angry with you. Stand your ground and honor
their passion, and they'll remain in open connection with you.

Transforming Your Destructive Patterns

If you are the Warrior, you can open yourself to others by
transforming your Conqueror tendencies. Consider the following methods.

- *Get off the Hamster Wheel of Achievement.* A Conqueror
  arrived forty-five minutes late to our appointment with an

ashen face. He was a large man with a prominent jaw, very rugged looking. "Sorry," he said, "I had a little problem. I couldn't breathe."

"What are you doing here if you can't breathe?" I asked.

"Oh, I didn't want to let you down."

Warriors are always pushing. Your tendency is to work until you keel over, and if you stop, you feel guilty. Rest is for sissies, right? Well, consider what happened to another Conqueror, fifty-year-old Gene. They found him lying across his treadmill where he had been jogging, having died of a heart attack. Earlier that day, he told a friend he was having chest pains. When the friend said, "Go to the doctor," Gene replied, "Nah, I don't need to." Like most Warriors, he tried to override his body. That's because Warriors believe in mind over matter. But you must understand that workaholism and continuous force put enormous stress on the body. It makes people old before their time and can kill them. Warriors often die a sudden death: stroke and heart attack. They also will have bleeding ulcers. It's as if they are burning themselves from the inside.

If you are a Warrior and tend to ignore your body's needs, you must cut back on your schedule. Mark out leisure time and vacations in your calendar. Do not allow yourself to work on Saturdays and Sundays. Turn your computer or TV off when your family is around. You don't need to watch every single sporting event. And consider cutting back on your consumption of alcohol. You probably use it to relax. Listen to family and friends who tell you that you need to take a break. Do not override them by telling them how much work you have to do instead. Remember, you are the type of person who races toward a future you won't be alive to enjoy. Stop. You are meant, and have the constitution, to live a long life.

Instead, try nonachievement-oriented activities that

calm your mind and relax your body, such as fishing, yoga and walking on a beach or in a park. Learn to still your mind through meditation or contemplation. Also ask yourself some personal questions, particularly when you notice that you're pushing hard toward a goal or you've set an unreasonable deadline. Step back and put your task into a new framework: If I don't get this accomplished by Friday, will I care at the end of my life? Is it really so important? If you answer no, stop pushing so hard. Take a breather.

- *Soften and Pull Your Energy Down.* You normally look like a bull moose in springtime ready to charge. Your eyes are intense. Your elbows are on the table. Your forehead is forward. Instead, sit back in your chair. Cross your legs. Put your arms in your lap—uncrossed. Imagine that everything you've been pushing out, you're now going to pull back and send downward into the ground. Speak to, rather than push at, people when you're conversing. Know that you're enough.

  Make an internal decision to "soften." This is important for women, but useful for men, too. Warriors never need to worry about strength. That's an innate quality. When a female Warrior feels she's become soft "enough," in fact she's only beginning her journey to renew her femininity. Here's a perfect example of the results. Over months of consciously working on myself to become softer, several men came up to me and said, "Donna, you look great. You've lost weight!" But I knew I hadn't lost a pound. They felt my approachability now that I'd dropped my outer layers. One of the ways I softened was taking "hot" yoga classes several times a week—it penetrated my physical and energetic armoring.

- *Demonstrate Respect.* You probably are the smartest man or woman in the room. You see how things should be said and done that others don't seem to see. You have great gut instincts and can shoot verbal arrows that knock the apples off people's heads. But if you do, the apple polishers you've outdone will hate you for it. Remember that you can create situations where you get stabbed in the back because of your lack of deference and respect for other people.

If you don't like what George says in a staff meeting, don't roll your eyes and say, "That won't work," (with the subtext that he's an idiot evident in your tone) or snort in contempt or look to the side. Don't tap your pencil while others talk, pace around the room or read paperwork while someone is talking to you. At least aim to appear that you are giving others the respect of your focus. Also take a beat before answering a question. Warriors frequently make up their minds before others are through speaking, then raise their voices and interrupt.

Since Warrior/Conquerers think they are right and don't want to lose—they're competitive—their Achilles' heel is to lose sight of the big picture. They go in for the kill. The solution is to get softer and push less. Slow down. Receive. Recognize that people are not "trying" to be idiots; they just don't see the world the same way you do. Remember not to take everything so seriously. We are all like kids in a sandbox who want to be seen and heard. If you sit back, breathe, cross your legs, give your attention to those around the room and take it easy, you will be surprised how much respect you muster in the long run. You just may be the person everyone turns to at the end to ask, "So what do you think?" If you demonstrate respect, you'll be honored for your wisdom and followed like a chief, because you have the clear sight of an eagle.

- *Lay Down Your Sword.* It's to your benefit to learn how to settle conflicts peacefully. Emotional interactions and disagreements do not have to be win-lose. They can be resolved so they are win-win. But your stubborn pride may get in the way. You've got rules about behavior, and your habit is to think, "I'm right, and you're wrong." Conquerors normally pick an enemy and go after that person. They seek an enemy to fight; otherwise there would be no conquest. Now you need to learn to find the gray areas in disagreements.

You need to stop picking fights and stop being a bully. If you have been in several lawsuits or have an emotional graveyard filled with old loves, friendships and jobs you killed off, this advice is for you. Your anger will ultimately result in isolation and poor health. Your soul work is to learn to forgive, apologize and let things go.

Forgiveness is not "losing." Forgiveness means you accept reality and accept people as they are. When you forgive, you free yourself of having to continually fight the past. It does not deter justice, and it does not mean you have to reconcile with someone who has hurt you. It enables you to move on.

An apology is not "losing." It means you take responsibility for the impact of your words and deeds on other people. It is childish to believe that it's only our intention that matters. Even when we mean no harm, sometimes people are hurt. When we apologize, we mend the hurt we cause and show maturity. It helps other people to move on in their lives and reopens the flow of connection with them.

Letting go of a thought or feeling is a decision. Once you decide to let go, you may have to reinforce the decision actively with gentle reminders to yourself. But it is done. Unless you go back and stir yourself up again, you can be free. This will lessen your stress and enable you to approach life and relationships freshly.

CHAPTER 5

ᛏHE VISIONARY/PERFECTIONIST

ᛏf you are the Visionary, you are passionate about excellence. You live your life with a sense of purpose. Ideals
always pull you forward toward higher evolution of your
goals and the perfection of your being and everything you
touch. You have the capacity to imagine an ideal, as well as the
discipline to manifest it in form. Everyone around you recognizes your total commitment and absolute integrity. You
understand how to inspire others to do their best, achieve
more and expand their minds. Because you have amazing
charm and finesse and always pay close attention to detail, you
can make a great boss or subordinate on the job. You are goal-
oriented, punctual and tidy. You honor your word by doing

what you say you're going to do—and on schedule. Your noble qualities also make you a wonderful romantic partner, parent and friend. As your operating style is assertive and proactive, you have considerable "stick-to-itiveness." You're able to delay gratification in pursuit of your long-term objectives, and you have the willingness to complete even the most tedious tasks when the outcome seems worthwhile. You work most effectively within rule-based organizations and systems. People and businesses thrive under your guidance and encouragement, as you lead them toward the highest ground. You are an innovator of ideas and solutions that positively transform the world.

Your shadow side is the Perfectionist, a wounded fragment of your greater being that has low self-esteem and overcompensates through self-obsession. As the Perfectionist, you are fixated on your appearance and how your behavior comes across. It's all about looking good. Everything you do is to gain validation for your mask. Whether it's donating to a cause or being on a board of directors, you're not actually giving for the sake of giving. You are giving to be seen a certain way. You are desperate to create a perfect facade, as you *need* people to be impressed. *What can I do to hide my flaws?* you wonder and worry. Since it feels critical to you that no one figures out how "ordinary" you are, you go to extraordinary lengths to hide your so-called imperfections. This starts with your physical body. You might be a size 2 woman or a man with six-pack abs. You will twist like a pretzel and jump through hoops for small confirmations of your worth. Your daily routine is likely to include—other than being best dressed, of course—gym time, lean chicken, green tea and salad (hold the dressing).

As the Perfectionist, your sexuality is based on looking good for other people's focus, meaning you also *must* have a "perfect" partner—a piece of arm candy. Of course, no one can measure up to your inflexible standards. Even models remove their makeup at bedtime, and muscle-bound athletes sometimes catch head colds. Sadly, at your worst you put so much energy into defending an ideal image that you rarely allow true intimacy to blossom. You live as your mask, and you don't have much contact with your core essence, so you can't share true, long-term intimacy. Instead, you have shallow relationships with superficial people.

Emotionally, you're such a reined-in person that you may be choking your own life force to death. "Think positive," and "It's all good," are two of your favorite mottos. Negativity is a no-no. You are a Dale Carnegie, Stephen Covey and Anthony Robbins superstar. In addition, your personal high standards make you intolerant of other people's behavior. If you can be on time for every appointment, why can't they? To you, being late shows disrespect. Similarly, since you're able to follow restrictive eating programs impeccably, you don't understand why the rest of the world just can't get it together.

Relationships with Visionaries can be exquisite, surprising and pleasurable. At their best, Visionaries are high-energy individuals who manage their lives with artistic flair and grace. Everything they do, they aim to do well. If a Visionary cooks for you, you'll receive a nutritious, delicious and elegantly presented meal. If a Visionary makes love to you, your toes will curl and your satisfaction is guaranteed. If you vacation with a Visionary, the itinerary will be planned in minute detail so you can rest and enjoy. If you hire a Visionary accountant or lawyer, you can be assured of quality service — down to the last penny. No stone will be left unturned on your behalf. Every *i* will be dotted and every *t* crossed. However, when Visionaries feel underappreciated or run up against too much opposition, their Perfectionist tendencies are likely to rise to the surface. Then you're in for trouble, as they can just as easily pour their energy into defeating you.

Perfectionists can nitpick you until you want to scream. They are hypercritical, fussy and relentlessly infallible. Their lives are run according to such tight schedules that it doesn't feel like there's any room to fit in or, if you're "in," to breathe. They expect you to mind read their specific rules and accommodate their standards and foibles. They insist on being correct, and must have the last word in every argument.

Giving love and affection to Perfectionists can be tough, because it's not easy for them to receive. If you give a gift to a Perfectionist, you'll likely feel that it was unwelcome or inappropriate. What's going on under the surface is that Perfectionists feel your gift has to be equaled by as good or better a gift from them. Only receiving might mean that you believe they're "needy" or "dependent." Those are insulting, dirty words to such folks. Perfectionists are motivated to be superior. You may find yourself advising Perfectionist friends to "live a little" or take a "walk on the wild side." But it's unlikely, unless they can be wild where no one can see them.

Like the Warrior, the Visionary passion signature develops during the teen years. It is a defensive layer built on top of earlier ones. The Visionary-Lover is a common Combo Platter. Of all people, these may be the most exceptional nurturers when they've done their healing work. Likewise, a person who embodies the Visionary-Creator Combo Platter has an ability to produce and make forward progress that a pure Creator might not. Such people are highly creative individuals whose efforts can sustain entire communities. By the way, Combo Platter Visionaries might not fit the physical profile. They can be out of shape, yet use qualities of this passion signature to run aspects of their lives. Remember, every passion signature has specific gifts. To survive different challenges growing up, we develop multiple sets of skills to help us function as best as we can. We adapt.

Visionary/Perfectionists often grow up in homes where there are dark secrets. They know that something is wrong that must be hidden, such as alcoholism or drug addiction, a bitter divorce, sexual abuse, an emotionally disturbed or physically ill parent, slovenly, chaotic conditions or extreme poverty. The teen assumes responsibility for closeting the family issue so that public humiliation or another consequence, such as the family splitting up, won't occur. The teen believes that if he or she can figure out the "rules" and follow them to the letter, then everything should be "okay." There's such a desire to conform that these youths tend to mature too quickly. They are good boys and good girls who toe the line for adults. They learn to compartmentalize the "bad" and the "good" to keep things orderly. Sometimes Visionary/Perfectionists are the children of other Visionary/Perfectionists, parents who raise them with so much emphasis on fitting in or looking good to sustain the family image that the children lose connection to the truth of who they are at the core.

There's a sense of desperation in Perfectionist teens' need for approval and their struggle to create an ideal world. It disallows human flaws and idiosyncrasies. In a culture riddled with popular images of hard-bodied music idols, models that look like prepubescent boys and athletes pumped up on steroids, teens have plenty of images of so-called perfection to imitate. Although, as dependent children, they are powerless to control the world, they soon decide that they'll control their bodies. Because they believe they should have been able to fix the home environment, but couldn't, they feel shame. Inside they feel they're "bad," "wrong" or "flawed." Outside they project an ideal.

If you are the Visionary, you possess the kind of intelligence that enables you to assimilate information, synthesize it, and present it in a simplified form that other people can understand and use to good advantage. As we live in a chaotic world, this ability makes you enormously valuable. You have the potential to be an innovator of ideas and systems—a trendsetter. However, you may be trapped in a pattern of rigid adherence to old systems and beliefs. This tendency limits your freedom.

Flexibility, self-acceptance and the willingness to admit your fears, failings and feelings are the keys to your personal growth. As soon as you surrender to the flow of life, develop tolerance for nonconformity, and learn to value and receive the gifts that others have to offer, your relationships will deepen and your life become richer.

Go to *www.thepassionprinciple.com/passiontools* to receive a free handout on the Visionary and other passion signatures.

The Story of a Visionary/Perfectionist Couple

Audrey came to see me for counseling when she was grieving over the recent breakup of a six-month relationship. Although she was American, her ex-boyfriend Sam was Japanese, and hadn't planned to stay permanently in the United States. Now he was using this as an excuse to keep his distance from her. But the more she told me about him, the more evident it was that she truly loved him, and also that their defensive patterns had locked. I'd seen the phenomenon many times before. Both were Visionaries whose Perfectionist streaks were activated by getting close in a romantic relationship. As they put up masks to shield their emotional insecurity, they froze each other out and their connection gradually perished. On Audrey's part, however, embers of feeling for Sam were still aglow in her heart. She told me sadly, "I wanted to get engaged. He didn't."

"You know what?" I replied. "You only have one life to live. You need to put this relationship to bed so that a decade from now you're not still dwelling on it and regretting that you gave it up without doing enough to salvage it. It's common for me to hear older clients say—twenty years down the road—that they loved their first spouse or someone early in life and now they realize it only was fear and some limiting behavior pattern that got in the way. It's three relationships later, and they wish they'd stayed together.

"It would require an act of courage, Audrey, but if you believe that you can deal with the possibility that Sam might never call you back or could ask you to leave him alone, then consider phoning to explore a reconciliation. Accept that you're having these feelings, and trust that it's good for you to go after whatever you want. No matter what the outcome is, at the very least you won't have to live with regret."

Audrey bravely called Sam. It turned out he was having the same feelings. They decided to come in together for couple's counseling as well as doing individual therapy.

It wasn't a smooth ride. Over a period of time, the relationship had many stops and starts. Sam revisited his decision to immigrate.The couple broke up and reunited on a few occasions. Mostly the process was about me guiding each of them deeper inside and then helping them to share the real self with the other. Gradually the relationship intensified and became more fulfilling.

In her sessions, Audrey focused on how she could expand her world so that she was not exclusively relying on Sam for her happiness. Her core fear was that she was not lovable. "I'm discovering how inadequate and insecure I feel," she told me.

"Have you told him that?" I asked.

"No."

"Why don't you try telling him in a simple way."

When Audrey shared her feelings, it brought Sam closer to her. He said, "Honey, I didn't realize," and from then on made a point of complimenting her more.

When I spoke to Sam, he told me he only wanted to share happy stories with Audrey because the other stuff in his life might depress her. Before they met, he'd had a high-paying job, but then he got demoted. This posed a huge challenge to his sense of self-worth. His core fear was that she wouldn't think he was valuable.

Sam told me, "I'm interested in having intimate relationships in my life, but I haven't spent a lot of time with my emotions. I'm numb, and I don't know how to share my inner self with Audrey. I'm great at details and duties and doing the right thing, but I just don't know how to connect."

Unmarried Perfectionists often fixate on the image of a perfect mate, so anyone in the flesh turns out to be a disappointment. I told Sam about another client, a man whom I'll call Fred, then fifty-two years old. Fred never married, although he'd participated in a series of short-term relationships in his twenties and thirties. No woman ever measured up. Now worth millions, he was lonely and desperate to find Ms. Right. Life was passing, yet he didn't have a clue as to how to live in the present moment, get "real," share his feelings and cultivate true intimacy. As Fred once reflected, "I met a nice woman the other day, but she has too much baggage. It seems all women have baggage—either kids or personal problems. As always, I got out before she tried to attach to me and it was too late. I try not to get too emotional and generally avoid sex. Otherwise, women get attached."

"Sam," I said, "Up 'til now, in my view, you've been going down the same path as Fred. The fact that you and Audrey connect with each other so well and have love is not something to take for granted or trade casually for public validation." He heard me and later would refer back to those comments as a personal turning point.

Sam and Audrey started taking walks together and having long conversations about their experiences and feelings. They began to be truthful with each about their hopes and fears, their ideas and revelations, and as a result, they fell even more deeply in love. Within a few years, they were happily married with children.

How to Recognize the Visionary/Perfectionist

As adults, Visionary/Perfectionists can be recognized most easily by the superb condition of their bodies. They are usually slender with toned muscles and extremely health conscious. Generally, they count every calorie they eat. They're the classic fat-phobic "gym rats" who train fanatically, even during illness and through injury. A Perfectionist friend of mine once mentioned, "I go to the gym every night after work. I spend about an hour, sometimes longer, on the treadmill. I've been working with a personal trainer. But I am very frustrated that my knee is hurting me because I want to do more."

Lance Armstrong, the champion bicyclist who led his team to victory in the Tour de France for a record-breaking seven years in a row, is an example of this passion signature at its best. After beating the odds and surviving testicular cancer, he then designed a training regimen so specific that his body still responds like a finely tuned instrument to his commands. He uses his sense of purpose and success to inspire others. Through his books, public appearances and a private foundation, he assists cancer patients and their families to face their challenges and is a role model of dedication and enthusiasm for the world. Montel Williams is another such person. Despite his grueling schedule, he has made time to take care of his fitness and overcome tremendous personal health challenges. His personal journey inspires others.

Visionary/Perfectionists set the standards of perfection for the rest of us. They are the kind of successful people who always wear the right smile covered over by the right veneers put on by the right dentist. They have the right suit, the right waistline, the right manicure, the right makeup, the right shoes and the right purse—and everything is color coordinated. They always hire the right experts for assistance. They have a personal trainer, if they can afford it, and a life coach. They buy the latest bestselling book on health or diet, and they're the ones who follow it. The rest of the population buy the book, start the program on Monday morning, and by 3 P.M. they're cheating. By Wednesday most people give up. Visionaries follow the rules.

In the extreme, the Perfectionist is the control freak who overdoes everything in the quest for excellence and drives everyone else crazy in the process. Perfectionists have an infatuation with themselves that excludes other people, and they sometimes pursue their own gratification and ambitions ruthlessly. As narcissists, Perfectionists exhibit exaggerated confidence and self-esteem. These all-consumed idealists have trouble leaving well enough alone and often drive a wedge between themselves and others because it's so hard for regular mortals to measure up. You've noticed people like this watching their reflections in shop windows as they walk down the street or posturing in front of the mirror at the gym as they do bicep curls. Step out of the way! And for God's sake, don't criticize this person in front of the boss unless you are a glutton for punishment. That score will be settled in public view, and you won't come out of it untarnished.

Perfectionists need to appear perfect and beautiful at any cost. Their complete value is attached to the outside—the mask—and they have no connection to their inner being. This makes them slaves to other people's opinions about their behavior. They can deprive themselves of an opportunity or relationship that is absolutely right for them because of what other people have said about it or how it *might* be judged. They'll even stay in a hostile or loveless marriage if they believe a divorce would threaten their image.

The woman who believes she is supposed to have it all, do it all and be it all is a Perfectionist. She's the supermom who holds a job, coaches her kids' soccer team, supervises the ladies' auxiliary at church, prepares gourmet dinners and still manages to keep an immaculate house. She vacuums her closets and dusts on top of her door frames. She even knows how to fold fitted sheets so they're flat, as if they just came out of the original package. She throws parties that could inspire Martha Stewart's envy. Although she's given birth three times, she's got a tight body. That's because she gets up at 5 A.M. to work out.

The pop star Madonna is an example of a female Visionary/Perfectionist. Consider the women you know who are in their mid to late forties. In fact, consider the women you know in their twenties. I bet none has a body that's as rock hard as hers. She is highly successful and supremely fit for the same reason: She's got discipline. Anytime you see someone who can reinvent her appearance and redefine standards of beauty or of a profession for the rest to follow, you know you're witnessing a Visionary/Perfectionist. This person has the imagination and inner drive to break out of the usual boxes.

Perfectionist women in our culture are susceptible to the abuse of plastic surgery. Men don't yet turn to surgery as often as women do, although rates are increasing. Plastic surgery is not wrong per se; however, it can become a form of self-mutilation to keep going back for multiple face and buttock lifts, breast implants, liposuction, collagen lips and Botox injections. When I hear a woman mention her plastic surgery, I always suspect that she may attribute too much of her worth to her appearance. Underneath the mask, she may feel enormously insecure and lack knowledge of her authentic value.

The male Perfectionist is the high achiever who scorns those who are not up to his standards. He's Mr. Clean at home and in the office. Do you remember Felix Unger from *The Odd Couple*? That's him. He stands perfectly erect, has a fit physique and possesses the smoothest personality in the world. He generally knows how to say and do the right thing. But he does not allow in any so-called negative feelings. Emotions like sadness or anger make him feel too vulnerable to tolerate. They might impede accomplishment or mar an otherwise spotless reputation. That's forbidden territory for this fellow.

At a fund raiser for a fine arts museum, I met an affluent Visionary man and his wife. He was sixty, but looked a good decade younger: slender and fit. I shared a few details about the passion signatures with them, and his wife became animated. "That's him!" she exclaimed. "He exercises and eats fanatically. Everything within a hundred-foot radius is organized. In fact, my husband is so attentive to detail that he even keeps index cards in the pocket on the door of our SUV so he can take notes when he's driving. He also *really* knows how to talk to people. That's a main reason he's done so well in real estate."

Perfectionists have a tendency to tell you how to think and feel. They are the positive reframe masters, seeing through the proverbial rose-colored glasses. Like supermen covered in Teflon shields, Perfectionists put a positive spin on anything you say to them. They cut you off by not allowing you space for your real feelings and experiences in the moment. Visionaries, however, have the ability to open your mind about the topic at hand.

Visionary/Perfectionists are very good at handling anything that has to do with form, function and structure. They assert themselves through practical measures. Here's an example of what I mean. At a conference, I attended a seminar along with numerous high-functioning businesspeople. To explore the different ways that people collaborate, we were broken into smaller groups by the facilitator and asked to complete an exercise. Our task was to put a series of pictures in a row based on their connections to each other. A woman seated to my left jumped in immediately, as did two men across from me. All three were Perfectionists. Being more of a Creator-Warrior myself, I was content to sit back and watch, comfortable to let them handle the details.

On entering a room, Perfectionists scan it for space. They live in tidy homes decorated with minimal furnishings. Books may be shelved alphabetically, in categories, or both. Their closets and dressers are well organized with special storage pockets, racks and bins for shoes, sweaters, pants, shirts, suits and dresses. When they clean, they don't just dust, they disinfect. The chrome in the kitchen and bathroom glistens. At day's end their desks are immaculate. Paperwork has its place, as do office supplies and reading matter. Their invoices are filed and bills paid on schedule or ahead of time.

If you would like to discuss an idea or an opportunity with someone to determine its viability, Visionaries are the ideal people to seek out. Visionaries can open your mind to new and greater possibilities and perspectives. What is the next and highest level of expansion? What are the steps to reach a goal? Visionaries are list makers extraordinaire. They do planning for themselves, and they can do it for us, too. We need them.

At their best, Visionaries of both genders make exceptional parents, spouses, friends and professionals. They can see the highest potential in everyone and every situation, and they can figure out the cleanest, most direct line to a goal or destination. Their enviable social grace and diplomacy enable them to communicate a vision of the possibilities to the people around them and establish a group consensus, and furthermore, they know how to set up the supporting structures that can help others stay on course. Healed Visionaries, those who've integrated their gifts and let the narcissism drop away, are fun to be around. They're team leaders who help everyone achieve excellence.

Perfectionist Relationship Traps

If you're a Visionary, you are a highly refined, well-functioning person, so it can be hard to distinguish a line between what's working and what's not working in your favor. The key is to notice where you are restricting opportunities and adhering to a narrow vision. Seek expansion and flexibility. There are three main ways that you impede the flow of connection in relationships with family, friends, coworkers and lovers.

- *You Have to Make Me Look Good.* Have you ever watched any of those so-called reality dating shows on television? I caught an episode of one in which a clearly Perfectionist bachelor was given a choice of twenty-five beautiful women as potential wives. He told the interviewer he wanted "the total package." To please him, his mate needed to look sophisticated and dress like a cover model. He wanted her to be intelligent and speak well. On dates he seemed to enjoy being worshipped by the women, but distrusted those who worshipped him too much. Conversations with his dates were shallow and mundane—frighteningly so, considering he might spend the rest of his life with one of them! He cut every woman from the competition who was outside the stereotypical box in any way. Essentially, his decisions seemed to center on appearances: Would his wife make him look good when she was on his arm?

    If this sounds familiar, I've got news for you: There's

more to life than looks. Yes, we all want to be physically attracted to our lovers and spouses. Good chemistry is important, and it's exhilarating. However, we are beings of mind, body and spirit, and until you embrace each of those elements in yourself and in your partner, you're not going have the exquisite life of your dreams. The most painful Perfectionist relationship pattern is getting together with intimates you choose solely based on looks and "sex appeal." When it gets real, Perfectionists are not prepared. Freedom and passion are limitless and expanding, so when you rivet your attention on a particular ideal or expectation, that's all you ever get. You won't get the potential "more." People won't feel safe enough with you to reveal the treasures that are available inside them.

The same thing happens with children. Perfectionist parents want their offspring to look good, succeed in school and then the workplace, and be a positive reflection of their values. They are not as concerned with whether or not their children are enjoying themselves or having fresh and original experiences. It can be tough for children who want to please their parents to feel they can't measure up. The older kids get, the more they'll keep a distance and reserve what's sacred in them for someone else.

The essential ingredient of successful relationships is whether you enjoy the inner qualities of people. Are they fun to talk to, share your life with, deepen and grow with, and laugh with? I see human beings as mansions with many rooms. To have good relationships you must be able to get to another person's core and share your core with someone. If you spend all your time at the gym and never explore your other dimensions—the many rooms inside you—by having different experiences, you'll only have limited access. You'll never know your true depth of being, and so you won't be able to share it with someone. When you do this exploration, you'll discover that some of those rooms are messy, and you may feel uncomfortable investigating them. But the outcome is continued growth and an expanding ability to be intimate.

• *Let's Be Positive.* On the job, as well as with friends and loved ones, you are a perennial optimist. No negative feelings, thank you very much. In fact, you can manufacture positive feelings better than anybody. Being around you is like living in a "rah-rah" camp. You are a one-man cheerleading squad: YAY! GO TEAM! People frequently appreciate this approach when they're striving for their goals; however, it shuts down intimacy when you deny the reality of their most vulnerable emotions.

There are occasions when life is sad or difficult. At such times, I have seen Perfectionists strangle back their true emotions so they can get out phrases like, "You're going to make it through. This is the bottom, and it can only get better." They seem afraid that they will fall apart if anyone else shows vulnerability. As a Perfectionist you do what's right and are a good person, but when others need to feel, you try to stop them. This can put a damper on relationships. If you expect people to fake it, they'll avoid you. Ultimately you can't have emotional depth or intimacy without feelings. Feelings are how we experience life. If you spend too much time manufacturing feelings, you will lose out on the original moments of life.

• *Picky, Picky, Picky.* You're so picky about the way things are done that you create situations where nobody wants to help you. For instance, a client told me how he helped a Perfectionist pal move into a new apartment. Due to his friend's past generosity, my client was glad to be at his service. But the friend was so controlling my client couldn't move an inch without his direction. His friend hovered nearby as he unloaded boxes in the kitchen, saying, "Don't do this, don't do that." Every chore was accomplished under pressure. The message the friend communicated was that my client couldn't do *anything* right and just wasn't good *enough*. After a few hours, my client exploded with anger.

One time I was waiting for my order to be filled at a crowded coffee bar. The young woman making drinks behind the counter seemed to be in charge of training new coworkers. Mistakes were rampant. But in spite of the long line of customers—or because of it—she refused simply to correct the problems and instead announced them to the store at the top of her lungs so she wouldn't look bad. "Jim, you wrote this order down wrong!" Now fifteen people can see poor Jim is inept, and he's red-faced. The next drink is ordered, and she loudly corrects the person manning the cash register, "John, you're ringing that up the wrong way!" Ironically, as she kept drawing our attention to her coworkers' errors so demonstratively, she made herself look bad. Nobody wanted to be around her because she was so bossy and loud.

A friend told me how his mother used to make him go back and forth from the supermarket at the age of six to buy one particular item. "Get milk," she'd instruct. But then it had to be 2 percent or skim—whatever he brought home wasn't correct. His mom believed she was teaching him how to function well in the world. In fact, her pickiness was such a common pattern that he grew up unsure of his judgment. He internalized her pickiness by developing a habit of continually questioning others for more details, so he would never again fail at a task. Mistakes were too painful.

Visionary Opening and Closing Formulas

Verbal appreciation is a major opening formula for Visionaries having a Perfectionist moment. Speak directly to their intelligence and higher selves, rather than their limitations. It is tricky to talk to Perfectionists about areas they need to grow in, as criticism shuts them down. Furthermore, they're afraid of something going wrong or looking bad. So you must be gentle and honor their abilities if you plan to start such a conversation. Otherwise, you'll face denial and resistance.

Perfectionists need to know that they'll be likable even if they reveal their fears, insecurities and inadequacies. They need to know they are valuable and that you'll stick with them even after you see who they are underneath the masks they wear. Say, "No matter how you feel, I'm going to stay here." Let them know that you find them perfect and beautiful and worthy. Another Perfectionist friend finally admitted to me that once a week he drinks beer, eats fried chicken and smokes cigarettes. He felt certain that I would shame him for this and toss him overboard when I knew. Of course, I didn't.

In order to help Perfectionists feel safe to express their feelings and be intimate, you may have to coax them out of denial by telling them how you imagine you might feel in a similar situation. Mirror a possibility by saying, "If I were you, and that had happened to me, I would feel . . ." Even if you're wrong, this type of phrase can help Perfectionists open up more. Also give them feedback about the clues you're reading from their appearance. Point out the obvious. One evening, for instance, a Perfectionist friend came over to my house upset and curled up in a ball on the couch. I asked, "How are you doing?"

"Lovely," she replied.

"Sweetie, you don't look it," I said. "Your eyes are bloodshot, and your skin is flushed. There's sadness in your face."

Then she admitted, "Okay, I'm not lovely," and was able to talk about it.

You won't always be able to open up Perfectionists, because, like Conquerors, they have a powerful need to be right. Therefore, when you're in a conflict, a key to connection is to let them know that you recognize and understand their point of view. Keep your tone of voice soft and your body language receptive. They cannot hold up resistance when you do not push your energy or challenge them. When Perfectionists talk about a subject they know well, they have a tendency to become fixated on facts and what is right. They are so mentally facile that you cannot win an argument in the same field of facts and hairsplitting. Instead, speak from your heart, and center your comments on mutually beneficial outcomes. Avoid comparisons or judgments; those are closing formulas for Perfectionists.

Some subjects that arise in relationship cannot be resolved in the moment. It's okay to go home or step away for a while. Come back later and calmly address those issues in a state of repose. An opening formula for such conversations is: "I want to talk to you about something, because this is how I felt about what happened and what was said. I know you didn't mean for that to occur. I just want to let you know."

One woman had to relocate in a hurry, so she asked her Perfectionist sister for help. Even though she'd invited her sister, the woman dreaded her arrival. She was afraid her sister would try to control and dominate her and would expect her to follow a rigid set of rules. But she also had been sitting around on the floor depressed and in a stupor, feeling completely overwhelmed. I said, "Hey! You're locking your Perfectionist qualities against your sister's. You're trying to beat her at the same game. I have a better idea. Surrender. Let her help you. Tell her you need her, and follow her instructions when she advises you what to do. Eighty percent of the time a Perfectionist knows what to do in situations such as yours. So don't give her any guff."

The woman phoned me from her new home ten days later. "Donna, I had the most enriching time of my life using the opening formula you suggested. Right when she came in, I told my sister I was scared, overwhelmed and depressed, and I didn't know where to begin. Historically, we would have fought the entire time about who was right and how to do everything. But I surrendered. I let her be the boss, and in a few days my house was cleaned and packed, and we had FUN doing it! I thought she'd go home and believe I was worthless. Instead my sister wrote me a letter telling me how valuable I am to her and how enriched she felt by the experience. Our connection is much stronger now."

Transforming Your Destructive Patterns

If you are the Visionary, you can transform your Perfectionist patterns using the following approaches.

- *Surrender to Life.* As a Perfectionist, you live confined in a self-made box of habits, routines and rules. It's as though you're covered in Teflon. Nothing penetrates the barrier. This legendary ability to control keeps people at a manageable distance. As a Perfectionist man told me, "I was sitting on a park bench one day, feeling isolated, when I began to notice the running conversation in my head criticizing the passers-by. This one wasn't fit enough. That one wasn't tall enough. Another wasn't dressed well enough. Suddenly I realized that I was alone because in my mind I made myself superior to everyone. For years I'd said that there were only a few people to whom I could connect. I had a walking list for my own behavior too — about food, fitness, clothing and reading this or that book.

The end result was: I made myself lonely."

Have you ever wondered what might happen if you stopped considering yourself superior? Well, there's a three-stage process to silence inner judgments. I've seen many people go through these phases and feel happier. Stage 1 is where you believe you are the mask you're wearing. You haven't yet identified that you have an inner observer, a part of you separate from your ego. You also believe that everything you think is reality. Stage 2 occurs once you begin to realize that you're full of baloney and that you're judging other people based on a critical inner voice. At this point, you clearly see the difference between the ego and the observer. You are aware that you have blind spots about the nature of reality—and that reality isn't the same for everyone.

Stage 3 comes when you learn to silence your critical inner voice. It may require meditation and a variety of similar experiences to connect with your being beyond the mind chatter. This ability can take years to develop. So the process is to observe the voice sounding off, and then, instead of letting it rule your behavior, taking a deep breath, blowing it out and returning to neutrality. Criticizing the voice won't help. Then you're only at war with yourself and resisting what's true in the moment.

Don't miss out on your life. It's happening now, now — and now. Yet judgment, which is a form of control, puts you at a remove from it. If you can surrender, you'll feel more truly alive. How? Put down your books (including this one) and concepts, and go have a new experience. I know a middle-aged Perfectionist who learned how to partner dance. He turned down offer after offer to dance for at least an hour until a leader finally wouldn't take no for an answer. Afterwards, having felt totally out of control, the Perfectionist told me it was "transformative" to discover that it was "okay not to know how," to stumble along and make mistakes.

There's a whole category of "reading Perfectionists" known to devour books to become expert on different subjects, yet they rarely have a direct understanding of anything. Often these mentally oriented folks join spiritual communities and show up at psychological seminars where they typically seek validation from the facilitators that they're highly evolved and more advanced than average, and so on. If you're this type—be honest—make a point to humble yourself and be a beginner.

Empowering your inner observer may not happen in the next ten days; however, surrendering to life can happen in an instant. Take a new route home from work today. Put yourself in an emotionally volatile scenario this weekend, such as going to a workshop at a retreat center where the goal is to uncover core issues. Next month go on a walking safari in Africa. Make a dinner date with a man or woman you believe is the "wrong" age, height, weight, race, religion or profession for you. Go to the park and walk barefoot on the grass. Talk to strangers at the grocery store.

- *Make Friends with Your Feelings.* Feelings are how people know life. When we're not feeling, it's as though we're not really in the body. If you're a Perfectionist, a big lesson is to learn what feelings are. You have a mass of numbness inside, as your tendency is to *decide* what your feelings are rather than checking in with your heart. Sadly, if you manufacture feelings and hold them in submission, it makes you a boring friend or life partner because you have no experiential base upon which your personal expansion can be built. When you expand the dimensions of who you are and how you feel, however, you can bring your discoveries

back to the people in your life. You then become an interesting person to be around and to know. If you regularly
suppress your feelings and oblige the people around you to
suppress theirs, understand that they've got to come out
somewhere. The stress of denial can literally damage the
body. Internal pressure is going to build up until there's an
explosion.

The antidote for numbness is an exploration of your
feelings. Spend quiet time in connection with your core
self. Seek to balance your mind and emotions. Allow so-
called negative feelings, like emptiness, fear, sadness, guilt,
shame and loneliness, to arise, as well as so-called positive
ones. I say "so-called" since feelings are transient. If we
don't resist them, they flow through us and aren't so
painful. Then share your feelings with another. Share
them with the world. Let those in front of you know your
innermost thoughts and feelings. Because you will enjoy
the process, as you continue making and sharing discoveries with the world, your core will be enriched. From then
on, your accomplishments and relationships will have
greater meaning and depth.

- *Be Real.* Much as you might prefer it, being genuine is not
something you can fake. People are like bloodhounds. We
can sniff each other out of a foxhole faster than the foxes
do. You're not fooling anybody. When you don't like
people, or you're hiding your true feelings or discomfort,
they know it. You may feel like a deer caught in the headlights when someone asks, "How are you?" and you're not
doing well. In an appropriate, well-modulated voice, you'll
reply, "I'm fine," and then continue with your current
résumé. Your kids are doing well in school, you and your
spouse have made many accomplishments, business is
booming and so on. Perfectionists can be grandiose. What

have you been doing lately? "I'm writing a novel." "Something fantastic is just about to happen." If it hasn't already happened, it's *just about to*.

Try asking: What if my worth is not defined by my appearance and accomplishments? If I do not strive to attain more, am I valuable? If I didn't put my life on hold waiting to sell the novel, get the promotion and so on, then what would my life actually be like? It's okay not to know the answer. The point of asking is to open your mind to new possibilities. Allowing others — and you — to know you are uncertain can be great healing for the Perfectionist.

Come out from behind the mask in your relationships. Get "real." Let another human being really matter to you, and learn to connect in a meaningful way. Lean on someone. Let someone help you. Let someone else be right. Watch how this deepens your sense of intimacy. Take a break from exercising. Go out without makeup and dressed in a T-shirt. Tell someone how empty and scared you feel. Talk about your deepest shame. Let an imperfect person love you. Start a relationship because you admire another's inner qualities.

Share your core essence with the world. All this requires is to stand in place at a cocktail party or church coffee hour and say, "Hi, how are you?" Then receive what is offered in return. You are a natural visionary, role model and inspiration for others. As you let them in, they feel uplifted and naturally cycle back good feelings. In this way, you and they are enriched. So contain rather than assert your energy. Wear a gentle smile. Soften your eyes. You can't fool me. I know there's a being behind your mask of perfection and overly correct voice that wants to be seen, valued and loved, and would enjoy connection. Now it's time for you to reveal that being to everybody else.

• *Look Deeper.* I once heard actor/activist Christopher Reeve give a speech. From the dais, he said that after he broke his neck he saw people through different eyes. Before the accident he'd been an elitist and, among other qualities, judged people by the level of their incomes. He was always chasing a goal and felt that he had no time to waste on the "little people." Afterward, when he was lying in the hospital unable to move, he was very grateful for the cleaning man who came to his room and spoke with him. Now he understood the man's human value.

The Achilles' heel of the Visionary is the belief that if it looks good, it must be good. Visionaries can be suckers for the superficial, and that's why flatterers and snake oil salesmen often find you easy prey. Be aware, therefore, of your tendency to throw out the message when you don't value the appearance or communication style of the messenger. Avoid falling into an old trap.

In romance, let yourself have a relationship with someone who isn't a trophy. Hang in there long enough to let things get real, and keep working at it. What grows may surprise you. Receive love, and trust that you deserve it. By allowing someone to mirror your wonderful qualities to you, you'll begin to believe they have merit. In the workplace, aim to evaluate people on their contributions rather than on how smooth talking they are. If people need your help to become better communicators, train them. Most people have the ability and desire to grow, and they're worth the effort.

• *Lower the Bar.* As a Visionary, you set goals and you attain them. So you keep raising the bar. Although your life is filled with accomplishments, these never seem like enough. You can't rest until you arrive at some ideal future that never comes. You may be a doctor, attorney or other professional at the top of your field, and nonetheless, an anxious voice in your head tells you that you never measure up to a high standard. Thus, you're a sucker for approval and likely to do backflips for a boss or anybody else from whom you want praise and admiration. Whether or not you have a good or bad day depends on how closely you've met your expectations and if you've noticed minute imperfections, like blemishes or fractional weight changes.

Slow down. Take a break from achieving and instead practice living. Smell the roses, take in the sky and play with a baby. Give for no reason. Let go of wanting a particular result. Join a race, come in fifth and enjoy the experience. Just because you feel inadequate from time to time doesn't mean you are, my friend.

Even as you read and study the information in this book, please remember that your capacity to deepen, and share that deepening with others, is infinite. It takes awhile to penetrate the layers of the Perfectionist mask. When you think you've gone deep, you've probably only dipped your baby toe into your core essence. Since this process is a journey of revelation of the self, if you haven't taken the journey, you've missed out. No brownie points are awarded for speed. There is no ranking. Just life.

- *Soften Your Energy Barriers.* You probably spend so much effort projecting energy through a pearly white smile and everything-is-great image that you've established a barrier reef around yourself. Overblown happiness is intimidating to ordinary folks. Stop, take a breath, soften your eyes, pull your energy in and down, and allow your beingness to peek through. Let other people in. Practice taking off your mask of positivity and infallible excellence, and instead allow how you truly feel in the moment to reveal itself. People will warm to you naturally once they can sense your humanity.

CHAPTER 6

ꝗHE PROPHET/ESCAPIST

ꝗ f you're the Prophet, your passion is higher knowledge. You ponder the cosmos, explore esoteric concepts and tap the unseen more than other passion signatures. As a seeker of spiritual wisdom and unity, your life's purpose relates to the evolution of humankind. Your remarkable intuition gives you access to realms beyond most people's understanding and ability to experience. In order to further the development of our species, personal freedom and inner peace, you are motivated to speak the Truth (with a capital T) as you perceive it. Once you've embraced the esoteric gifts you possess, your presence brings healing and solace to everyone around you. Using powerful insight, you guide others to connect with their passion and make progress in the creation of a better world and quality of life. At your best, you are an earthly angel, a radiant messenger of God and of goodness, and a spiritual teacher.

Unfortunately, your tendency as the Escapist is to disconnect from everyone, including yourself. It's as though you can't stay present in your physical body. Often you feel unsafe and mistrustful. You imagine that the world is out to get you. Let's say you're standing in front of your boss, who's reading you the riot act, and you feel like a deer caught in the headlights. Next thing you know, a blank stare covers your face—you're gone! When you feel vulnerable, you literally can withdraw your consciousness and personality through the top of your head. In this scattered state, someone can be speaking directly to you, and you won't hear because you've gone bye-bye. As a result, you can be very forgetful. Your memories also are often confused and fragmented. At your worst, pervading feelings of emptiness, meaninglessness and emotional flatness haunt you. You may also suffer from panic attacks. It is generally hard for you to make commitments or follow through.

Being in intimate relationships with Prophet/Escapists can be difficult unless they've taken proactive steps to anchor themselves in the body. When you hug Escapists, they can feel limp, cold and devoid of energy. Their sexual drives can be minimal. You may feel as though the lack of connection is a judgment on you. It's really not! Due to extreme emotional sensitivity, Escapists prefer to isolate and so, although they enjoy one-on-one companionship, they might not be willing to accompany you to social events. If you like parties, it can be a drag to show up—once again—without an Escapist partner or to feel obliged frequently to accommodate a partner's unusual discomfort or alienation.

On the plus side of the score sheet, Prophets are attuned to subtle energy to such a high degree that they serve as vessels of divine love and inspiration for those in their lives. Once they've made peace with their fear of being annihilated, they feel at home in physical form. Then they delight in the pleasures of the five physical senses and in expressing soulful communion through the body. This makes them excellent lovers, as they perceive deeper levels of reality beneath the world's surface and know how to blend with the energy field of another being. Open access to divine guidance makes them uncommonly astute advisers. If you've got something you want to hide, however, you might as well fess up because the Prophet won't be fooled for long.

The Prophet/Escapist is the earliest passion signature to develop, and its patterns incorporate some of the most intangible elements of human experience. For many of us, including those who identify more closely with other passion signatures, the Escapist is the defense of last resort when none of our other survival strategies seem to be getting the job done. A Warrior/ Conqueror, for instance, who is normally a fighter, one day might find himself in a situation where that option isn't available. Powerless in the face of a threat, the Escapist mode kicks in. Suddenly he can neither focus nor process what people are saying. He's so blank-minded that he can't hear or understand.

The Prophet/Escapist passion is created in the womb or at birth. Perhaps there is a physical crisis during delivery, such as the umbilical cord wrapping around the neck. Or perhaps the mother is under stress or filled with doubts throughout her pregnancy, or the father or mother truly doesn't want the baby. On an energetic level, the infant senses a lack of welcome in the world or the threat of outright danger. Thus, the tiny Escapist keeps a foot in the world of divine spirit, even on entering the three-dimensional world. Such babies are quieter than average and have glazed eyes or a vacant facial expression. It's as though they're having an in-and-out-of-the-body experience. They're not all here yet.

A few additional types of experiences can contribute to the emergence of a strong Prophet/Escapist passion in a given individual. One of these is a near-death experience (NDE), especially if it takes place in childhood. People who've passed away and come back report similar phenomena, including traveling through a tunnel toward a bright light and being met and guided by loving family members. When they awaken from the NDE, they also typically say they feel they have a purpose on Earth and are absent of fear. Although they look forward to their reunion with their loved ones in the light at a later date, they relish having the ability to see, hear, taste, smell and touch the world. While many Prophet/Escapists have fragmented personalities, the NDE survivors I've met are generally highly integrated—calm, centered and compassionate. They can recall the sublime oneness of life outside the body and tap into this sensation—perceive this high-frequency field of energy—at will. They live with a quality of euphoria that is most commonly enjoyed by those who regularly meditate or pray, such as monks.

Another experience that prompts the emergence of the Escapist is emotional, physical and sexual abuse or terrible violence, such as you might find in a combat zone. These circumstances are psychologically and physically threatening to such a degree that a child—and sometimes an adult—evades them by disassociating from the body. People experience this self-protective state as fragmentation. Later on, when a post-traumatic stress response kicks in, it's as though the Escapist is viewing himself from under water or at a distance, while another personality inhabits his familiar shell. It's a numb and unpleasantly dreamlike state that feels as though the world is being warped or stretched.

In adulthood, the challenge for the Prophet is to experience

READER/CUSTOMER CARE SURVEY

We care about your opinions! Please take a moment to fill out our online Reader Survey at **http://survey.hcibooks.com**.

As a **"THANK YOU"** you will receive a **VALUABLE INSTANT COUPON** towards future book purchases as well as a **SPECIAL GIFT** available only online! Or, you may mail this card back to us and we will send you a copy of our exciting catalog with your valuable coupon inside.

(PLEASE PRINT IN ALL CAPS)

First Name   MI.   Last Name

Address

State   Zip   City   Email

1. Gender
❏ Female   ❏ Male

2. Age
❏ 8 or younger
❏ 9-12   ❏ 13-16
❏ 17-20   ❏ 21-30
❏ 31+

3. Did you receive this book as a gift?
❏ Yes   ❏ No

4. Annual Household Income
❏ under $25,000
❏ $25,000 - $34,999
❏ $35,000 - $49,999
❏ $50,000 - $74,999
❏ over $75,000

5. What are the ages of the children living in your house?
❏ 0 - 14   ❏ 15+

6. Marital Status
❏ Single
❏ Married
❏ Divorced
❏ Widowed

7. How did you find out about the book?
(please choose one)
❏ Recommendation
❏ Store Display
❏ Online
❏ Catalog/Mailing
❏ Interview/Review

8. Where do you usually buy books?
(please choose one)
❏ Bookstore
❏ Online
❏ Book Club/Mail Order
❏ Price Club (Sam's Club, Costco's, etc.)
❏ Retail Store (Target, Wal-Mart, etc.)

9. What subject do you enjoy reading about the most?
(please choose one)
❏ Parenting/Family
❏ Relationships
❏ Recovery/Addictions
❏ Health/Nutrition
❏ Christianity
❏ Spirituality/Inspiration
❏ Business Self-help
❏ Women's Issues
❏ Sports

10. What attracts you most to a book?
(please choose one)
❏ Title
❏ Cover Design
❏ Author
❏ Content

TAPE IN MIDDLE; DO NOT STAPLE

BUSINESS REPLY MAIL
FIRST-CLASS MAIL PERMIT NO 45 DEERFIELD BEACH, FL

POSTAGE WILL BE PAID BY ADDRESSEE

Health Communications, Inc.
3201 SW 15th Street
Deerfield Beach FL 33442-9875

FOLD HERE

Comments

the oneness of spirit while remaining grounded inside a separate human body. The Prophet/Escapist must journey along the continuum of fragmentation to reach the flow of wholeness. Because of flipping in and out of the body so frequently, Escapists must learn how to draw back the edges of their personal energy field, which is so powerful that it covers a broader area than do most people's. They must learn to filter out negative thoughts and feelings. Otherwise they'll remain hypersensitive to the fields of energy emanating from other people and may begin to feel polluted and overwhelmed.

If you're a Prophet/Escapist, your sense of fragmentation is a direct result of your disconnection from your body. When you learn to ground your energy, it won't feel so diffuse, and you will be more present in the moment. That's when your true power will emerge. You have great gifts to share as a spiritual teacher, counselor, healer, artist, scientist or advocate of new thought. You may see auras or have psychic abilities, like clairaudience or clairvoyance. Your incredible power may seem as frightening to you as physical danger. Because you sense energy fields as palpable waves of emotion and light, you may have a fear of getting swept away by them, as if on an ocean current, and drowning. Your concern of being overwhelmed keeps you searching for the trapdoor out of your experience. You worry that you'll be caught out in the open with nowhere to hide.

Honestly, Prophet/Escapists have a fear of annihilation that's partly rational. If they speak publicly about their perceptions of ghosts, auras and psychic phenomena, they run the risk of being misunderstood, ridiculed or even attacked. Our society undervalues the gifts of the Prophet, so these individuals are often labeled with clinical diagnoses. People who are schizophrenic may be accessing other realms of energy and consciousness, although the experience leaves them fragmented and overwhelmed. Chemical imbalances in the brain can cause people to suffer from paranoid delusions. We have to distinguish real mental illness from spiritual access.

So what's the difference between a person having hallucinations caused by a chemical imbalance in the brain and someone else who's hearing messages from angels? Both may be Prophet/Escapists, albeit on different ends of the continuum of integration. Fear, paranoia, the inability to function and take care of oneself, and posing a danger to oneself or others are signs of ill health that need to be addressed with professional help. Spiritual help is also available to those whose gifts of prophecy are emerging. Indigenous cultures, such as the Native American nations, seem to understand the signs of spiritual opening better than we do in the Judeo-Christian world. You could seek out a shaman, a nontraditional psychotherapist or a meditation group for support. People who lack energetic boundaries might seem as though they have an emotional illness. What this type needs, however, is training in skills to manage this unusual spiritual gift.

Unchecked, a pattern of Escapism could prevent you from manifesting the life of your dreams. In fact, of all the signature types, this is the most likely to be heard saying, "I'm tired of this life. I want to go home. I feel like I don't belong in this world. I would like to leave." One Prophet said, "I don't feel like I have skin or protection. It's like other people's thoughts and energy can hurt me." They talk about death as though it is the time when they will go back to where they came from and feel they truly belong. Other passion signatures may have no sense of their existence beyond this life, whereas this type is certain of their existence. In fact, that's the place that is seen as safe, while this world is seen as unsafe.

As a psychotherapist, I hear in private about spiritual phenomena from clients of all walks of life. Many are devout,

Bible-reading, conservative professionals who attend church on a weekly basis. They've helped me understand that we should study altered human consciousness and not automatically identify it as the work of "Satan" or "evil." Rational people aren't afraid to talk about intuition. Likewise, these phenomena are part of the realm of human life, and so we should seek to understand them. Although they may seem extreme to you, and outside your own experience, doesn't it make sense for us to explore them the same way we would explore outer space or the ocean's depths?

Go to *www.thepassionprinciple.com/passiontools* to receive a free handout on the Prophet and other passion signatures.

The Story of a Prophet/Escapist

Meredith was a detective with a high rate of success in uncovering criminals that other investigators were unable to locate. Besides being intelligent, she had an uncanny knack for intuiting who was honest and who wasn't. When she contacted me several years ago for therapy, she was agitated because of recent, strange events in her life that had thrown her mind into turmoil. As a person who relied on scientific evidence to make her cases, she was now keeping a deep, dark secret from her family and colleagues.

"Donna," she said, "there's something people don't know about me, and I'm not sure if it means I've gone crazy. I can see weird things, and one of the most extreme things I'm seeing is dead people." She was like the lead character in the TV series *Medium*.

While washing the dishes after supper one evening, Meredith noticed the ethereal figure of her neighbor standing beside her. The woman's funeral had been a week earlier. "What are you doing here?" Meredith asked.

"I need you to give a message to my son," said the spirit of her neighbor. "Promise me you'll tell him that I love him, and the papers he needs are underneath the carpet in the corner of the closet, along with $5,000."

Meredith promised. Even though she felt uncomfortable doing it, in the morning she phoned her neighbor's son and asked him to come over for a minute. "I know this will sound weird," she said, "but . . ." and then delivered the message. When the son got over his shock, he went home and checked under the carpet. Lo and behold, the papers were right there.

One of the problems Meredith faced was her shame about her intuitive gifts. The women in her family lineage had a long history of "second sight," and they'd faced disapproval from other family members because their gifts defied their religious beliefs. It was no joke how thoroughly these women had been persecuted. Meredith was concerned that as her secret came out she might lose her job, be clinically diagnosed, get pumped full of drugs or locked in a mental ward or, at the very least, be humiliated. She felt her ability to communicate with the dead and to receive messages was an aberration of nature.

In our work together, I helped Meredith understand that her astonishing abilities and perceptions were God-given. We discussed at length how she could discern when it was safe and appropriate to share the guidance she received with others. Just because she saw something did not automatically mean she had to speak about it. After all, the rest of us do not always talk about everything we see or hear, do we? As we mature, we accept the information provided to us by our senses and make choices about when and with whom we prefer to share. I felt she was capable of deciding when the information was urgent to pass along, such as the papers under the carpet.

How to Recognize the Prophet/Escapist

Pure Prophet/Escapists are usually thin and reedy with
wispy muscles. They have a hard time keeping on weight.
Sometimes they forget to eat or take care of their bodies. They
will have very few friends and sometimes only one. They can
seem awkward and out of place at typical gatherings. Unlike
social butterflies, they rarely feel at home in the midst of
groups. Instead, they hesitantly come forward and soon
retreat, like wild animals or skittish domestic cats. Escapists
often leave parties early or sit on the sidelines where they can
avoid engaging in conversation. They also talk about being
overwhelmed by the energy of groups. Unless they've overcome the fear of people and annihilation, they're unlikely to
hold eye contact with anyone, so they come across as a bit odd,
nervous and spacey. Conversely, healed Prophets establish and
hold eye contact that feels as if they're looking through you
into your soul—and beyond. The penetration of this experience makes many people feel uncomfortably exposed.

While most of us are Combo Platters, the pure Prophet/
Escapist generally lives outside the mainstream. Whether or
not you believe in their abilities, they are conduits of higher
frequencies of energy. The local psychic who hangs up a shin-
gle and reads tea leaves or Tarot cards for a living is probably
such a being. But so may be a scientist working in the field of
quantum physics.

I know a young man who is a natural remote viewer. Once
he told me he'd visited the rings of Saturn and felt their vibra-
tions. It would be easy to dismiss this anecdote as a fantasy if
several respected former military personnel hadn't publicly
acknowledged their participation in our government's remote
viewing experiments. In books and lectures, these individuals
describe similar experiences taking place in a laboratory. Such

abilities to travel beyond the bounds of the physical body have been scientifically verified.

Once, when I was still based in Texas, I visited a former NASA engineer, a scientist-turned-energy-healer, a Prophet who lived way out in the country like a hermit with his wife in a metal barn. He'd designed an octagonal room to house an enormous, flat bed that teetered on and spun around a single point at the center of this space. The device was said to balance the flow of the energy fields in the body. Just as I arrived, another psychologist was leaving after his own treatment. While I prepared for my session, two physicians called to refer their patients to him. They knew this man might succeed where traditional medicine had failed.

As I lay upon the healing bed, the Prophet gently spun it around and played ethereal music. I went into a trancelike state of relaxation and do not remember much of what happened, except that he touched my feet and a feeling inside me shifted. I didn't understand this Prophet's work; however, it was clear that he was a genius and an eccentric. He had integrated his spiritual gift with his knowledge of engineering and lived the way he wanted to live and contribute to the world.

One female Prophet drowned at ten and was pronounced dead on the table in the emergency room. While she was dead, she went to the Other Side, and she returned with full memory of the experience and access to spiritual beings she'd met there. After ten minutes, she suddenly took a breath and came back to life. During her near-death experience, time did not exist, and she experienced a full world and consciousness.

According to her, "On Earth, we're so lucky! On the Other Side, it's as though you're making love with people all the time because you exist in a web together. But they don't have these magnificent bodies we do. Just to be able to take one finger and touch your hand is amazing. That's something they cannot do." The other realm is so beautiful that she now finds it hard to live among people who cannot perceive how connected we all are. As a result, she spends much of her time communing with nature: walking on the beach or in the woods, hugging trees and doing anything else she can to connect with the physical world.

For those who are Prophet/Escapists, a typical problem is being afraid the people in their lives won't accept them or might believe they are crazy. They worry that they will be annihilated for expressing their truth.

A man or woman who never seems to have any money may be an Escapist. I once knew a Prophet/Escapist, an exquisite, intelligent and sensitive woman who spoke of inspiring communications from archangels during meditation. She filled page upon page in her journals with divine messages of hope and healing, which she shared with her close friends. Those who knew her always came away from their conversations with valuable insights about life and purpose. Although she was a loving mother and deeply committed to the well-being of her twin sons, there was a serious disconnect between her uncanny spiritual intelligence and the day-to-day requirements of life in the third dimension. Due to negligence, all the lightbulbs burned out in the house. She blew out her car's engine because she forgot to fill it up with oil.

Escapists may turn to substance abuse of alcohol or drugs to deaden their second sight and make them less sensitive to pervading fields of emotion and energy. They may turn to chocolate, cola-flavored soda and cigarettes, as well. All these consumables can make one's energy feel denser, flatter and more solid, less blissfully connected.

The defensive aspect of the Escapist is related to anxiety and fear. It feels like being fragmented but is useful for self-protection. As one Prophet/Escapist said, "I grew up in a dangerous community. When something would trigger me to feel unsafe, such as someone yelling at me or trying to start a fight, I'd go out of my body, but some other personality would come into me and throw his energy right back at my antagonist. It would be a character, not me. This character is sarcastic and gets off on violence. Because I'm slender, when this fierce aspect came out of me, people were surprised.

"Today, I have an Escapist episode—an experience of fragmentation and leaving—every month or two (it used to be more often), but now my sense of not being safe is triggered by feeling unsupported, lacking intimacy or even boredom. It's as though I have a village in my head, and I'm in charge, but I'm not a good leader. Abandonment, separation, rejection—these are my triggers. As an Escapist, the incisiveness of making agreements is beyond me. I can't decide what I want. At worst, I feel suicidal.

"Don't get me wrong, though; it can feel good to be able to fuse or merge with people so thoroughly. It's a visceral 3-D type of experience. Holographic. My imagination seems totally real when I'm in this state of being. I lose myself in people. For instance, I was sitting on a subway once, and there was a girl there with hair hiding her face. I started tuning into her energy, and I began to feel how she felt. I associated with her until it was as though I became her. I am a psychologist/artist/philosopher. I found words to describe the relationship of the self and reality. In my mind I flowed out a poem. I was connecting to her through my writing. I love this part of being a Prophet."

Escapist Relationship Traps

Prophets need to be aware of three traps that prevent them from making meaningful connections with others. Understanding these patterns is the first step in feeling safe in the world and making those connections.

- *The Houdini Maneuver.* You are the ultimate escape artist when there's an emotional conflict. You can be standing with your spouse or lover, your parent or child, a boss or coworker, and if this person has a complaint—*whoosh!*—you disappear up the chimney like Old St. Nick on Christmas Eve. All that remains for this antagonist to confront is your empty shell. For others, it's incredibly frustrating trying to relate to you when you've popped out the escape hatch. You're a wishy-washy rag doll who gets moved around by external forces. You can't decide where to go to dinner, which movie to see or what food to eat. And then you won't even listen to them when they've got a gripe. Forget you!

  Do you ever find yourself meditating for hours a day, rather than getting up and going out of the house? That's also the Houdini Maneuver. While meditation is essential for peace of mind and to cultivate focus, sitting and stewing in the balmy bathtub of spiritual energy is not a substitute for life. If you go out of body too frequently, you become a burden to others who have to pick up the pieces and take care of your business. Your lack of drive means they always have to provide the assertive energy in your relationship. They never get to rest. You lose track of time, and they watch the clock to make sure you show up at work. When you're skittish, they serve as your grounding rod and security blanket. I knew a mother who sat in her closet weeping every afternoon about her inability to function. Her kids found her exhausting, and when they were old enough they got away.

- *Life Is But a Dream. Nothing Matters. It's All Meaningless Anyway.* As a Prophet/Escapist, at times you may feel as though you've lost your voice. You'll be enthusiastically moving forward, and suddenly you cease caring about the outcome that used to motivate you. You drop into a state of emotional paralysis, simply cannot focus and lack enthusiasm. Words won't come. You have no desire to pay your bills on time, to finish the screenplay you're writing or to interact with anyone. What's going on? This trap is about hiding from power and an underlying sense of unworthiness to exist or embrace your purpose.

If you entertain your power, what feelings come up? If you accept the opportunity to stand in your power, are you afraid you won't be able to handle the energy? Perhaps the very thing you seek will destroy you? Perhaps the truth you want to speak is not real? Perhaps you'll be exposed as a fraud? Due to these types of fears, you hide in a hole of neutrality. You believe that once you step out, the door will close behind you, and there will be no sanctuary. Therefore you are committed to resisting your own power and to staying isolated.

Here's the thing though. The Prophet/Escapists I've met have secretly longed to reveal their spiritual power. They knew they had it and were sometimes even a little bit smug about it, especially if they were being stingy and withholding it from others. Those who have revealed their abilities seem to be granted ever-increasing access to unlimited supplies of supernatural energy and assistance. They have thrived on bringing higher wisdom and spiritual guidance to ordinary people.

Once you face your fears and step into your power, you can bring the force of the cosmos into everything you do, like the Prophets before you did. If you're a musician, your music will lift people into other worlds and expanded states of being. As a scientist, you will develop new theories that take humanity to a higher evolution. As a spiritual teacher, you may bring new interpretation to ancient spiritual texts or become a channel for higher frequencies. Connecting with higher states can be an ecstatic experience. That sounds pretty great, doesn't it? Wouldn't you like to share that experience with others? You're going to discover that people are immensely grateful for the depth and meaning you bring to their lives. Remember, you wouldn't have been given your gifts if you couldn't handle them.

- *I Don't Fit In.* Yes, you have special gifts. In fact, the rest of us are waiting for you to embrace your power and share your higher truth and spiritual teachings with the world. Since hiding keeps you disconnected from your passion, your soul will continue to nudge you to step out. You know you want to, right? You feel your greatness. You may even feel a bit superior to "mere mortals," who in many ways just don't see the whole picture. In your head, you may live in a kingdom or fantasyland. This makes you feel as though you do not fit in. But, oh, my friend, you do. We need each other. Connect with one person in a deep relationship of love or friendship, and through this grounding rod you can feel safe enough to begin bringing your gifts to the world. You need more grounded folks to bring you into the third dimension. We need you to open us to the stars.

Prophet Opening and Closing Formulas

Prophet/Escapists tend to feel safest with spirit. Because they fear obliteration, a leading desire is for physical safety. At the same time, they hunger for acceptance and belonging. If you're in a relationship with an Escapist, remember that the mental and emotional disappearing acts that take place do not result from conscious choice. They're also not personal. When an Escapist's eyes glaze over, don't make a big deal about it, as that would be shaming—a closing formula for the Escapist. Be aware that it's just a response to being threatened in some fashion. Whenever there's a perception—even if it's not factual—that danger is at hand, the nervous system takes over. To help the Escapist return and reconnect, an opening formula is to create a safe space around him or her for a few minutes. Say, "It's okay, you're safe. I'm staying with you." Encourage the Escapist to take deep, slow breaths.

Do not badger Escapists when they're "out" or try to make major conversation until they're back. Pull your energy inside you—and wait. Without knowing it, you may have been doing something that was scaring the person in front of you. You need to view this as a moment of crisis for that individual, and respect the Escapist's needs.

An acquaintance of mine is a rape survivor with Escapist tendencies. When her husband got strident one evening about politics, it triggered her fear of being attacked. Her efforts to calm her beloved down backfired and only made him angry. Thus his voice grew harsher, and his eyes got fierce. No matter what she said or did, he was adamant. He refused her rather inarticulate request for support. Instead he continued asserting his point of view, which only made the environment seem more menacing to her. As a result, she started pulling away from her body. When he saw her upset, he told her to "toughen up." He interpreted her fear as criticism and believed they were having a fight. It got ugly.

If this normally loving husband had recognized the activation of his wife's nervous system, an opening formula he could have used would have been to get quiet, be still, remain neutral and yet stay connected with her. Escapists in the middle of a threat response need to be taken care of and guided on their path. They're in a hopeless state where they cannot communicate properly and actually lose the ability to function. At such moments, they need a compassionate person to take charge and offer protection.

Another opening formula for extreme moments is to create an energy bubble around Escapists. Because their personal energy fields are so wide open, while merely walking down the street or sitting in a movie theater they can sense everyone else's negative thoughts and painful feelings. They are human lightning rods. If they are hit too many times, their circuits get fried. While some Escapists like to be embraced lovingly and feel securely held on such occasions, often being touched is too much. So ask, "Would you like me to hold you?" If not, imagine that you are an angel spreading your wings to surround the Escapist. Hold both of you safely inside a protective cocoon.

When Prophet/Escapists get stuck in the Houdini Maneuver trap, give them space. Mr. Elusive Man or Woman, who is noncommittal, not returning phone calls and doesn't want to socialize, probably feels overwhelmed by life and, thus, is withdrawing. Examine the facts. Is the Escapist injured? Afraid? Exhausted? Undergoing a major transition, such as a new career, new home or new relationship? What does he or she need? Probably space. The Escapist may try to provoke you to annihilate him or her. And you may even get to the point of fantasizing about slapping the Escapist silly. But don't let it under your skin. Just do your own thing. Feel free to go out, socialize and have fun.

A Prophet who experiences profound states of oneness, rather than fragmentation, may be a blissfully connected lover — and this could push the edges of your own envelope of comfort. Communication with a Prophet partner is the key. Keep honestly sharing your feelings about the deep fusion you're being invited to enter. Because it's hard for the Prophet to put the feeling of oneness into words, don't ask open-ended questions during lovemaking and expect complex responses. Be simple and give yes or no choices. This enables you both to remain connected on a level your partner can access comfortably.

Help the Prophet/Escapist to be grounded in the world and remain open to tangible, earthly experiences by supporting this individual in developing disciplined behavior and pursuing physical activity. As Prophets integrate their gifts and spiritual abilities, the world seems less threatening and so does the energy they sense. Communicating safety and acceptance are important opening formulas.

A final opening formula is simply to acknowledge their gifts. Prophets are concerned about being destroyed for revealing the truth of the spiritual world they can access. They know what they're going through may be beyond your experience. (By the way, everyone perceives energy differently—there's no single way to perceive it.) Mirroring the truth of their being means they can begin to let down their guard, and don't have to expend themselves on proving the unprovable.

Transforming Your Destructive Patterns

If you are the Prophet, you can overcome your Escapist tendencies and become more grounded in the world. Try the following suggestions.

- *Find Someone You Can Trust.* A relationship with a compassionate, open-minded person will enable you to ground in the world. You can then build upon this foundation to share your gifts. As your sense of trust and the initial connection grows stronger, you can return to this friendship, alliance or romance as you would a secure home base, making it easier for you to establish even more relationships.

  No matter how alienated you may feel on occasion, I assure you that I've never met a Prophet who wasn't surrounded by a sizable group of friends and acquaintances. It is fine for you to accept that you are interdependent on other people. Everybody needs the support of diverse gifts. Since your gift is a special access to divine energy, try asking for spiritual guidance in meeting the companion you most need. You'll receive assistance. The soul generally guides us into our relationships, literally drawing appropriate people into our lives.

A Prophet who is a professional medium was horrific in financial matters, mostly because she had no sense of proportion. When she had ten dollars in the bank, she'd charge $200 on her credit cards. When she had thousands in the bank, she'd complain that her accountant wanted to be paid a couple of hundred. Until she found a life partner, she felt vulnerable and susceptible in the world. Then with her mate's support, she came into her own and became a huge success.

A painter I know who is an Escapist used to have similar issues. He could not make tangible plans for selling his work and often failed to deliver on his promises to the art gallery that represented him. With the help of a devoted friend, a Visionary-Creator, he began to develop discipline. Until he received feedback from this trusted companion, he didn't know his behavior had an impact on anyone else's life. Because he believed he was living in a dream world, he viewed other people as "illusions."

His friend explained to the painter that people are real to themselves, and you have to take their third-dimensional reality into account, or else you risk hurting and losing them. Once he absorbed this message from his friend, someone whom he didn't want to offend, he began to function, and his circumstances turned around. His new allies invigorated his career.

- *Create Energetic Boundaries.* If you do not learn to contain your energy, you'll always feel easily fragmented. So practice pulling your diffuse energy field closer to your body. If you think it, it will be so. Imagine there's an opening in the crown of your head through which you are connected to the divine energy of the cosmos. On an inhalation, visualize a beam of 100-percent pure light connecting to your heart. When you can hold this energy in the heart and transform it into world service, you will be an integrated Prophet. Giving from the heart is the essence of your power. By turning your attention away from self-protection, you can become an open conduit of love and compassion. Then others will mirror your value to you.

- *Ground Yourself in Your Body.* You are prone to flights of fancy and imagination. So how can you learn to stay with the reality in front of you? Try anything that brings you more awareness of your physical form. For instance, go to the gym and do aerobics, or take a run in the park. When you feel your feet pounding on the ground and your breath deepening, that's going to move energy down into your lower body where it needs to be. Dancing is an especially great practice for the Prophet/Escapist. As you move around the room, notice how you feel. What does it feel like to move your torso? Your arms? Your legs? What does centrifugal force feel like when you spin? What is it like to connect with a dance partner?

  One Prophet/Escapist acquaintance of mine, a man in his midtwenties, joined a dance class where people are encouraged to explore their emotions. For the first few classes, he stood still in the middle of the room and cried. He was in extraordinary resistance to committing to movement. Soon he started dancing a little bit and allowing the music to affect him more. As the months went on, it was like watching a balloon that had shriveled up gradually inflate again with life force. He explored the room and his body, and he began to interact with the other participants. To get to the freedom to connect, he had to pass through the initial experience of being unsafe.

You can learn to catch yourself as you're going into fear-override mode, or after—when you're actually gone. In either case breathe rhythmically into the lowest part of your abdomen. Imagine that you are cycling energy in from the top of your head and moving it down to your feet—top down. Also imagine that you're a tree, and your roots come out from the base of your spine and plant themselves in the earth. Breathe down into your roots.

Part II

CREATING A
PASSIONATE LIFE

CHAPTER 7

DISCOVERING YOUR PASSIONATE SELF

efore you can deepen your relationships with others, it is vital to deepen and improve your relationship with yourself. As a signature expression of life, your job is to be *you* as much as you can, to learn to accept—even admire—yourself as a work in progress, and to give yourself the permission and support you need to have the life, love and success of your dreams. The power of your soul is a radiant beacon burning like a star inside you, and once you tap into this amazing, expansive life force there truly are no limits. You'll find that it's your constant source of fresh energy, inspiration, creativity and joy. Passion is a clear indication that you have opened up a channel of love for and within yourself.

If you've read this far, you can now identify the mind-sets and habits of the five passion signatures. You learned about the narrowest, most restricted and fear-based pattern of each (the Vamp, the Martyr, the Conqueror, the Perfectionist and the Escapist). You also learned about its highest, most expanded and fulfilling evolution (the Lover, the Creator, the Warrior, the Visionary and the Prophet). But what can you do when you feel yourself falling into an old trap and shutting down? How can you stop repeating the same patterns in your life? In this chapter, you'll learn to recognize when your survival mechanisms have been activated—and why—so you can remain open and connected.

You Are Probably a Combo Platter

You are one *or more* of the five passion signatures. In fact, most people—with only rare exceptions—are Combo Platters. This means you may be a Visionary-Creator or a Warrior-Prophet on the job, and then be a Visionary-Lover or another combination in your marriage. Different life situations and different relationships will bring out different talents, abilities and attitudes. They'll also activate different survival mechanisms.

When the defenses of a passion signature are activated, it's like an automatic pilot switch has been turned on. Suddenly, you're not in control anymore—your "machinery" is. That's because the human nervous system by adulthood becomes a filtering-out, rather than an allowing-in, system. The primitive brain cannot distinguish between the threat of death and the threat of asking someone for a date or of seizing a career opportunity. It does not have a value system. It is neutral. It only intends everything in your life to stay the same so that it will know ahead of time how best to respond to protect you. Such responses are programs, like the software in a computer. Unfortunately, you cannot have anything more or different than the program says you can when you live by the rules of your defenses. You'll only get placed back into situations similar to ones you've already experienced. If you shift direction, your program will try to bring you back on course.

In order to break a pattern, you have to reprogram your nervous system. You have to train yourself to operate from the motivations of your highest self, rather than your survival instincts. As a Combo Platter, you may spend periods of your life as a wounded Conqueror evolving to a Warrior, then a wounded Vamp evolving to a Lover, and then a wounded Escapist evolving to a Prophet, and so on. Such periods can be years long, weeks long or only hours long, depending on what life tosses your way and how you choose to respond. Luckily, there are quick and easy ways to unlock the defenses.

It is not wrong or bad to be one passion signature or another. None is the best. They all have special qualities that are useful and necessary, which is why they tend to be mixed together inside us. The signatures that develop earliest in childhood (the Prophet and the Lover) are more passive than the three that develop later. The Creator can be either passive or assertive. The Warrior and the Visionary are assertive. The need for self-assertion is a major reason we add extra layers of defense on top of the ones that develop earlier in childhood. For example, a Creator, superb at generating ideas, also needs access to the discipline typical of the Visionary. If a Creator is a Combo Platter who possesses both energy styles, that individual is going to be more capable of follow-through than a pure Creator. It is very common to see Combo Platters who are mixtures of a passive and an assertive passion signature.

On the plus side of the Combo Platter healing equation, as

you become familiar with the characteristics of your inherent passion signatures, you'll know when you're drawing upon one set of abilities or another set. The more integrated you become, the more available those gifts will be whenever you want them or as circumstances warrant. You can invoke the power of your inner Lover when you are wooing a romantic partner or draw upon the leadership skills of your inner Warrior to build consensus at a business meeting. You can expect your inner Visionary to architect your career and rely upon your inner Prophet to provide your children with spiritual guidance.

In theory, a completely integrated person would have access to the gifts of all the five passion signatures and would never go into a survival mode. While it is rare for such an evolution to occur in practice, it's a compelling possibility—well worth aiming for— and a very good reason to continue your journey of expansion and transformation throughout your lifetime. Until the day you leave your body, you have the potential to keep learning and expanding. Lots of people give up, shut down and stagnate, but you do not have to be one of them.

On the minus side of the Combo Platter healing equation, survival-based passion signatures can be powerful saboteurs. If you haven't healed the wounded aspect of one of your passion signatures, its version of pain and limitation is very likely to color your perceptions and drive your behavior, particularly when you feel the stakes are raised.

Here's an example. Let's say you are a Warrior-Lover Combo Platter. Although you may possess the gifts of the Warrior, when life feels challenging you are more likely to respond as a Vamp because challenge activates your fear of abandonment. And if so, until you integrate the Lover's gifts and higher nature, a yearning, Vampish personality will rise to the surface from time to time unbidden, sort of like Mr. Hyde did from inside Dr. Jekyll, where it can succeed in undermining your Warrior nature.

Then let's imagine you subsequently do heal your Lover/Vamp pattern. Suddenly, you may discover yet another layer of defense—one that was previously camouflaged—ready now to overwhelm your progress. That newly revealed level might start popping up all over the place until its fears are addressed. Wounded personality fragments are like the trip wires attached to tiny land mines. They explode whenever our survival mechanisms get activated.

It's a clue that your defense programs are involved when:

- You're confused or upset, and there's no earthly reason.
- You're sabotaging a loving relationship due to knee-jerk responses.
- You're a successful person and suddenly don't care about anything you do.
- You're an intelligent, capable person holding down a boring job for which you are overqualified.
- An unhealthy pattern of behavior emerges out of the blue, like suddenly becoming accident prone, taking unnecessary risks or going on a drinking binge when you're usually a teetotaler.
- Your highest ideals lie in one direction, but you nonetheless keep going in another.
- You take a sudden left turn in life, like having an affair when you're in a great marriage, or sabotaging the job you just got.
- You feel a severe degree of constriction in your body.
- Your mind informs you that you have only a few options.

Are You Being Activated?

The simple way to begin shutting down any subconscious autopilot programs running your life is to determine whether you are in a state of passion or activation. To do so, take a few seconds to check in. Is your energy focused on self-protection, or is it focused on enriching your life? Use the qualities listed below as guidelines to help you determine where your energy is going.

Qualities of Passion: I Feel . . .

Adventurous	Full of possibility	Loving
At ease	Generous	Oneness
Available	Graceful	Open-minded
Centered	Grateful	Optimistic
Clear	Growing	Peaceful
Connected	Hopeful	Radiant
Contented	In flow	Receptive
Courageous	Inspired	Relaxed
Creative	Intuitive	Resourceful
Deserving	Joyful	Strong
Enthusiastic	Learning	Transformed
Expanded	Liberated	Willing

Qualities of Activation: I Feel . . .

Aggressive	Inferior	Spacey
Angry	Isolated	Stale
Apathetic	Jealous	Stubborn
Bored	Judgmental	Superior
Close-minded	Needy	Tense
Confused	Not good enough	Tight
Critical	Overwhelmed	Tired
Diminished	Pessimistic	Trapped
Disconnected	Resistant	Unacknowledged
Dull	Restricted	Undeserving
Fearful	Sad	Unseen
Hateful	Selfish	Useless
Incapable	Separate	

If you are feeling passionate (you identify mostly with the feelings listed in the Passion box), that's fantastic. There is nothing you need to do at the moment except enjoy yourself and go on about your daily life. Maybe you'd like to take a deep breath and remember this feeling for future reference.

If you are feeling activated (you identify mostly with the defensive feelings in the Activation box), I suggest you find a quiet, safe space where you can be alone and connect with yourself as soon as possible. Consider which pattern may have been triggered. Could it be the Vamp, the Martyr, the Conqueror, the Perfectionist or the Escapist? Depending on which one of the survival patterns you sense is being activated, go back to the appropriate chapter in Part I and review its transformational strategies.

Remember, everyone gets activated. That's only human. What separates soul-based people from survival-based people is how they choose to respond when it happens. Bottom line, the five passion signatures are different ways of using personal energy in relationships. Those who embrace the secrets of managing that energy are more able than others to develop and sustain exciting, life-affirming, and mutually supportive personal and professional relationships because they ultimately become passion-driven.

Activation Can Be a Sign of Progress

Until you are in the driver's seat of your life, you have to go where the chauffeur goes, and unfortunately, that may be a ride off a cliff. But a few bumps in the road can also indicate that you're on the first leg of a delightful adventure. I highly recommend you take nothing for granted and just keep your attention on what is right in front of you.

After years of avoiding intimacy, one woman I know did so

much healing of her Creator/Martyr isolationist tendencies that she finally permitted herself to start actively dating. That's when her Lover/Vamp surfaced. At first, she was distraught. Then she realized it was a sign of progress and felt immensely grateful. Her life had expanded and become richer. As a result, her new experiences were triggering a different set of fears.

The woman shifted her attention to transforming her Vamp tendencies and soon found she could connect to men without as much anxiety and activation. Then she began using the qualities of passion as her guideline, noticing that with some dates she felt more deeply connected to herself than with others. Those were the relationships she pursued.

Often it is exactly when we make a positive change or move toward something we want most that our survival mechanisms get activated. The nervous system aims to filter out everything new or different because our mental and emotional programs are always scanning the world around us, expecting the worst. The mind tells us, "Don't do this or that." But we can override it by embracing our passion rather than our fears.

What's in Your Recycling Bin?

Recently, I facilitated a weeklong course at a retreat center on breaking defense patterns. The following exercise was one of the most powerful tools the participants used to heal the wounded aspects of their passion signatures. It is based on the principle that we can transform entire patterns of activation running through our lives by releasing stuck emotional energy that's anchored by a few specific instances from the past. Whenever we break a survival pattern, energy is freed and begins to circulate in a more flowing way.

You can be sure that a pattern truly has been healed when there is an actual, tangible shift somewhere in your life. For instance, if you've been recycling a pattern of debt, compulsive eating or romantic betrayal, a tangible shift would be getting out of the red, dropping some weight or entering a relationship with a truly committed partner. Or your pattern may be an intangible quality like a continuous sense of deprivation or loss, in which case a tangible shift would also be abundance in many forms, including new friendships, increased earnings and so on. The "impossible" may even begin to seem probable once your energy is no longer anchored in place.

The guidelines for this exercise are simple.

Step 1: Write down your life history using a few short bullet points for each of five periods that correspond roughly to the development of the passion signatures. Don't rigidly adhere to these time frames. Estimates are fine, and the periods may overlap.

- *Conception to Birth.* Is there anything you know or were told about your mother's health and emotional state during her pregnancy with you? What was going on in the household before you were born? Was your mom happy, sad, angry or experiencing another emotion? Was she sick or healthy? Was she excited about your impending arrival or scared by it? Did she have family support? Were your parents happy together or at odds? Was your father involved in your mom's life and happy about your arrival?

  Is there anything you know or were told about your birth? Were you delivered vaginally or by cesarean section? Was your arrival relatively quick and easy? Was it drawn out and painful to your mother? Were you a breech? Was the umbilical cord wrapped around your neck? Did the doctor or midwife use forceps or another kind of technology to pull you out of the womb? Were you welcomed? Were you rejected? This is the period when the Prophet/Escapist passion signature is established.

- *Birth to Age Two.* Is there anything you know or were told about your relationship with your mother during your infancy? Was your mother nurturing or removed? Were you breast-fed or bottle-fed? Did you get held and cuddled a lot, or were you often left crying alone in your crib? Was your mom nurturing to you but angry with others? Was she emotionally deprived in some way and using you for her own comfort? Did she have a good relationship with your father? Did your dad leave her or support her? This is the period when the Lover/Vamp passion signature is established.

- *Ages Two to Six.* What do you remember or what have you been told about your parents' relationship to each other and their relationships with you during your early childhood? This was the developmental stage in which you were first exploring your creativity and beginning to have an identity separate from your mother. Do you recall if she felt like a strong or a weak presence? Was she supportive and encouraging? Were you close? Was she distant? Did she leave you in child care to go to work? Was she a stay-at-home mom? Were your parents happy together? Did you have siblings? Did they get more or less attention from your mother than you did? This is the period when the Creator/Martyr passion signature is established.

- *Ages Six to Twelve.* In this period the opposite sex parent has considerable influence. Men and women both should look closely at recollections of their fathers, however. Usually Dad has increasing influence on development after early childhood. What do you remember or what have you been told about your parents' relationship to each other and to you during your preadolescence? Do you recall if Dad felt like a strong or a weak presence? Was he supportive and encouraging? Were you close? Was he distant? Was he around or gone a lot? Were your parents happy together? Did your siblings get more or less attention from your father than you did? As your body began maturing sexually was there a shift in the way you were treated? This is the period when the Warrior/Conqueror passion signature is established.

- *Ages Twelve to Eighteen.* What was going on in your entire family system when you were a teenager? Was there chaos, violence or sexual abuse in your household? Was there alcoholism or drug addiction? How about extreme poverty? Was there shame in your home and an unspoken agreement to hide details about it from the world? Were your parents extreme perfectionists? Was there a strong emphasis on "looks" and achievements? Was your family very religious and highly concerned with "correct behavior" and "being good"? Did you experience any traumatic events that made you feel out of control, damaged or unworthy? Were your parents supportive of your friendships, activities, lifestyle choices and future goals? Or were they denigrating? This is the period when the Visionary/Perfectionist passion signature is established.

One man in my course who did this exercise reported that he'd been told that an X-ray was taken during his birth. It showed that he was literally wrapped in the umbilical cord, which was like a python trying to choke the life out of him in his mother's womb, and that he had his feet first, refusing to come out, as if he knew life would be the death of him. He still has recurring nightmares where he is in the darkness and hears cracking and crunching sounds—possibly a memory of his birth by cesarean section. He also recalls being told that his mother was yelling at everyone in the family during her pregnancy. From these three bullet points, we determined he would definitely have a streak of Prophet/Escapist in his Combo Platter. On top of that defense, other incidents in his life history revealed layers of Lover/Vamp and Creator/Martyr. To cover these he was the Visionary/Perfectionist. As a result, he was an excellent boss of over thirty happy employees who found him to be a man who not only helped set up structures for everyone to follow but also did a great job of listening, solving problems and nurturing them. What was causing him so much trouble was that he was great at being there for others but didn't know how to be there for himself.

Once you've identified the probable layers of your Combo Platter, be assured that you've incorporated these passion signatures in your life somewhere. If you haven't located them already, that doesn't mean they don't exist. You may have been blind to them until now, or perhaps they've been dormant. Step 1 alerts you to their presence in your energy matrix, so their defenses can be anticipated and their gifts integrated.

Step 2: Your soul will lead you to what needs to be healed. In general, it is most helpful to work on whatever problem or issue is right in front of you because that can shift you out of a state of activation and into your calm and passionate core. In this step, your purpose is to retrieve a part of you that is locked into a particular defense pattern.

Decide which of your passion signatures you would like to integrate. For this illustration, let's say it is the Prophet/Escapist. At the top of a blank piece of paper, write down the question: Where am I being an Escapist? Then, on the left-hand side of the page, create a column of the three or four bullet points from Step 1 that you wrote for the period "Conception to Birth." Consider how each one makes you feel. Allow the feelings to exist in your body. Just breathe deeply and feel.

To work on the Lover/Vamp, use the bullets from "Birth to

Age Two." To work on the Creator/Martyr, use those from "Ages Two to Six"; for the Warrior/Conqueror, "Ages Six to Twelve"; and for the Visionary/Perfectionist, "Ages Twelve to Eighteen."

Next look at your current life and any aspect of it (e.g., your job performance, an intimate relationship) that isn't satisfying you or is somehow causing you grief. On the right-hand side of the same page, create a new column of bullet points listing these, or use the space to describe a scenario in which your Escapist tendencies are activated. For instance, taking the case of the Escapist man in Step 1—whose bullets were (1) I felt choked and refused to come out, (2) I was scared by loud sounds, and (3) My mom was very angry at everyone—he might describe this scenario: "When my girlfriend gets angry and raises her voice, I feel overwhelmed or choked, go passive and retreat."

After writing your own description or list of bullets on the right-hand side of the page, consider how this makes you feel. Again, breathe into the feelings.

For the purpose of this book, I designed this retrieval process as a written exercise; however, you also can do it by sitting quietly and visualizing events in your imagination. In my seminars, I usually set up physical conditions that help participants achieve similar insights. It doesn't matter how it happens. What's most important here is that you begin to notice your habitual responses to certain triggers and experience your feelings about them. Those triggers are your personal closing formulas, like the archetypal ones we explored in the chapters in Part I.

Step 2 is all about connecting the dots between the past and the present: identifying themes that run through your life. Often awareness is enough to foster a cascade of insights, liberating you from a whole series of ingrained responses. You know you've found a link when the pattern loses its power over you. Suddenly:

- You feel free.
- You are not fighting someone in your mind.
- Physical tension evaporates.
- The opportunities in your life change.

Emotional Release

Emotional release is a sign of a significant breakthrough. It shows that pent-up emotion, or stuck energy, is being rerouted, and your nervous system is essentially reprogramming itself. You could liken a release to taking a logjam out of a river so the water can flow smoothly. If you're on your own, music, or something you have seen on television, may serve as the catalyst. The body has many sometimes seemingly strange ways it releases pent-up energy. A deep release can take the form of uncontrollable crying, laughing, shivering as if from the cold, yawning or burping. But while the onset of awareness can be like a powerful rocket blast, it also can be gentle and gradual, especially if you're open to transformation.

Visit *www.thepassionprinciple.com* for information on the care and tending of your energy, which includes activities that can assist in emotional releasing.

Crying is the form of releasing that you or others are most likely to try to shut down, fearing that you are feeling bad. Quite the contrary, it is a positive sign. Therefore, one of the greatest gifts we can do for one another is to hold the space for someone to go as deeply as he or she needs to go into an emotion. Holding space may look like sitting silently with a person with an open heart, while expressing comforting words from time to time. Or it may take the form of asking if he wants to be held. If so, hold him and stroke his hair while he cries. When you feel like you need to do something, this is often the best thing you can do. Let the tears subside naturally.

We may forget that we're on a journey of evolution for as long as we live and breathe. Most of us do not come into full emotional maturity, self-acceptance and integration of our beings until we are well into our midlives. Nonetheless, experiences continually come along that help us grasp insights and expand into our potential. Who sends them? Perhaps it is God, the soul, the universe or fate. To me, it doesn't seem accidental. Sadly, however, too many people fail to seize the opportunity to evolve past their childhood pain and the programmed behavior it elicits. Everyone I know who has died accidentally or tragically of self-destruction experienced at least three preceding events that could have shocked them into awareness and led them to take an action that would have prevented death.

Not everyone dies from his or her defenses, of course. But defenses are the major source of pain and limitation in our lives. For almost a decade, I watched a gentle-natured, good-looking, highly lovable male friend—a Perfectionist-Escapist-Vamp Combo Platter—struggle with an aching personal issue: his desire for love. He prayed for love to enter his life, talked about it and did his best to open up to it by neutralizing his defenses. In fact, he made a lot of progress in his life. He evolved and integrated many of his gifts. Yet I also saw him push love and intimacy away by being guarded.

One summer evening, a small group of us went to see *The Notebook*, a movie about the love and devotion of an elderly married couple. The wife, played by Gena Rowlands, has Alzheimer's disease, so the husband, played by James Garner, spends every day reading a journal to her so that by day's end she might remember, just for a few minutes, how they met, fell in love and committed their lives to one another. Seeing this film was the equivalent of taking a two-by-four and cracking my friend in the head—and the heart—with it, waking him up to the love he'd been depriving himself of having. "Here it is," the movie said. And he got it! He also had a revelation of what stood in his way.

As we were leaving the theater, my friend broke down in tears. He was filled with regret. He told us how every time he had wanted to reach out for the love he so intensely desires he experienced terror and shame about not being good enough. "It was like I had Alzheimer's and forgot what love is. But love is not as big a deal as I've made it into by blocking it. It's just two people caring and sharing and giving their lives to each other." To me, it appeared as though a reversal had existed in his nervous system that told him he was not worthy of love, and it had suddenly flipped back into alignment with reality.

In the ensuing months, my friend went through a major shift in consciousness. He reported, "In the past, I would try to control how others perceived me. Now I know it is safe to be me. I wasn't stuck before, I was growing, and yet I couldn't accept myself. What broke my heart that night at the movie was seeing absolutely clearly that I am the one who has deprived myself of love year after year. I put an enormous mountain in front of having it by giving my power away to anyone who might validate my worth. Underneath it all, I did not feel deserving.

"The revelation that led to my emotional release allowed me to start being more authentic in every part of my life: at work and with my friends and family. I faced my fear of revealing myself, then being judged and possibly rejected. It's a risk. Day by day, I've been learning to feel safe, to be okay when I'm alone and quiet, to stop looking to achieve something because I'm not where I am 'supposed' to be and to open up. The more I stop yearning for love, the more I can see how ridiculous my mis-judgments were. It's given me permission to bloom and really take in all the places I am already loved."

When you have an emotional release after recognizing a pattern in your own life, trust that it's an opening that needs to happen—even if you are grieving. It can feel brutal to see how much you've restricted yourself from having what you want. You may fall into a space deep inside yourself for a few days. You may feel exhausted. Like frostbitten toes thawing out as blood circulation is restored, there's an ache as the life surges back into your emotionally numb places. But the ache will go away, so don't run from it. This is an important stage of transformation. If you need to sit at home reflecting for a week, do it. Journal. Share your revelations with trustworthy friends, and ask for honest feedback. Pain can be the catalyst for an enormous amount of growth.

Amazing techniques, such as bioenergetics and other body-centered therapies, are available today to diffuse traumatized emotions stuck in the nervous system. These are part of the emerging discipline of energy psychology. Research has shown that feelings of trauma held over from early childhood are not always accessible by talk therapy. They must be accessed experientially.

Generally, we grow for a while, and then we plateau, as though we're going up a set of steps. We expand and transition, and then we stabilize. When emotional releases happen, they catapult us to new levels of understanding as well as freedom from previous constrictions. They are the launching pads for the next phases of our lives as more integrated beings on the path to fulfillment.

Taking Your Power into the World

There is another important question to consider when you're working to neutralize the defenses of your passion signature, which is: What are they actually defending? For sure, they were created to guarantee your survival. But since everyone interprets how to survive in a unique way, yours are defending the rules your parents taught you to live by. Your defenses inform you through emotional activation that you're going the "wrong" way or doing the "wrong" thing, even when it runs counter to your conscious decisions, like my friend's decision to have love. His nervous system knew that love was dangerous, and his broken heart from years past proved it. His defenses were trying to protect him from further harm—he felt they were sabotaging him with activation.

Our fathers teach us to achieve, to reach out and take what's ours, to stand on our own two feet in the world and to speak our minds. They show us how to assert ourselves. Whether we are male or female, we need to be initiated by Father. He needs to hand us a symbolic torch that gives us permission to succeed in life. But, sadly, he may not be able to, perhaps because he never picked up his torch or his father never gave a torch to him. Some fathers refuse to pass along a torch, for instance, by competing with their children. Other dads are not around to provide a role model. When you were young, perhaps your own father left home due to divorce, death, abandonment or workaholism. If so, there's a chance you'll need to face the father living inside your head and take back your power from him before you can truly be at peace with yourself in the world as an adult.

If you remain on autopilot, the energy you received from your father determines in large part how you assert yourself. Growing up, you'll either embrace or reject his style of assertion. If your father was a passive man, you probably won't be assertive because you won't know how. If your dad was aggressive, you may become aggressive like him, so you can stand up to him. Or you may become passive on purpose because you're afraid of making others feel the way your father made you feel.

A couple came to see me for counseling. In her private session, the woman said, "I love my boyfriend—but like a brother. He doesn't give me a sexual charge anymore." In his private session, the man told me, "I give everything of myself to her." From these two comments, I knew that the problem they were having originated in his father energy.

His father had been a stern taskmaster, whom he perceived as an "enemy." I helped him heal this pattern in a matter of weeks by leading him through a line of questioning that helped put him inside his father's skin instead of judging him. As he reclaimed his assertive energy, he realized that he wanted to be in a different relationship.

Unblocking Your Receiving Channel

Perhaps you want tremendous love, a great job, a ton of money and a new house. Abundance. Fantastic! Those are reasonable goals worth your attention. However, if you aren't open to receive, they won't be able to come into your life. In every moment, each of us actually has all that we are capable of letting in. Remember that the human nervous system is a filtering-out machine with instructions encoded into it of what to block. If we want more, we must go back to our early life programs and carefully rewrite the code.

The source of our receiving and nurturing patterns is Mother. How she physically and emotionally nurtured us in childhood becomes the way we nourish and receive in adulthood. Thus, if you remain on autopilot, the code you received from your mother in large part determines how you receive from others and how much you are willing to give to yourself. Growing up you'll either embrace or reject her style of receptivity and self-nurturing. If she herself was unmothered or undernurtured, in emotional distress or felt trapped, you instinctively mirror her situation. If your mom put up walls around herself, you may have trouble letting in support and affection because you won't know how. If she was overly dependant, you may keep looking for support instead of taking responsibility for yourself. Also, if you didn't feel nurtured by your mother as a child, you may not feel you deserve to receive. You may find many ways in adulthood to deprive yourself personally, on your job and in your relationships in order to sustain this familiar pattern. In this case, the child in you believes, "I am deprived *because* I am unworthy."

Carol was an extremely bright, unmarried woman living on a subsistence wage. She'd spent seven years in a job that bored her. When I asked her questions about her assertive code, I discovered that her father was an entrepreneur bringing home a six-figure income. That told me she had the capacity and instructions to be a go-getter and entrepreneur. So why wasn't she? Her feminine receptive code had to be involved. We turned our attention to her mother's messages to her about support and career.

Carol's mother was a homemaker who had never finished school, and she hadn't ever really taken on life. She leaned on her kids to do things for her and had been unhappily single for many years. She focused most of her attention on looking perfect so she could attract a man to take care of her. From this information, I knew that no matter how smart Carol was, her feminine energy was out of balance. Her receiving channel was blocked. She could assert herself, but she didn't because, like her mother, she was waiting for a man to marry her and make her life okay. We discussed how, on some level, she didn't understand that it was all right to nurture her own talents and abilities. As a result, she'd put a lid on her dreams for a better life.

In a burst of insight, Carol awakened as though from a long sleep. Within a few months, she went back to school for an advanced degree. Then she began a new career investing in real estate. Five years later, she was earning $200,000 a year. She contacted me to let me know how much she loved the creativity of her job.

CHAPTER 8

THE SECRET POWER OF YOUR FAMILY

Anything that is recorded by your psyche as painful when you're growing up is flagged for avoidance and as being a threat to survival. Your imprinting system is not interested in having a relationship, a career or a house. It is only here to keep you alive. The trouble with this is that by the time you are an adult your essence is riding around in an armored vehicle. Although you may step out to have a relationship or an original moment, all that the world sees and responds to is your armoring. Meanwhile you wonder why you can't get what you want. That's your blind spot: *You do not know what you do not know*.

Here's an example. If your heart has ever been broken, your nervous system has no interest in love from then on. Love would be counter to survival, wouldn't it? "Love hurts," is the message you've imprinted. If you don't confront this imprint and reopen your nervous system to the possibility of love, then it will do everything it can to make your relationships predictable, even cause them to fail, in order to keep your heart safe. During your lifetime your world will continually shrink as you keep repeating painful experiences over and over, narrowing down your possibilities. Reenacting patterns only validates the know-it-all nervous system, which chimes in, "See! I was right."

The secret power of your family members—particularly your parents—is that they are the quickest routes to transforming your survival-based patterns. They can help you figure out what you do not know—yet—about your unconscious behavior. Family was the source of your original pain, and it taught you a specific model of how to respond to that pain, so you could say your parents and siblings installed the triggers that activate your defenses and extinguish the fire of your enthusiasm. In this chapter, we'll look at the healing role that you and your close relations can play for each other. Besides being the shortcut to naming your blind spots, your family members are also the key to reopening your nervous system to passion and enriched, deepening connections.

As I was finishing this chapter, at the local coffeehouse, of course, it was Thanksgiving weekend. I sat next to a man in his thirties and his parents who had just come into town. The mother and son, who had obviously engaged in a lifelong relationship of comfort, immediately began engaging in a deep conversation, all but leaving the father out. The son briefly glanced over at his dad, while directing most of his comments toward his mother. Meanwhile the father sat there fidgeting uncomfortably, until his cell phone rang and he had something to do. Having lost my own father, the energy of this dynamic affected me powerfully. The father was the only father this young man would ever have, his master teacher for manhood. Yet he was ignoring him, as he and his mom prattled on. He was missing a huge opportunity. It wasn't until I lost my father and then my brother that I began to understand the gifts family members are for us. For better or worse, our mothers and fathers are the source of most of the key programming that runs our lives as adults. Thus they have the capacity to help heal us in ways not available to us through other individuals.

Often the trouble is that we freeze our family relationships. We tend never to allow ourselves to grow up in the presence of our families, and we also don't allow them to grow and evolve through the years. But if we can allow growth, evolution, forgiveness and the gifts of our family members to emerge in the present moment, they can become our greatest allies. Our parents can initiate us into adulthood and teach us how to take our rightful place in the world in a powerful way few people realize.

Family Members Can Uplift Each Other

Everybody in a family unit basically functions in his or her own world. But most folks have individual emotional hiccups that relate back to their family hiccups. Just like balancing the wheels on a car or getting a tune-up, all their lives become so much richer when these common patterns and mutual areas of difficulty are smoothed out. The advent of the conference call and inexpensive travel has opened a whole new possibility for family transformation. Doing weeklong, intensive sessions of therapy also makes this possible.

Many people are surprised when they learn that I do therapy with entire families, including those with adult children and aging parents or with members living in different states. Some of them imagine that sharing a therapist or doing joint sessions would be an embarrassing prospect. Or that sharing their authentic feelings with relatives would provoke trouble. They'd rather "let sleeping dogs lie." Others worry that I'll take sides against them, and they'll be manipulated. Still others believe their family of origin isn't relevant to any current personal issues because they're already grown up and have left home or their children are long gone.

There is also the misguided belief that therapy is only for "sick" people. On the contrary, I deal with highly intelligent, forward-thinking people in these sessions. Years ago I realized that it takes a visionary to understand that not only could things be better but that it is essential to reach out and ask for assistance. It also takes humility.

To me, concerns about doing family therapy are smoke screens sent up to obscure the root issues that therapy and relationship coaching intend to address. A main reason that mutual counseling sessions work so well is that when people describe their behavior and motivations, the description frequently differs from the reports of the people closest to them. Families are capable of revealing keys to healing and truths that people are unaware of about themselves. The presence of a therapist or benevolent coach makes it safe to do so.

We are thoroughly enmeshed with our families of origin. Relationship patterns from our families show up in every other area of our lives, from our romances and marriages to our business interactions and friendships. We may see and respond to our co-workers as if they were our siblings and to our bosses as if they were our parents. Similarly, we may see a boyfriend or a girlfriend as a parental figure. When we get strongly activated in a relationship or a circumstance, chances are good that a family pattern has been triggered within the nervous system. Then we go on automatic pilot.

Often survival-based patterns are multigenerational. The entire family can be blind to the existence of a specific pattern, since as a group they've uniformly embraced it, and often wholeheartedly. For example, a woman who is raised with the belief that she is less valuable than her brothers is probably going to grow up undernurtured. A part of her nervous system would get frozen into a dominant feeling pattern of "yearning." When she grows up and becomes a mother herself, a part of her would remain a child, and she would pull on her children to get the love she didn't get from her own parents as a child. A woman like this becomes the unrealized Lover, or Vamp. Her children find her needy. As children, they probably give themselves up to take care of her emotionally. In adulthood, they are wounded Creators, or Martyrs, who are so afraid of engulfment that they avoid her. But they also avoid any situation that seems reminiscent of their mother's energy. This intergenerational pattern will affect them throughout their entire lives.

Of course, the woman would never do anything to push away her children if she knew this was what she was doing. Her children, similarly, long to have a better relationship with her. But they do not know that the nervous system does not grow up; that it fixates on certain issues and only evolves through a process of new learning. In the relationship between a mother and her children, even though in truth they love each other, they could easily miss out on a lifetime together. They also could miss out on fulfillment in their individual lives. An extremely valuable gift they could give to each other would be to heal the pulling and pushing of energy in their family.

People adopt the culture of the homes and communities within which they were raised. This includes taking on the value systems (judgments about what's "good" or "bad"). Unmet childhood needs, which I also call nurturing wounds, create our relationship energetics, the patterns with which we connect to others from then on. For instance, if, as in the story above, the household value is that "men are better than women," an accompanying energetic might be: "Men push energy; women pull energy." Another value might be that "women are better than men." Its corresponding energetic could be: "Women give away energy; men pull energy." Everyone's energetics are different. What is significant is that the core fears, and feelings that result from them, are less real or tangible than the movement of the energy in any situation.

Although I didn't set out at first to do coaching with entire families that incorporates an understanding of the passion signatures and relationship energetics, I regularly suggest it to my clients now because it's very direct and much more rapid than traditional individual therapy. In family coaching, if I can persuade everyone to take responsibility for transforming their portion of the group energy dynamic, this redirects the flow of energy through the family system and liberates all the members. As Mom begins to understand what she "feels" like to her grown son, she practices making changes such as not saying such classic one-liners as: "Why don't you ever come to visit?" or "I guess you're too busy to call your mother." Instead, she learns to stand on her own two feet and create a life for herself outside her life with her children. In the process she communicates self-reliance when her son calls and does not complain about her life and how much her son is or isn't calling. He learns to be available without feeling engulfed or ashamed for having a separate life.

As one person goes free, a new pattern is established as a model for the next person. It works because we are naturally empathic as human beings. We hurt for each other as much as we heal for each other. Most folks don't actually clean up their old business with living parents. It is actually done in individual therapy through imagery and emotional release work.

However, I believe that when we are adults, a living parent is God's special gift to us. We have an opportunity that is available only as long as they are alive. When our family members suffer, we feel a subconscious pull to suffer—in the same way a pregnant woman's mate feels sympathetic labor pains.

When a sister transcends a family imprint, such as a pattern of pushing away love, and suddenly allows herself to receive the love she has been seeking all of her life, her siblings often will be inspired to reach toward the same fulfillment in their own lives. They begin to permit themselves to have what they want. It's a strange paradox, but yearning after anything you want blocks it and keeps it at arm's length.

We can get stuck in a pattern of yearning when the very thing we want in our lives goes against deep, formidable imprints. For instance, if a woman never saw signs from her mom and dad of enjoying an emotionally intimate and affectionate bond, she will probably possess an imprint that says, "It's not allowable to fuse in a loving connection." Then as she and each of her grown siblings can't find someone to love, or can't find the "right" partner, the real obstacle remains hidden. In families that hold such imprints, each sibling hurts for the others in some forgotten internal place throughout the passing years.

Among siblings another common dynamic is that one feels guilty for "leaving the others behind" if one achieves success or happiness and the others have nothing comparable in their lives. Unknowingly, each sibling has been living out a version of the same relationship energetic around love, success and so on. The guilt is misguided, however, because it only serves to keep the unhappy, unsuccessful yearning and lacking energetic in place. In fact, a personal breakthrough can initiate a domino effect of transformation for the entire clan. Piggybacking one person's healing on another's is the quickest road to personal transformation I have ever found. Siblings can illuminate hope and fresh possibilities for each other because they come from the same background and share energy patterns.

Parents are the foundation in a house of cards. Any movement from them has the power to collapse the entire house. Then a new house can be built on a much firmer foundation. Although people can heal without their parents' involvement, parental involvement makes things go much smoother. Parents have special access to the subconscious minds of their children. When children—even as full-grown adults—see their parents make a decision to confront their own emotional issues and participate in an evolutionary process, it gives the grown children's own transformational work a boost. In ways we shall explore presently, parents are offspring's most significant role models. On a fundamental level, they are eternally influential. When a forty-one-year-old man works on himself, and ultimately, his sixty-three-year-old father makes himself available to work on himself, this can double the progress made in the son's life almost immediately. It just makes it happen. The elder family member is sending a message to his son's subconscious mind, "I am humble enough to accept that I might not know everything. I could need help. I am smart enough to know when to reach out."

Families can free each other, and it's my belief that we actually have made soul agreements with our close relatives. After all, the difficulties we experience in childhood contribute to the formation of our passion signatures—the positive attributes as well as the defenses. Every family poses different challenges and teaches different life skills. One family is open and affectionate, and its children learn that fusion and intimacy are a natural part of life. Another family can't stand each other, and its children learn that it is not okay to fuse. So they fight and create petty skirmishes or seek connections that will deprive them of the intimacy they crave. One family learns one set of lessons. Another family learns another set of lessons. But nothing can truly conquer the human spirit. Depending on how we play the cards we're dealt at birth—if we make the effort to heal our wounds—we can end up with tremendous gifts.

A deep sense of family loyalty exists, even among people from dysfunctional families or unhappy homes, and my clients have shown that the journey of personal growth is easier when we sense that we're not leaving anyone behind. We may feel like murdering our relatives on occasion, but we love them. Generally, when we're on the shadow side of the emotional continuum, we see ourselves as the victims of life history. On the passion side, we see our families as our greatest teachers and honor them in our hearts. Living with family is like mulching and weeding a flower bed. It can be tedious and difficult work, but folding in manure enriches and fertilizes the soil. Then we can grow beautiful flowers or nourishing vegetables. Difficult work, even pain, likewise makes way for a passionate life of beauty and fulfillment—if we choose to plant those seeds.

You can be a powerful agent of change for your family. By transforming your own role in the group's intergenerational patterns you can uplift the others. No one gets left behind. You can be a model of inspiration for your parents, siblings and children. You can liberate stagnant energy that has been enmeshed with yours. Even if you haven't spoken to relatives for ten years, you came into this world with an invisible connection to these people, and you'll probably feel a deep sense of peace and relief as you sense each of your family members moving toward a better life.

I cannot count the number of times a client has come to me to address a work or personal problem, and in our initial session together, I learn that he or she hasn't spoken to a mother or father for many years. Usually the client brushes this off, saying it's not significant, but I know better. This is like saying the undertow of the ocean I am standing in isn't pulling me off balance. In the process of addressing their presenting problem—the work or personal issue—I make sure to include creating a resolution with the estranged parent. Although at first I get resistance, once the individual understands the connection between the subconscious mind and how it projects the images of family members into other relationships, the client gets on board. The result is not only the transformation of the presenting problem, but the transformation of the client's life.

The Influence of Parental Defenses

Your parents' defenses and passion signatures match yours like a key fits a lock because their personal energy made indelible marks on you at various stages in your development. The patterns below are some of the most common I've observed over the years. A main reason why you're probably a Combo Platter is the dual influence of your parents. By no means is this list comprehensive—it is provided here merely for insight.

- *Vamp Mother = Martyr Children.* A mother who is unnurtured herself feeds off the energy of her children. This pattern is normally passed down for generations. No one teaches us how to parent. The undernurtured child grows up to have children, and the cycle repeats. Since mother energy teaches children how to be receptive, they lack the ability to self-nurture.

- *Vamp Father = Martyr Daughter + Conqueror Children.* A father who is unnurtured himself feeds off the energy of his daughter. Because father energy teaches children how to be assertive, however, children of both genders may become aggressive to compensate for their father's lack of assertion or because they feel they must fight to sustain their own life force.

- *Martyr Parents = Martyr Children + Perfectionist Children (especially if the parents are very overweight).* Parents who leak energy generally teach their children to leak energy. The exceptions are children who reject the parental model and do the opposite, which is to contain the energy under inflexible control.

- *Conqueror Mother = Conqueror-Martyr Children + Escapist Children.* Mothers who dominate their children energetically either cultivate resistance—the kids fight back—or trigger their children to disconnect and check out mentally and emotionally. Their children do not learn to self-nurture well or how to be assertive.

- *Conqueror Father = Conqueror-Martyr Daughter + Martyr Son (with a hidden Conqueror).* To survive the domination of aggressive male energy, daughters of a Conqueror father often reject their feminine energy and wholeheartedly adopt the masculine mode. Since they often felt energetically violated by their father, they resist connecting with male energy. They do not learn to self-nurture because they reject the maternal model. Since the father model is so painful, many sons of Conquerors reject their masculinity and lack assertion. When pushed to the wall by their circumstances, however, they can lash out like the father.

- *Perfectionist Parents = Perfectionist Children + Martyr Child.* Perfectionist parents control their children very carefully with their energy, and the children usually fall in line with the same mode. The children know that it is all about how they look and that they must make the family look good if they want to have value to their parents. For whatever reason, however, there's often one slovenly or overweight kid in the household playing the role of family pattern-breaker.

- *Escapist Parents* = *Conqueror Children* + *Vamp Children.* The energy of Escapist parents is so diffuse and unassertive that children often survive by mustering their own assertive energy. Another possibility is that the lack of calm, consistent nurturing will create a child who grows up yearning for nurturing and yet is attracted to people who are disconnected and unfulfilling.

Having a Healing Conversation with Your Parents or Children

Our real healing power lies in turning around and facing what's behind us. That way we have full access to our ability to feel. Our feelings are how we experience life. Having a conversation with our parents or children is a practical way to clean out the unwanted or stuck energy patterns in our family system, restoring our freedom to feel. At the end of this kind of talk, both people should feel at least a little bit better or more understood.

Imagine you're the daughter of a sixty-year-old woman who comes to visit you, your husband and your new baby. Her arrival makes you nervous because, historically, she has sapped your energy, so you hold up a hand against your mother to keep her at a distance. "Don't come too close." It doesn't matter that she's been to see a therapist, because she has never made much progress with you. Now she's obviously trying to be positive and loving, but you don't trust her motives. You set up obstacles to prevent her from coming near. Why? When she was less conscious, her energy made you into a Creator/Martyr, and now she must deal with the fact that she taught you to fight her engulfment.

Now imagine that you're the sixty-year-old grandmother, and your daughter has acknowledged neither the inner work you've done nor the changes you've made in the way you use energy. It's making you a tad angry that she's still keeping you at a distance. But you've committed to healing your relationship, as you recognize that as a matriarch your energy can affect multiple generations of people in the future. In this case, instead of blaming your daughter for the disconnection between you and making her "wrong," you'll look at the accumulation of stuff you didn't know in the past that prompts her to resist you today. You'll decide to invest in some professional coaching so you can bring a more conscious being back to her and create the possibility of future openings between you. A woman I counseled on a similar issue told me, "I earnestly want to leave a legacy behind me of love, growth and family enlightenment."

The mother in the example above could approach her daughter and say, "When you have a moment, I would like to talk to you." And then later, "I've recently had some realizations. One is that when you were growing up I thought I was protecting you, but I was actually pulling you too close. I don't blame you for wanting to push me away. I am sorry." This kind of communication creates openings.

When the adult child comes to a parent willing to engage in healing conversation, it is vital for the parent to remember that it is difficult for the child to truly move on and set a frozen part free without acknowledgment from the parent. Acknowledgment can be as simple as saying, "I get it. I can now imagine what I must have put you through when I was raging (or abandoned you or smothered you or sabotaged you and so on)."

Never assume your parents or children are broken and need to be fixed. Show respect. Remember that they are on their own soul paths and living their lives as they see fit. If your mom lives in a messy house and complains about being lonely, unless you see her reach out in the world to do something about it—to heal herself—she is actually more attached to her dilemma than to the concept of freedom. She is not stepping out of the pattern because she is inured to the fight. You can offer help, but you must allow her to be where she is. Treat your family as whole and empowered people.

You can have amazing conversations with your parents. It doesn't always have to be in person. It can start out over the phone as well. For an opening, try the approach I used with my father: "As I have gotten older, I've had some realizations. One is that one of us is going to die some day. There are ways I don't know you, and there are things about my childhood history that I don't understand. I would like some time alone with you so we can talk." Except in cases of mental illness, I've never seen a parent reject that approach.

Conversations about the present can be fruitful. A client of mine told his mother, "When you talk to me about Dad behind his back, it puts distance between me and Dad." His mother got upset, but that was okay because it needed to be said. He didn't attack her with it. She denied his comment, but he stuck to his guns. "I need to know Dad and connect with him because he is the only dad I will ever have, and one day he will be gone. I love you, too, and don't want to feel like I am betraying you by getting close to Dad." By having this conversation, he broke an unspoken family agreement.

The most conscious person is responsible for the destiny of any conversation between two people. Your parent may surprise you and say everything you have always needed to hear, especially if you tell your parent what you need from him or her. However, if that is not the case, realize that the person you're speaking with is a wounded child. You may need to end the conversation and find emotional healing elsewhere.

The worst atrocities in families are usually passed down through generations. Monsters can be made. Everyone is born an innocent baby, wide open and ready to love. So remember that your parents, like you, are wounded children walking around inside grown-up bodies. Sometimes the most that parents can give you is an understanding of what made them the way they were. This in itself can create tremendous healing because you will finally understand that you weren't the cause of your parents' behavior.

My father died from the complications of diabetes. For many years, he went through a degeneration process. I had always perceived him as very unhappy. He drank as he and my mother struggled to keep the family store afloat and feed six kids. My image of him was that he was always angry and never home. The kid inside me felt sad because it felt like I'd never be able to get what I needed from him.

The decision to understand my father and his feelings for me before he died was the greatest gift I ever gave myself. It seemed to bring him peace as well. He was more open to speaking than I expected, and over the next few years I asked him every imaginable question about his childhood and what happened to him growing up, and how he felt about his own children. He surprised me. This gruff, silent, once-angry man seemed eager to be understood, eager to cross the gulf to reach his daughter. Part of the magic was that I did not "confront" my father as if he were a toxic parent. I approached him with the goal of understanding him.

On the day before he died, he gave me a blessing that I cherish to this day and that I would have missed if I had not faced my fears and reached out to him. I thanked him for building us the best tree house in our neighborhood. He said, "Thank you, Donna. I never thought I did anything for you kids, and I regret that now. But God will bless your life because you are a good person, and I am proud of you for who you have become." No matter what I had told myself through the years, his words were a healing balm to my soul. Soothing warmth

spread through my heart on hearing them. I was in my late
thirties and although I had told myself I didn't need my father's
respect and acknowledgment, I'd been fooling myself.

Try using your understanding of the passion principle to
help your family open to new possibilities of relationship with
you. If they're receptive to information about the passion signatures and survival mechanisms, you can include them in the
deeper process of healing. If they're not, it's okay. Your willingness to connect honestly matters most. It is a sign of emotional maturity to deal with your parents or siblings without
attacking them. Improve your relationships if they're available.
That's the basic goal of this work.

**If you are the parent of young children, you can go to my
Web site *www.thepassionprinciple.com/passiontools* and get
free information on raising passionate children.**

When It Doesn't Go So Well

A twenty-five-year-old male client of mine kept sabotaging his
professional opportunities because he was enraged at his mother. I
raised one eyebrow and, with the sliver of a grin, said, "You know
what I think? You like making your mom a bit nuts." He looked
down and chuckled under his breath like a kid whose fingers had
been caught in the cookie jar. "Yes, I enjoy torturing her some."
Then he realized, "Wow! I'm failing at this in order to punish her.
When I was a boy, I tried to get her to come home and be with me,
and she wouldn't. She went out playing cards and left me to take
care of my brothers. Now she tries to be there for me, and I'm fighting her involvement in my life."

His insight that he was fighting his mother inside his mind
and resisting her actual nurturing was an important first step.
He saw that the boy inside him was still so angry that he was
holding her hostage. Until he went back to her and talked about

his feelings there could be no redemption on her part. "If you don't change this pattern," I told him, "at age thirty-five you could be doing the exact same Creator/Martyr dance with your mom that you're doing now." Then I coached him how to have a productive conversation with her.

Most children are raised by parents who are barely adults themselves. The parents mess up, lose their way and later suffer regrets. As they get older, the greatest mistake parents make with their adult children is trying to compensate for the past. An angry child is running around inside the skin of their offspring like a ravenous monster. No amount of giving on the parent's part will ever satiate its appetite. The only way to get things back on track is for the child to address the place where the anger began with the parent.

On her side of the dialogue, my client's mom realized that her Perfectionist-Vamp tendencies activated her son's anger and passivity. It was tough for her to do at first, but she decided to back off and stop micromanaging his activities. She'd been trying to make up for the years when she'd neglected spending time with her son, but he hadn't been ready or willing to forgive her and heal, and so he'd acted like a small boy.

Your parents or children may resist conversing with you honestly, or they may flat out refuse to engage in a discussion. Typically this happens when folks go to their family members acting angry, blaming, shaming or attacking. Then the walls go up, and things go nowhere. So be very careful that you aren't trying to lacerate the person you approach. Between any two adults, even a parent and a child, it should be considered a favor to converse about important issues. Wait until you are less activated to initiate a dialogue. Then be as respectful as you can, and take a time-out if you feel agitated.

In communication with your family, avoid the following closing formulas. No one responds well to any of these strategies:

- Trying to change/fix them
- Blaming/accusing
- Superiority
- Minimizing emotions
- Denying history
- Impatience
- Threatening disengagement
- Punishments

If in the worst-case scenario you try to talk to a parent or child and things don't go well, at least you'll know you've tried—so you won't need to have any regrets. Then you can move forward more lightheartedly on your personal path of growth and freedom. You might also seek out some relationship coaching to help you try again. Sometimes there are too many hot buttons between family members to handle a conversation on your own. It's like operating on your own kidney. Know when to reach out and ask for help.

What if your parent is deceased, mentally ill, a hopeless alcoholic or you were adopted? Are you hopelessly stuck? No. That is the blessing of being a spiritual being having a physical experience. The following spiritual process is the key to finishing emotional business with parents and other family members, even if you've lost contact or after they've died. By serving as a surrogate in the following exercise, the participant is released from childhood pain in a more profound way than anything I've seen in the world of traditional therapy.

Finishing Business—Even
When They're Gone

On a daily basis in my practice, I have observed that there is much more to us than anyone understands. Ordinary people from all walks of life—housewives, managers, lawyers and shop clerks—are equally able to draw upon a special ability to tune in to relationships in ways that defy the rational mind. Perhaps they are tapping another state of consciousness or have found a way of *really* getting at the ghosts living in their heads. I believe this exercise is effective because we are spiritual beings who are connected to each other beyond the space-time continuum. Whatever this intuitive or imaginative capacity may be . . . it has the power to set us free of wounds that have been holding us back for years, keeping us recycling our old patterns. As one man put it with a sigh of relief, "I feel like I have finally gotten what I always needed from my parent. Now I can move on."

Here's how finishing business works when I do it in my office with clients. I say a prayer, often under my breath. I ask for spiritual assistance that whatever comes through in that moment for that person will be what is needed for my client's transformation and freedom. You could say a prayer on your own behalf, or otherwise set an intention for healing, if you are so moved. Then proceed with the following three steps.

Step 1: Imagine the parent (or other family member) who lives in your head seated in a chair across from you. In detail, describe out loud what your father or mother looks like—what he or she is wearing, the look in his or her eyes—and what it feels like sitting across from him or her. Let yourself see not only the person you know or once knew, but also the spirit or higher self of that person coming from the other side of the veil, the spiritual realm beyond our world. This is the aspect of your parent that can understand issues so much better now that he or she is free of an earthly life. It is the part that can help you understand why the parent was as he or she was to you, and can say anything the parent would like to say now from this new viewpoint.

Step 2: Say everything you've always needed to say to your parent (or other family member) seated in the chair. Be completely honest and direct. Keep going until you have really cleaned out the barrel of your feelings.

Step 3: Change chairs. Go sit in the chair where you envisioned your parent (or other family member) sitting. Close your eyes and breathe deeply, imagining that you can open a hole in the top of your head. You can breathe the spirit of the parent down through this hole into your body, until your legs become your parent's legs, your torso becomes your parent's torso, your arms become your parent's arms and so on. Also imagine that your thoughts move aside to give the spirit of your parent a chance to speak through you honestly and intimately. Talk to the chair you were just seated in about the subjects you raised.

Some of the statements I have my clients begin with are:

- "Hearing that, I want you to know . . ."
- "Hearing the pain I put you through, I want you to know . . ."
- "Now that I can see so much better, I want you to know . . ."

An important piece of this process is to have your parent explain what happened in the parent's childhood that made the parent how he or she was.

Another way to finish business is through a deep meditation. Sit peacefully with closed eyes and ask your parent's spirit, or higher self, to come and sit in front of you. As you see your parent in your mind's eye, imagine yourself in your parent's skin. Feel what the parent's own emotional wounds are like, see what your parent got from his or her own parents growing up, and imagine what the wounded child inside your parent feels it lacks. Your understanding is the first step in true forgiveness. It can be a powerful salve.

CHAPTER 9

UNLEASHING YOUR ROMANTIC PASSION

Romances and marriages can be the source of our greatest joys and deepest heartaches. Sadly, society gives us more instruction on brushing our teeth than on how to build strong relationships and keep them running smoothly. Even the most significant relationships can stagnate or fall away if somewhere along the line we get stuck and, without realizing it, relate predictably to our lovers and spouses. Due to our defenses, we create problems by tending to hook up to our partners in unhealthy ways. However, we are not condemned to keep blindly following our old, troublesome patterns if we bear in mind that the true source of our love and fulfillment resides within us rather than within the partners to whom we are emotionally attached. Integrating this knowledge alone can eliminate the need for pushing, pulling, leaking or blocking the energy we exchange. With determination and compassion, we can develop the intimacy skills of passionate partners and begin actively building more expansive relationships.

Passion in a romantic relationship comes from sharing a deepening connection with another being. Arguably, this journey is the greatest adventure that exists on the planet. A supportive mate becomes a companion, a lover, a teacher, a healer, a child, a parent, a collaborator and a spiritual guide. Whereas our defenses only serve to keep our lives narrow and unchanging, dropping our personal shields to allow open and equal exchanges of energy with another person, who may ultimately become family and home, expands our horizons and generates new and exciting possibilities in our lives.

Are Your Defenses Blocking Your Love Life?

An unattached person may activate a defense pattern when meeting a potential mate. Let's say we met at a party a day or two ago, and there was a mutual attraction, a spark between us. We enjoyed a wonderful initial conversation—we felt open and connected—and both of us agreed that we wanted to get to know each other better. Down deep, at the core level, we are already prepared to love one another. But staying wide open and connected from now on could be a tricky prospect because of our habitual styles of self-protection. These have enormous potential to dampen our mutual spark.

Before I go to sleep on the night of the party, I have fabulous feelings toward you. Then overnight it's like a switch is activated in my brain. Even though I want to know you and love you, by the morning there's also a sense that it's actually dangerous to be wide open and connected to you. Depending on my past experiences, I may wake up fearing suffocation, abandonment or domination. It could feel as though my very life is being threatened. Wherever you are, you're going through a similar activation process. This is entirely natural, and it's unsurprising. Unfortunately, the next time we see each other it will feel different than it did when we first met—less spontaneous and joyful.

Today we decide to get together again, perhaps for coffee or dinner. During this rendezvous, some of the things you say and do open me up. Some of the things you say and do close me down. Your words and behavior alternately put me at ease or trigger my anxiety. Unwittingly, you've hit upon my opening and closing formulas. The point is that the self you first met isn't really showing up right now, and so we are not having a truly connected conversation. We are not in control of our relationship. Rather, my defense patterns and yours are playing a game of strategy that's not unlike chess. I make a move. You react and make a countermove. Then I react and make a move. And so on. Because the moves are so predictable, if we stay unaware of them our interactions will also be predictable.

Later—if we manage to get that far—the relationship we develop probably will have striking similarities to relationships we've had with other partners. As Jeff said during one session, "I met a woman at a party and liked her, but by the time I woke up the next day, my mind had already raced ahead to marriage, kids, responsibility and the 'T' word—trapped! We went out once, and I called her again, but I didn't have as much fun on our second date. It's so frustrating. I tell myself I want a relationship, but when a potential girlfriend shows up I always run."

Clues that invisible energy patterns intended to block connection are present early on in a romantic relationship include the following phrases. You may hear these kinds of statements being said to you, or you may find yourself saying them to someone else. Be aware. In the moment, they will seem perfectly legitimate and true. The issue is neither that they are truths or untruths, nor that the person who says them is "bad" or "good." The issue is that these phrases often reveal survival-based patterns of behavior:

- "I'm too busy/too late/too tired to get together."
- "I really *need* to go to the gym instead of seeing you."
- "I've decided I don't want a relationship *right now.*"
- "Sorry, I just couldn't find an opportunity to phone you."
- "It doesn't matter how close we get. The day will come when I will leave you. I don't want you to be hurt, so let's not get involved."

Behaviors that are similarly designed to block connection include:

- Frequent tardiness (People who keep you waiting are somewhere doing something—they just have a different priority than you.)
- Canceling get-togethers, especially at the last minute
- Dishonesty, by omission as well as by outright lying
- Failing to keep promises
- Forgetfulness
- Refusing to answer the telephone when it rings (aka screening someone out)

If you catch yourself or a current love interest saying or doing any of the above, it's time for an honest appraisal of your feelings. Reflect on whether or not anything is triggering your fears, as they may be clouding your judgment. Are you running on autopilot due to your defenses (the Vamp, the Martyr, the

Conqueror, the Perfectionist, the Escapist)? Are you seeking validation, security, submission, domination, an outstanding image or infinite bliss? Is your love interest available (or unavailable) to you? Is your attention continually drawn to this individual because, in fact, you two *cannot* connect in a deeper and more enriching way? Did you choose the person explicitly because there's a low risk of success (or failure)? What fear does the prospect of setting this love interest free trigger? How do you feel about seeking someone else more available or whom you would prefer? Does the idea of being alone activate you?

After consideration, if you believe that you and your love interest are both available to each other, and you would like to preserve the relationship, moving it past any blocks that have arisen, ask your love interest to sit down with you for a face-to-face conversation. Be clear about your intentions for the relationship and about your feelings. Speak in the "I" voice, be specific, ask for clarification and offer appropriate praise:

- "I would like to spend more time with you and get to know you better."
- "I like you a lot, and if you are interested, too, I want to date you."
- "I enjoy your company, and I also need you to pick me up on time. When you come late, I feel disrespected and resentful."
- "Because you have forgotten to call when you said you would more than once, I wonder if you are still interested in me. How do you feel?"
- "I liked how the connection between us felt when you responded to my request. Thank you for making the effort."

Keep in mind that you are having a dialogue—a two-way conversation—with your love interest. Listening, therefore, is just as important as speaking. Honoring this person's sense of reality is vital to the relationship, as acknowledgment creates safety for people to reveal themselves and emerge from behind their masks.

Remember, of course, that you cannot change another person. You can only change yourself. So if you are not interested in pursuing a romance with someone, set that person (and yourself) free to seek a different partner. And if someone seems disinterested in pursuing a relationship with you, the best decision may be to let that person go. Often people have mixed feelings about relationships or lack the communication skills that would enable them to express their unwillingness to go forward. They are afraid and freeze up. Nonetheless, you can read their lack of availability through their behavior. A major sign is that words and actions do not match.

Pulling energy is another pattern that often comes up on dates. In the search for love and belonging, many of us expose our Vamp tendencies. For example, a friend of mine went for coffee with a man she contacted through an Internet dating service. In the course of an hour, he told her anecdote after anecdote about the painful experiences from his childhood and how his parents abandoned him. Then he described how one woman after another had hurt his feelings on comparable dates because they wouldn't trust him—a complete stranger—in their cars or at his home on the first date, or because they wouldn't phone him right away to talk more and set up a second meeting.

Although the man appeared to be a sweet, gentle guy with a decent job, my friend told me afterward, "I knew right away that I didn't want to see him again. With a man like that you have to tiptoe around his feelings. There's no room to breathe. He was too intimate too quickly. His own desire was so important to him that he couldn't understand that when women ensure their physical safety it isn't a personal comment. It was as if he was looking for proof of love or an immediate commitment. So I told him that even when people are nice, everyone doesn't always fall in love with them. That put on a damper."

From my perspective, my friend's date provoked rejection so he could recreate a pattern of neediness with women. Vamps may appear to be seeking fusion, yet they are actually committed to fighting abandonment, and so they block true connection. This guy may also have had some elements of Martyr-Perfectionist mixed into his Combo Platter. It is often tough to know which set of defenses you're meeting. It is much more critical to focus on yourself and learn to trust your responses. As my friend reported, "There's no room to breathe." It was evident that there was an unhealthy dynamic between them. She discerned that she wanted to be with a man who didn't have this particular issue.

Of course, you don't have to be "healed" to begin a relationship. While it's important to honor the processing of your wounds and the wounds of others, don't wait to love somebody until a time in the future when you're "perfect." You can go out and enjoy relationships even when you're sad and imperfect. Somebody can be with you where you are, and you can be there for somebody exactly where he or she is. You and your partner can grow together and catalyze each other's growth processes. If you know each other's passion signatures, you can draw upon the wisdom of their opening formulas.

In one of my own relationships, a boyfriend helped me heal childhood wounds through his acceptance of my immature tendencies. Growing up in a household with six children, mealtimes were usually chaotic free-for-alls to get food. As a result, my fear of deprivation was triggered when my boyfriend reached over for a bite off the serving plate when we went out to dinner and decided to share a dish. I could have stabbed him with my fork. Seeing my discomfort, he gently said, "Hold on, let me divide it up so you can relax and eat." Because he didn't shame me for it, I learned not to hate my narcissism, selfishness, "me-first-ness" and fear of losing. He opened a new window in my life.

Perfection is not essential. There always has to be room in a relationship for transformation. In fact, an opportunity we miss all too often is the chance to allow the relationship to be the container to heal our past wounding experiences. A loving and devoted partner can help us heal the pain we carry from childhood. What's important is that you are willing to address your issues and those of your mate. Blocks feel restrictive. Connection feels expansive. Keep your eyes on the prize. As long as you and your partner have basic human chemistry, and as long as you're with someone who is on a growth path, you'll be fine.

Are Your Defenses Threatening Your Marriage?

A young couple, Tony and Melinda, came to me for counseling. Tony was so handsome he could be a *GQ* model. Ever since he got married, his female friend Janet suddenly wanted to spend more time with him. She was a tall, skinny, model type and knew how to make the most of her looks. Although ostensibly she was coming over to talk to him about her daily struggles, "just as friends," she always wore tight jeans and full makeup. Melinda felt uncomfortable when Janet was around. Her behavior seemed inappropriate. But when Melinda complained, her husband said, "Why don't you like her? She's so nice to me."

Janet was a classic Vamp, a wounded Lover chasing after an unavailable man. Her body language and special interest in him got Tony hooked on being around her. That's the intoxicating power of the Vamp. But until I pointed out that his wife wasn't making up a problem, one *actually* existed, he was happy to go along with Janet for a thrill ride. He hadn't observed the pattern or how much he was being sucked in by Janet's allure, and so he dismissed Melinda's feelings and shut her down, thinking she was just acting "bitchy and jealous." His denial was snuffing out his wife's light. In addition, it gave him an excuse for maintaining the hookup with Janet.

When Tony complained to me, I pointed out to him, "Your job in this relationship is to help your wife blossom. Her job is to help you blossom. If she's irritable and 'bitchy,' is it possible that you might be doing something to provoke her to be that way?"

Once he saw what Janet was doing, and how positively he responded to it, Tony realized that there was a woman at his office who was doing similarly seductive things to get his attention—and she was succeeding on some level. This coworker was a sort of Stepford wife type who always agreed with him, smiled at him, laughed at his dumbest jokes and crossed her legs seductively while leaning against his desk. He found himself fantasizing about her when she wasn't there. "How can Melinda compete with that?" I asked him. "And why would you expect her to? It isn't serving the health of your marriage."

In my 50,000 hours of counseling people (many now in second or third marriages), a disturbing number have told me flat out, "I wish I'd stayed with my first wife/husband. But I didn't value our relationship or understand how important it was to me. Someone else came along and I got distracted, so I lost my spouse." From my observations, I'd estimate that 25 percent of marital conflicts are triggered by energy hookups indulged in with outsiders.

Tony was a survival-driven Creator-Visionary Combo Platter and, as such, was highly attracted to the validation he got from women outside his marriage. Like a typical Creator/Martyr, he felt engulfed after making a marriage commitment and desired a taste of freedom. Like a typical Visionary/Perfectionist, he also loved being showered with praise and was quick to deny Melinda's hurt feelings. Unconsciously, he saw them as threatening his fulfillment. He couldn't see how much his defenses were coloring his perceptions.

Tony didn't understand how to make his union with Melinda grow and bloom because his parents hadn't had a happy relationship, and their marriage ended in divorce. He was unconsciously following their model. They had lived in a survive-the-years, children-oriented marriage, so that's what his internal programs instructed him to create.

I suggested he start watching Janet and the woman in the office through more objective eyes. He came back to me saying, "Ohmigod Donna, you're so right."

I replied, "Now, save yourself some heartache. You can become a fifty-year-old man with three ex-wives because seductive women lead you around by the nose all the time. Or you can look deeper inside these particular women right now and consider if you would rather connect to either one of their core beings or to the core being of your wife. Ask, 'Which woman and relationship has more depth, value and meaning for me?'"

He said, "Hands down, I choose my wife."

"Then you're going to have to come to terms with the fact that Melinda's not always in a good mood or perfectly dressed. Sometimes she's tired and not listening. Sometimes her hair gets messed up. She might have bad breath or be grouchy in the morning. Although these other women have no panty lines and always wear the latest fashions, they do not have the essential qualities that you love in Melinda. And even though you were friends with other women before your marriage, if the women make Melinda uncomfortable, you need to listen and create more distance from them. You've been selling out the woman you love for a hit of validation. Until you learn to value yourself, no amount of female attention will ever be enough.

"Melinda clearly perceives the energy you and these other women exchange. She sees that you play along even if you haven't crossed 'the line' of physical contact. You want less sex and you're less available to her because you want to spend more time at work or have Janet over. She feels unloved and threatened. But when she talks to you about it, you invalidate her feelings and call her names. From where I sit, Melinda is not destroying your marriage. Your defenses are."

One person alone cannot establish a connected and mutually supportive relationship. It takes two. Marital closing formulas include:

- Maintaining energy hookups outside the marriage
- Denial or trivialization of your partner's feelings
- Failure to listen
- Withholding your feelings and information
- Unwillingness to discuss problems

Look Beneath the Surface Issues

In my practice, I often counsel married couples. At first they usually want to vent about surface issues that are making them angry. "He works too much." "She doesn't listen." "He's throws his clothes on the floor." "She won't touch me anymore." The entire time they're talking about the details of their lives, I am listening for the hidden code. If I actually started by addressing what they were saying, I'd be lost like a rat in a maze. Instead, I seek to understand their relationship energetics.

To salvage a troubled marriage, it is essential that there was an original spark of passion between the partners. Without that, their connection is lifeless—and probably always was.

Some people heard an inner voice before they walked down the aisle saying, "Don't do this," but ignored it. Later they recognize the consequences of their decision and want to reverse it. As best I can, I've helped such couples end their marriages with dignity and compassion. Most times, however, a couple comes in and wants to regain a flame that's been lost. When they walked down the aisle, they got an internal green light. They loved each other. They felt it, knew it and were excited about their union. Now ten or fifteen years later, they're acting distant toward each other, and one or the other is planning on leaving. My role is to guide them to peel back the defensive layers covering up their core essence, heal their pain and renew their passion.

First I ask them to tell me about their parents' marital relationship. If they have children, I also ask them to describe their parents' marriage at different phases. How was the parents' marriage when my clients were the same age as their children are now? A wife may answer, "My dad left home when I was seven." If so, this informs me that she has no internal map for a thriving marriage. As long as her unconscious machinery stays in charge, something deep within her will initiate conflicts with her husband. Suddenly she'll feel cold and aloof and begin making exit plans. Inside, a voice asserts, "I'm going to leave him before he leaves me!" Usually the parents' marriage aligns with that of the clients'.

If the husband's parents stayed together, yet his father was only rarely at home, his unconscious programming probably guides him to be a workaholic. Ironically, his long hours at the office then may be activating his wife's defenses against abandonment. Because he is often not around her and the children, he accidentally aligns with her perception of men and escalates her fears. On his side of the story, the husband doesn't have permission to come home and enjoy a rich, flourishing, loving and sexually hot marriage. He's missing out, and so is his wife.

I almost married twice. In both cases, I ended the relationships before it was too late, and I am grateful for the inner voice of wisdom that stopped me. After I understood the power of family imprints, I could see that my relationship with my first fiancé mirrored my mom and dad's marriage exactly. Even though we were both therapists and to the world looked good together, we were Conqueror-Perfectionists dedicated to being in a war together against the outside world. We built a business together, just as my parents had built their carpet business by working long, stressful hours and without being particularly nurturing to each other. My second serious relationship was with a compassionate man whose unhealed Martyr tendencies activated my unhealed Conqueror tendencies. Whenever he would implode, he provoked me to go on the attack. After two years of being shut out, I lost respect for him.

Here's a point about which I'm confident. You must have permission, both consciously and subconsciously, to fuse in a marriage. Otherwise, you and your mate may continue to need therapy and other forms of practical assistance to manage your marriage for years to come. If you do not understand that your real issue is about feeling that it is okay to fuse and be happy, then you may end up in an endless stream of minor skirmishes with the same result—distance—which behavior, after all, fits your love map even though you hate it. If this permission to connect deeply does not exist in the relationship that your parents modeled and that your nervous system imprinted, then you need to go inside yourself and change your marital and romantic instructions.

Because the need to love and be loved exists at a depth of the psyche that is so close to the core of your being, so closely allied to your earliest memories, the issues that arise in your marriage can feel absolutely primal. Just by virtue of loving you and being the object of your love, your mate is an incredible catalyst for your activation and thus a reflection of your wounding. When you look at your significant other, you can clearly see your own projected fears and blocks. You may end up resisting your relationship when you're activated if you blame your partner for unwanted feelings instead of claiming them as yours. On the other hand, by providing a safe haven and supporting each other's process of moving from activation to passion, you can be each other's greatest teachers.

The Worst of the Old-Style Relationship Traps

Men and women are different by nature and thus much of our cultural behavior is divided along gender lines. Women have long been the nurturers, caretakers of children and home. Men have been the providers, responsible for income and world affairs. Blended together in respectful partnership, these male and female roles are complementary and sustain families. Yet there's a historical perception that one sex is taking advantage of the other. People joke about the excesses common to the genders—e.g., women are "gold diggers," "manipulators" and "spendthrifts"; men are "sex-crazed," "simpletons" and "power hungry." In fact, there is a basis of hostility and deep mistrust behind these jokes. They expose the worst of the old-style relationship traps.

In our society the stereotypical unhealthy masculine role is as a verbal abuser. For the most part, this man's attacks on the woman in his life take place behind closed doors. To everybody else who knows him, he probably seems like a great guy, but he exerts power over his significant other, putting her down to compensate for a lack of self-worth. His abusive comments may take the form of discounting her feelings; topping her complaints with complaints of his own; withholding information and refusing to answer questions put directly to him; calling her derogatory names like "dummy," "bitch" and "idiot"; criticizing her; trivializing her interests and enthusiasm; and intimidating her or threatening her either with abandonment or physical violence. When confronted about his abusive comments, he'll usually deny them.

Psychologist Patricia Evans clearly explains this dynamic in *The Verbally Abusive Relationship* (Adams Media, 1992). A verbal abuser is a crazymaker for the woman with whom he's in relationship, as she is relating to him from within a different reality. He is operating in the realm of power. She is operating in the realm of collaboration. Therefore, they aren't speaking the same language. The victim of abuse comes to believe she's a poor communicator, because the man she loves just doesn't seem to get it when she explains how hurt she feels. She wants to work it out and make things between them function better. The truth is that he doesn't wish to change. If the woman begins to feel good, it is threatening to the verbal abuser—and he will try to suppress her happiness.

The stereotypical unhealthy feminine role is as a needy and grasping drainer of men's resources and energy. This wily schemer uses her sexuality initially to captivate and ensnare a man, and then she becomes his dependent for life. Although she has no financial power in this relationship, she influences her mate through subtle and overt means of manipulation that range from whining and pleading to teasing; to offering, withholding or seducing with sex; to complaining and nagging; and so on. It's a dangerous position for a woman to be in, especially if she has children to raise, as she could get bounced and lose her "supply line." So she has to be relatively indirect and never exceed the limit of her mate's tolerance.

In the old-style relationship paradigm men and women hurt

one another, and their fear of more pain causes them to be self-protective. Their nervous systems constantly get activated and reactivated. But the dual patterns of pushing and pulling can be stopped, even by working on only one side of the relationship. It takes two to tango.

The new paradigm of healthy relationships energetics is one of mutuality, reciprocity and personal expansion. According to Patricia Evans, "Mutuality is a way of being with another person that promotes the growth and well-being of one's self *and* the other person by means of clear communication and empathetic understanding. Co-creation is a consciously shared participation in life that helps one reach one's goals."

If you've never experienced a healthy relationship or good communication, give yourself a chance to develop the skills by working consciously on them with your mate. Particularly in long-term relationships, we teach others how to treat us. Relationship improvements take reinforcement and practice. Verbal abuse should not be tolerated. Everyone has a right to be treated with dignity and compassion. But even if you and your mate have a shipwreck of a day or week, if you both accept responsibility for your own blocks and activations, and both of you are authentically committed to changing the way you exchange energy, your connection can be improved. Willingness is half of the battle.

Transforming Your Marriage or Romance

Shifting an ongoing relationship from one where two people's defenses are interacting to one where their core essences are connected involves a conscious process. First the partners must establish healthy relationships with themselves, meaning they take responsibility for their own feelings and how they exchange energy through their hookups. They need to be able to recognize the signs of their own activation — even if they are blind to the reasons why it happens — and take care of it. Then the partners need to know how to request support from each other and de-escalate conflicts. The practices of the most passionate partners I know include the following strategies.

- *Employ Intensive, Patient, and Nonjudgmental Listening.* Good listeners always have the juiciest relationships, as they draw their partners out and make them feel appreciated. Here's how it can work. Put your full attention on your partner when you're conversing. As your partner finishes a sentence or thought, rather than jumping in with a comment in response, ask for more details about what he or she just said to you.

  I have a friend who is an expert listener. When I say, "I had a good day," he asks, "What was good about it?"

  "Well, I worked on my book and took a walk in the park," I reply.

  Then he asks, "What did you like about writing today?" and so on, staying with my experience and feelings until I have expressed everything I could possibly want to share. Only then does he take a turn. I never resent giving him a full turn after mine. His ability to listen makes me feel wonderful and never pressured to complete my thoughts in a rush or defend my point of view. It helps us avoid misunderstandings.

  We feel mutually fulfilled and safe to share our deeper thoughts, discoveries and revelations with each other.

  In long-term relationships, the ability to grow personally and share ourselves with loved ones is what keeps things juicy and renews love through the years. So many times in couples sessions, one spouse has sat in wonderment as I got the other spouse to talk about deep and meaningful aspects of himself or herself. It was a simple magic. I kept the focus on the spouse and continued to ask open-ended, explorative questions about what he or she was sharing. The sideline benefit was that the listening spouse felt a renewed interest, realizing that the "book" they'd been reading had more than one chapter. They just had not known how to gain access to the interior pages until then.

- *Discuss Your Opening Formulas Ahead of Time.* Before communication breakdowns, or misunderstandings and hurt feelings occur, it is a good idea to explore how you would prefer to be treated when you get activated. Review the chapters in Part I and come up with a few suggestions that seem applicable to you. Of course, the process of learning what works best in your relationship may involve trial and error. Good intentions count for a lot in a relationship; so keep trying if it's not yet perfect. If you notice your loved one clamming up, snapping back, getting angry, changing the subject or generally shutting down, you can trust that you have inadvertently used a closing formula. A simple question like, "Did I say something that hit you the wrong way?" could get you back on the road again. Let your partner speak fully then, without interruptions, and apologize. Then it's your turn to explain your thoughts.

- *Mirror the Value of Your Partner's Being to Your Partner.* One of the most incredible gifts you can give your significant other is the genuine truth about the qualities you love in him or her. Most of the time, we are unaware of our impact on those we love. The smallest things we do can be so special. Your loving feedback is like nectar from the world's sweetest flower. It nourishes your partner's soul and helps your partner to grow and blossom. What happens to most relationships that end badly is that after years of unresolved disagreements, misunderstanding and stubbed toes, the nervous system begins to associate the partner with pain. People begin to relate in habitual self-protective ways. That's the road to disaster.

- *Frequently Take the Temperature of Your Relationship.* Checking in with your partner on a regular basis will enable you to know when you have swerved off course and allow you to swiftly make a correction. For instance, when stress is high in your lives, you and your partner could unintentionally develop emotional distance by neglecting the daily activities, such as walks and meals together, that sustain your connection. Ask simple questions like, "How are you really doing? How are you feeling with me?" If you get a less-than-favorable answer ask, "Did anything I do help create your feelings?"

- *Pay Attention to How Your One-Liners Are Landing.* One-liners are those tiny comments, usually intended as amusing, that we fling over our shoulders as we leave the room or toss into the middle of a conversation like we would croutons in a salad. Unfortunately, you can all too easily say something that isn't heard the same way you intended it. Therefore, pay attention to your partner's reaction to your tiny comments. Did he look away or down? Did his eyes roll or dart? Did she blink abruptly or say something defensive? Stop and address it immediately. Apologize for any hurt feeling. Clarify what you meant. Clear the air.

- *Honor the Space that Lies Between You.* As two separate individuals who are presently sharing a life, an important part of your relationship is knowing how to give room to your partner when it's needed, just as well as how to come closer when your partner needs connection. You also need to know how to ask for the room and the closeness that you desire. No matter what popular movies and romance novels would have you believe, you and your partner are not becoming one person, or "completing" each other, through your relationship. That silly idea is a setup for disaster.

- *Anger Doesn't Give You Permission to Be Evil.* A little bit of poison can ruin a whole barrel of water, so you must be trustworthy even when you're fighting. You may never use your partner as a dumping ground for your toxic feelings, nor may you use the confidences your partner has shared with you against him or her. Using your partner's weaknesses and confidences as a weapon invalidates your partner — and it is difficult to backtrack and regain trust and connection once you've done it. If you catch your partner saying, "I can't trust you. You always use what I say against me," stop and pay attention. You can never have depth or true intimacy when there is lack of trust. When you destroy trust, no opening formula will work, because your loved one's nervous system will consider you a person who must be defended against. As one woman put it, "I never know when it is coming. I never know when he will turn on me."

  Watch out for "back at you" comments. If your partner says, "You seem withdrawn tonight," appropriately respond by saying, "Oh really? I did not know that's how I was coming across. Well, let me see . . . I am feeling . . ." Never say, "Well I think you are the one who is withdrawn!" Also monitor things like eye rolling, discounting ("It's not so bad!" "You're too sensitive.") or phrases beginning with the word "always" and its kin ("You always . . ." "Here we go again. . . ." "Not again!").

- *Accept Where Your Partner Is.* The subconscious mind doesn't recognize the past, present or future. So denying your partner's feelings or laughing off your partner's opinions by remarking, "That's in the past," is neither kind nor particularly useful. In fact, it's what I call an "accidental escalator" because you have just made your partner more upset than before by making him or her feel discounted. Just because you were able to shrug off an argument, for instance, doesn't mean your partner was. If you were able to get past it, then you are now able to help your partner make similar progress. Change your attitude. Remember, if you are in the process of retrieving parts of you that were frozen in the past, so is your partner. So if something you feel resolved about is brought up, deal with it. Amazingly, your acknowledgment may be the key that helps your partner move forward.

• *Give Your Partner Permission to Call You on Your Garbage.* Either partner has to have the right to speak up and say that something is wrong. One might notice the other partner becoming distant before the partner does, and the one who mentions it should be acknowledged for contributing to the good health of the union. You want to create safety above everything else. You both need to feel safe bringing up the smallest things. Remember, since the mind doesn't know the difference between fantasy and reality, your partner may have gotten activated over something that is completely inaccurate, not happening or made up. But unless you both feel safe enough to clear the air, those little festering items can mean death to the relationship's intimacy. It only takes one spark to start a fire that burns down a house.

• *Learn the Initial Signs of Slipping into Your Activation.* The sooner you see yourself getting stuck, the sooner you can take care of it, and the less potential harm will be caused by your behavior. If you believe you will escalate a conflict, you can remove yourself from interacting with your partner. Activation is an excellent time to retreat, be alone to reconnect with yourself (see Chapter 7) and

consider your options. When you develop a conscious per-
ceiver, a part of you that can watch objectively while you
do what you do in life, this part can help you stay on track
or get back on track if you've slipped.

Remember, when you're activated, your nervous system
is no longer dealing with your loved one. It is now projecting a past relationship onto this relationship, and you
are fighting your past. At such times, it's best to take a
breather. One woman was walking down the street and
realized that she was no longer having a fight with her
lover, she was fighting with her father. No wonder she
couldn't hear his objections to her issues! She took a few
moments in silence to gather her thoughts and return to
the present, and then she resumed the conversation with
her lover. When she was collected, she said, "You know
what I realized? I wasn't talking to you anymore; I was
talking to my dad. When that happened, I couldn't hear
you. I was overwhelmed with emotions from the past."

- *Hold the Space for Your Partner.* When we are activated, it is
  as though movie projectors in our heads turn on and over-
  lay a fantasy reality (nonreality) on top of events that are
  really happening. In essence, we are hallucinating. A loving partner can see the flash of disconnect in our eyes as
  we are spewing angry epitaphs. As we finish, our partner,
  avoiding his or her own activation by knowing not to take
  it personally, can say, "Honey, I am sorry. I forgot your
  Daddy died in a car accident on a road trip. I should have
  left my cell phone on or called you while I was driving. I
  can see that it really activated you." Your partner can then
  take you in his or her arms and mend the fears. What a
  lovely alternative that makes to a potential night of particularly nasty fighting.

  We underestimate the power we have to collapse

distortions by holding the space for each other to share them. When we accept our feelings and deal with them, they move and release, and we are freed to move on as well. It's the things we don't express that fester. We can hold space for our partners and they can hold space for us.

- *Back Away from Verbal Assaults from Your Mate.* As above, there are times when it is good to remove yourself from interaction. When your mate is trying to pick a fight, he or she is activated, and you should try not to allow yourself to be emotionally provoked. It would be easy to let your mate push your "hot buttons," but what good would that do either of you? To avoid the toxic dumping on you, create distance. However, don't just leave or shut down. You can say, "Honey, this isn't feeling good, and I don't think I can respond to you without starting a fight. I'd like to take a walk, a breather, a break so that I'm not so activated." You can also say, "It sounds like you are attacking me, and I'm getting defensive. Can we take a break so we can both calm down, and then talk about this tonight/later/tomorrow?"

- *Look in Your Partner's Eyes when You Apologize.* When you align your body language, voice and words to make a sincere apology, your partner will *really* receive it. Keep it simple. Don't explain or justify when you say, "I'm sorry." It makes a big difference that you stop to get your partner's full attention and then calmly express your regret for any hurt you have caused. This way you know that your apology has landed, and you can patiently wait for forgiveness.

Another magic part of this opening formula is to do reflective listening to what your partner is telling you has angered him or her. For example, if your partner says, "When you didn't come home until midnight after you said you'd be home by eight, I felt slighted, like I don't count." As your partner speaks, imagine yourself in the same shoes. Think about yourself sitting there, waiting for four hours, and how that would have made you feel. The first thing to do after that is to say, "I can imagine how you felt that way. If I had been in your shoes, I would have felt the same." Then stop, and give a sincere apology.

Most folks waste time telling a long story about how the boss kept them late, then the car broke down, and then the traffic jammed. But we all know it's a story. Unless you are stuck in a Third World country without a dime to your name and no cell phone, you could have called to say you would be late. So cut the defense and acknowledge that you were thinking of yourself, not your impact on your partner.

Magical Love Connection Opening Formulas

Whether you are married or dating, your love connection will be much stronger if you understand your beloved's passion signature. **(Visit the Web site *www.thepassionprinciple.com*.)** You can use these opening formulas for the rest of your life. These are special words you can say and special things you can do to open your mate to his or her passion over and over. Most of us are Combo Platters. Here, you will find opening formulas for the many dimensions of the one you love. You can even mix and match opening formulas from a different passion signatures. For example, the Warrior requires you to have integrity, but every passion signature appreciates honesty.

The Lover: Probably the number one opening formula for your Lover is to look him or her deeply, engagingly and lushly in the eyes while you speak together. One woman said, "I was leaning so far across the table while talking to my boyfriend last night that our noses were almost touching. In that moment, I wanted to unzip his skin and crawl inside. He loves it, too, so it works for us." This availability to fuse enables your Lover to achieve intimacy and opens the Lover's soul.

Of course, balanced Lovers also understand the need for breathing in after breathing out. They are able to pull their energy back inside themselves, rebalance, take care of their own needs and stand on their own two feet. They know that they cannot live indefinitely in a fused state with another person. They have learned to swing easily from closeness to independence.

Your Lover needs you to put your relationship ahead of your job, your friends and anyone or anything else in your life. Don't abandon these other connections; just keep your priorities in order. The Lover cannot thrive, for instance, with a mate who regularly works long hours. If you must work overtime or be away from home for a long period, call home and check in. Tell your Lover when you will return.

Whether male or female, your Lover will nurture you and create a sense of a "warm hearth" around which your family can flourish. Like the strong hub of a wheel, your life can span out into many different areas when it's supported by this loving connection, protection and safety.

Opening formulas for the Lover are making special time for vacations around both of you, and turning off your cell phone, computer and television after work. Your Lover blooms when you do things together and set up romantic encounters. Even if you have children or your Lover is the president of the United States, to the Lover your relationship comes first. Ronald and Nancy Reagan's marriage exemplified this type of connection. No matter how their lives branched out, the world knew their love was at the heart of what they did. In the truest sense, the Lover is connected to what is truly important in life. Honor your mate for that.

The Lover opens if you hold eye contact when you talk to him instead of glancing at the television or answering your cell phone in the middle of dinner. She opens when you leave special time for the two of you to languish in bed on a Saturday, physically touching, caressing and caring for one another. He opens when you remember Valentine's Day and special events. She loves when you do special little things throughout your day. Lovers also bloom when you encourage them to develop their gifts and talents, and stand on their own two feet.

The Creator: The Creator needs your nurturing and for you to explore his or her life. Even though your Creator mate will try to put the focus on you, shift it back. Ask your love questions about what is going on with him or her. Be the shoulder your Creator can lean on. It's in the Creator's nature to be the best counsel you could ever need. So do the same for your Creator.

Respect that your Creator is like a flower that opens and closes in cycles. Intensive engagement with you is often followed by a need for space in order to rebalance. The Creator senses the subtle edges of his or her boundaries as they diffuse and merge with the surrounding world. This interdependence may feel wonderful for a while, and then it will be followed by a strong desire for independence. So in loving tones, remember to ask, "What do you need right now? How about I give you some space? I never want you to feel obligated when you need to take care of yourself—there is always another day. You are free to do what you need to do to take care of yourself." Sensing the needs of your Creator relieves the Creator of pressure.

When two Creators get involved, there is an understanding that exists between them that makes this kind of communication more common. The Creator is the master of simultaneously seeing several points of view. Few others are so adept. Yet when you truly drop your self-involvement and make the attempt to get inside your beloved Creator's skin you will discover the capacity to deepen your intimacy in ways you never thought possible.

I went out to dinner with a Warrior-Creator who took me to a magnificent restaurant. Unfortunately, the maître d' seated us in the middle of the room. The cacophony in the bustling space felt like it was going right through me. I would have liked to be seated in a quieter spot, but looking around, I saw no other tables, so I decided to be polite and do the best I could. A few moments later my date excused himself from the table. He returned with the maître d', who moved us to a quiet nook in the corner of the room, where we proceeded to have a lovely three-hour dinner. When I expressed my deepest gratitude, my date said, "Donna, I could feel your distress, and I knew I needed to do something about it." This man demonstrated one of the most effective opening formulas for the Creator. He felt *into* my needs. I had spent a lifetime feeling into others' needs. I was moved when he cared enough to feel into mine.

If your mate is a Creator, chances are he or she has a people-oriented job. Creators often will be around people, talking, negotiating, problem solving and smoothing out rough edges all day long. The greatest opening formula and gift you could give your Creator is to stop and take your love in when he or she gets home. Ask, "How was your day? What did you have to deal with?" Give the Creator a full debriefing and then say, "What do you need right now? If you want to lie down and rest, take a shower or watch TV, just let me know." Since Creators easily feel trapped or hemmed in, make sure you encourage your Creator to take a night out upon occasion. Creators need time for themselves.

Since Creators are "nice" and feel guilty when they express their needs (especially if they think it will hurt you or that they are being selfish), don't get upset if it is a bit confusing to deal with your Creator. Creators are so used to giving themselves up that they often can't figure out what they need until they have already agreed to something. Later they realize, "Hey, this isn't what I wanted!" One wife told her husband, "I can't believe you are mad at me right now. You told me it was okay for me to go to the beach today. Therefore, I thought you were saying it was okay for you to stay home with the kids on your day off." In truth, both spouses were burned out. Even though he said yes, this woman could have helped her Creator husband by "feeling into" him and saying, "You know what? We are both tired. How about this plan? If I go to the beach today, next Saturday you can play as much golf as you want."

The Warrior: Keeping your word is the most important opening formula your precious Warrior has. A handshake is a deal. Since the Warrior is often misunderstood due to his abrasive style, he is used to betrayal. Therefore he values straight, open, direct talk. As one Warrior stated, "You can say anything to me. Just say it. I love that. It doesn't matter if it hurts. I can take it. I would rather know the truth." Consistent loyalty will open your Warrior. He would probably die for you. One woman said of her Warrior boyfriend, "When I saw the movie *Titanic*, I cried. My boyfriend is just like the character Jack. He would wait for me, stand up for me and protect me under any circumstance."

The Warrior needs your tenderness and understanding more than any other type. Because he or she often comes across much harder or harsher than intended, the Warrior may be touch deprived. Although your Warrior may not be used to it at first, experiencing physical touch that's given with the intention of nurturing can melt the stone that shields the heart. Touch does not always have to be sexually based. But Warriors' bodies are strong enough to tumble, so avoid using touch that's limp or passive. The Warrior needs to be able to feel you. Imagine that you are connecting with your own heart and sending your feelings through your hands as you are touching the Warrior.

Your Warrior attacks life like a battlefield. When he or she comes home, treat the Warrior with the respect due someone who's been out in the world fighting to support you and your family and preserve your well-being. The Warrior will feel appreciated and open to your softness.

This is a highly sensitive being with a big heart. The Warrior's armoring was put on to defend against a world that hurt too much. Connect with your own softness, speak in gentle tones, touch with tenderness and read between the lines. Direct disagreements will activate the Warrior's Conqueror aspect and a win-lose battle will ensue. It makes the Warrior feel wrong, defeated or stupid when you seem to win. Find what you agree with in what the Warrior says, let your love know and make any additional points you have sound like extras. You must ask yourself, "Do I want to win or open my Warrior to love?" Whenever possible, listen for what your Warrior intended to say, rather than how it was said.

When you must teach your Warrior what is not acceptable, try different approaches. Once I had to leave a boyfriend of mine warming a bar stool as his commanding tones and overbearing point of view became intolerable to me. After three attempts to stop him—to no avail—I finally told him I had to go. He was shocked. It made the point. Several days later we spoke, and in gentle tones I described how I had felt and how he was coming across. He began to change this aspect of his communication style.

If two Warriors make a love connection, they will probably be dedicated to each other. What may tank their love, though, is that they fight like gladiators when they're in conflict. As they switch to being Conquerors, they will do anything to win.

If there are too many spears to the heart, their love won't survive.

If your partner is a female Warrior, you must be strong on the inside and emotionally available to her, even gentle, on the outside. To feel safe, she is going to need to feel like she is in control. In her heart, she wants an equal with whom she can surrender. As she begins to feel safer in your presence, she will soften and open. It takes a man with a bit of intelligence to "read" into this woman's depths and understand her complexity, because on the inside she is afraid of men, having been overpowered or dominated by her father. She comes across as self-reliant, strong and not needing anyone, a tower of strength. But way down deep, at her core, she is the Lover with a deep desire to connect in an intimate and loving way. If you become too passive with the female Warrior, you will lose her respect. Even though you think it's okay for her to pay the bills and run the house after working all day, think again. Take over, even when you don't know she needs it, and she will melt in your arms.

The Visionary: Your Visionary is a good person whose presence feels light. There's nothing burdensome here. Treating your mate as though he or she is well-meaning will go a long way in your relationship. Your Visionary's generally upbeat nature responds to upbeat attention. Lavishing your Visionary with praise about how good he or she is at a task, what a good job was done, and how good he or she looks will open your Visionary up. Imagine you're in the presence of a person who just wants to be a good boy or girl and get your approval. Treat your Visionary mate with tenderness and appreciation, and your love will do whatever he or she can to please you.

The Visionary needs you to attend to the physical world of form. Your mate naturally responds to perfection and beauty, so when you take care of your body and live a healthy lifestyle, it communicates that you care about the Visionary. Since your Visionary mate tends to his or her own garden, keeping healthy and vital, the Visionary appreciates you valuing him or her enough to do the same. Aesthetically pleasing colors, style, class and sophistication open the Visionary, whereas harsh tones, ugliness, abrasiveness, classlessness, yelling and pointing out imperfections close this optimist.

Your Visionary needs you to role model being "real" in any moment. You can show your mate how to flow with feelings that are not positive. Encourage the expression of pain, sadness, guilt, anger, jealousy, inferiority, insecurity and all the other messy feelings we have as human beings. It's not "all good." Share your deep discoveries about self, your daily experiences and your humanity, and encourage the Visionary to do the same without shame. This will enable you to deepen your love connection.

One Visionary man, who had regressed into perfectionist tendencies, continually criticized his wife for little things she wasn't doing right around the house. He finally said, "I feel jealous that you get to stay home with our lovely children. You often talk about loving your life, and I hate my job—I don't love my life." His wife immediately opened. "I can understand why you would feel that way. The courage you have in sharing this with me is the reason I love you so much." They didn't have to have the answers yet; they only needed to feel the strength of their connection. Together they had opened a new possibility for depth in their marriage.

The Achilles' heel of the Visionary is the need to be right. Because you love your mate, try to tolerate his or her need to have the last word on just about everything. Imagine your partner as a friendly, tail-wagging dog who brings back the right answer instead of a stick. Being right includes being right about the way the coffee tastes in the morning and being right about the way the dishwasher is loaded. Everything in the garage has a right place, too. Remember that your beloved connects being right to being lovable and valuable as a person. So if you need to disagree, try doing so in a way that doesn't sound like a disagreement at all. Otherwise, you could have a long night ahead of you, with you ultimately giving up as soon as your Visionary exhausts you—after having championed the last word.

The Prophet: To open the deep, mysterious connection that is possible with your beloved Prophet, you must understand that the world you will share is yours alone. You have engaged an otherworldly creature with a rich inner world, one in which you can be taken to the rings of Saturn through the Prophet's imagination or to a castle in Camelot. Your Prophet has many secrets. Many places your beloved's mind goes are experiences that transcend the physical world. These are shared with no one, unless you choose to be the opening force in the Prophet's life.

An amazing opening formula for the Prophet is to ask gentle questions and explore the Prophet's inner world without judgment. Remember that this type believes they could be called crazy if the world only knew what went on in their heads. One Prophet told me about communicating with the dead, another described a psychic experience of reading someone's future, another telepathically read my thoughts while yet another spoke of channeling the archangels. These phenomena sound crazy to the rest of us. But if you call him or her crazy, your mate will shut down. If you humble yourself to the fact that there may, indeed, be so much more than we can perceive that exists in the nonphysical world, your Prophet may be just the one to take you there.

Although your Prophet may live in solitude, your beloved craves a sense of security. When you provide a grounding connection, your Prophet will open and can use your bond to feel safe emerging further into the world. If your Prophet alludes to weird or crazy experiences he or she is having, stop, get still and ask, "What's happening? What are you seeing? What are you feeling?" For over twenty years, my office has been a safe haven for many Prophets to speak what was in their hearts. I have been a nonthreatening listener. It is the Prophets who have come into my office afraid of being crazy who have taught me most about the invisible realms. Most often they have a private world they do not even share with loved ones. They have a sense of living one life in the ordinary world and living in another world as their truest selves. One Prophet said, "I feel like an alien in this world." Touching the Prophet's alternate world with your beloved will open your Prophet emotionally to you. In return, your Prophet can teach you to know God in love.

Never expect your Prophet to be the life of the party. Your Prophet is like a delicate gift from God, your own hidden treasure, a special jewel, and must be treated as such. You must be independent enough to be content on your own while valuing what the Prophet brings to you. Respecting the Prophet's need for time in seclusion will open your beloved. Another opening formula is to *see* your Prophet. Think of your mate as your own private Harry Potter. When the muggles look at Harry, they see a crazy person. He lives under the stairs and has strange powers. But he's really a benevolent wizard. Your Prophet is here to give a gift of spiritual teaching, higher science, psychic phenomena, clairvoyance, metaphysics and creativity.

When you open your beloved up, it becomes easier and safer for the Prophet to share his or her gifts with the world. One man who began channeling after a near-death experience lived in obscurity with his ability until a very grounded partner came into his life to serve as his trusted lover and companion. Through their love connection, this man started sharing the higher information he received with the world. Touch, tenderness, kindness and reassuring words are all opening formulas for your personal ET. Never hit your Prophet straight on with anger or harsh confrontation; otherwise, your love will blank out. Wait until you are calm before talking to your beloved if there is some conflict that must be discussed.

How to Know When to "Cut Bait" and Toss the Fish Back into the Sea

Unless a soul is willing to be involved with another, there is no hope whatsoever for a relationship. No set of skills you can learn from any book, seminar or TV program could create a breakthrough when the soul does not choose it. Of course, this can be terribly frustrating for a willing partner. It's painful, a lot like hitting your head against the wall. But all too often we do not listen when we are told no because we believe there must be something more we can do to fix it so our desires prevail. A part of us wants what it wants when it wants it. So we ignore the inevitable and keep on trying.

A man who says, "This relationship doesn't fit into my twenty-year projection," or a woman who tells you, "I leave everybody with whom I get involved," is telling you that he or she is not available. That's the truth. This person most likely has chosen your relationship, with its current limitations, because in his or her mind it does not have long-term potential. It doesn't matter how great the sex is, how attractively you dress or how well you get along, the day will come when you will hit that nasty wall of resistance. In fact, you will most likely hit the wall right after you attain an amazing state of ecstatic union. Then out of the blue, everything will come to a screeching halt.

Most likely you will stand there dumbfounded as you receive this bit of news from your love interest, because you've previously been told you are the most amazing person this individual has ever been involved with, yours is a connection beyond anything he or she has ever experienced, or your spirits have expanded into other universes. You may think, "Oh my God. It's so amazing. I am so glad to have this person in my life." Then suddenly, the very next time you speak to your love interest, he or she informs you out of nowhere, "It's over." It's very important to listen to what is being said to you and heed the messages. Otherwise, you are in for deeper disappointment.

"If only my partner changed, things would surely work out," we say, and ask, "How can my partner walk away from the potential between us?" An answer is that people walk away from others if they do not have a space within to hold love. Love can be too scary. Another answer is that people do not realize that relationships can help them integrate developmental tasks. Each unrealized passion signature has a self-destruct mechanism. When the autopilot is switched on, the nervous system is narcissistically motivated to avoid the pain of childhood. It doesn't see the potential for adult love through adult eyes—the potential this person is showing us to heal some wounded aspect or explore some unrealized aspect of self. It doesn't live in the moment.

The nervous system can be stronger than the human heart. As I've repeatedly said, its only interest is protection from anything unfamiliar or that has caused past pain. For some people, the possibility of establishing a profound connection poses perhaps the biggest threat anything could. The Vamp will feel "not good enough," the Martyr will feel "engulfed" and so on. Many people run from intensely connected relationships. The fire of passion is literally too hot for their nervous systems to handle. Without the soul choice to hang in there and face the fire, a connection doesn't stand a chance.

It doesn't matter which techniques you use in a relationship. Unless there is an awakening of consciousness and a desire to increase the level of intimacy, there cannot be a breakthrough.

You can easily spend ten years trying to get a Martyr to commit to you without ever succeeding. Martyrs are too concerned with what they'll miss out on later to commit today. Perfectionists have been known to spend thirty years trying to find Mr. or Ms. Right, and no one is ever good enough. You won't be good enough either. You can beg a Conqueror to come home from work and put your relationship first for twenty years, only to bury your mate before he or she has honored your request. You can consume five years trying to get an Escapist to join you in the three-dimensional world to no avail, and forfeit just as many years of effort trying to establish a significant relationship with a Vamp. To the unwilling partner, the moment you become available the attraction is gone.

Everybody carries invisible wounds that show up only in the light of love or when we are facing the possibility of expansion. As long as the status quo exists, these wounds are never revealed. But when our relationships trigger the wounds to rise to the surface, relationships also become the containers in which we can heal old wounds. As adults, relationships—and the special people with whom we choose to partner—are the resource that helps us come into wholeness. If she did not have a nurturing father, for instance, a woman might attract a gentle lover into her life to give her the nurturing she never received as a child. But that transformation could not occur if the lover were unwilling to participate or if the woman herself was unwilling to connect with another being and risk intimacy. For the process to begin, the first step is that two souls must choose to commit to each other in relationship—at least for a period of time.

In her audio program, *The Breakup Bible* (Sounds True, 2000), Daphne Rose Kingma talks about how most of us do not reach our full adult development until well into middle age. Along the way, our relationships serve to help us accomplish various developmental tasks that did not get done in childhood. Rather than indicating failure, relationship endings are often signs that a developmental task has been successfully completed. Many people cause themselves an enormous amount of heartache when their wounded personalities lock. Then instead of using the relationship as a vessel for growth, they cut bait (break up) and toss the fish (a partner) back into the sea.

One of the most maddening Combo Platters is the Vamp-Martyr. These are the type of people who cannot be with you because they are still kind of involved with a former partner or spouse, and when you try to get them to commit to you, they accuse you of trying to control them. In fact, they may have two or three friendly ex-partners. If something about this situation seems uncomfortable to you, take note. Do you feel connected to this person when you are together? When you are apart, do you feel as if this person is connected somewhere else? If you ask your love interest to choose between you and the other, do you come off looking like a jerk? If you can feel the tug-of-war, you probably will never win here. Let go! You deserve better.

Anytime you feel as though you are losing your mind in a relationship, it's a sign that your nervous system is up to its old tricks again. Furthermore, unless you figure out what is going on and find a way to calm it, the nervous system always wins. It only creates and recreates what it already knows. Period. End of story. One forty-five-year-old man grew up under the domination of an angry, controlling mother. As an adult, he continued waging battle against his mother by never committing to one woman. In a series of monogamous relationships, he provoked a long stream of women to become hostile and demanding, just like his mother, until the day came when each one could not stand any more and left him in disgust. What he didn't realize was that his Vamp-Martyr aspects were so ruling his life that love would elude him forever unless he dealt with his wounds. His latest girlfriend, a woman who wanted to understand her patterns, brought him to my office. She asked me to help her decide whether to stay in the relationship or break it off.

The man was the eternal "nice guy" who would do anything for his woman, except commit. Each of his previous girlfriends only knew this accomodating, chameleon-like guilt of his. His defiance of her was never put in her face. It was subtle, insidious, behind-the-back stuff, nothing she could put her finger on. He seemed to be there, in the relationship, except he wasn't really there. He told his new love interest that he was keeping his connections with the other women because he didn't like to hurt people. He insisted that he wasn't stringing anyone along—it was just that he had never found the one woman to whom he could commit.

My client was a Lover/Vamp who had been replaying a traumatic childhood scene of her own with the boyfriend. In relationship with him, she was trying to get her abandoning father not to leave. Her dad had walked out when she was a small child, never to be seen again. Both were full-grown adults, yet when it came to love, they were hopelessly locked in a painful cycle of tug-of-war.

Remember: There are no bad guys here. Sometimes we're ready for things, and sometimes we are not. A sign that you are personally not ready is that you continue choosing people who are also not available when you check below the surface. Or if they are available, you "make" them not good enough or tell yourself, "Not now."

If you are on the receiving end of a message of reluctance, hang in there for a little while in case your love interest becomes more comfortable. Seek help in processing your feelings if you must. But if you find your self-esteem draining from you as you wait, or you feel less and less valued by your mate, it is time to cut bait and walk away.

A Final Thought

If you are in a loving relationship, it is vital that managing the relationship and growing in the relationship become your two highest relationship priorities. You must be honest and diligent. You must take responsibility for your own energy, feelings, thoughts and defenses. And try to understand your impact on your partner. This last item can matter most when things are going wrong or you are aiming to deepen the relationship, for instance, because one or both of you believe that something more is needed. As was mentioned above, take unwavering interest in getting into your partner's shoes and seek to view the other as yourself. These are the keys to unleashing romantic passion, a powerful connection made between the cores of two individuals that produces joy and soulful expansion.

Chapter 10

YOUR KEY TO SUCCESS IN THE WORKPLACE

Years ago I was hired to give a two-hour lecture to the senior staff of a rural retreat center owned by a well-known author who also had a nationally syndicated radio program. With a crescendo of nervous anticipation, I drove onto the grounds of the sprawling, several-hundred-acre estate where bison and longhorn cattle were grazing in the pastures. The famous man himself greeted me at the door of a large, southwestern-style ranch house. Tall and thin, he had hollow cheeks and eyes that were buzzard-sharp and piercing. In his presence, I immediately felt uneasy. It was strange that people sought out this foreboding man for health tips when he looked devoid of spirit and energy.

My host leaned in too close as he shook my hand, bore his gaze into my eyes and with an icy tone that made my stomach turn over, said, "I've already covered everything. There's nothing left for you to teach. So I've cut your time from two hours to one." Then he opened the door to a room filled with waiting retreat attendees and added, "Have a good talk." Even though my success on that day would have been no threat to his own — he had published thirty-five books — I could feel him literally trying to drain my confidence and put me off balance — classic signs of a power stalker, the Conqueror-Vamp. In response, I thought, "Not this time, buddy." I reflected on what a shaman had told me about the invisible things people do with their energy to steal power on the job. Here it was in my face. I raised an invisible shield between my host and me, then stepped into the room and had a wonderful time giving my talk.

Power stalkers steal energy from others in order to build their life force — Conqueror-Vamps in the truest sense. It can feel as though you've been slugged in the gut after an encounter with one, as your self-esteem is drained. If you aren't savvy to their emotional tricks, you can end up being reduced from a confident adult to a tiny, insecure child in their presence. Disempowered people, usually Martyrs or Vamps, tend to surround these Conqueror-Vamps. On the job, they are bosses and managers who intimidate their employees. As teammates, they have insidious ways of condescending to their coworkers, who become less capable as the years go by.

Such Conqueror-Vamps may use their sexual appeal inappropriately to seduce you and drain your energy. You'll know a power-stalking Conqueror-Vamp has bitten you if you find yourself mixed up in an office relationship with a charismatic charmer who intoxicates you — until this person gets what he or she wants and throws you away. Or your colleague may keep you around for future feedings anytime he or she needs something. It's a sign that this is a Perfectionist-Vamp if you feel like Mr. or Ms. 007 has you in a spell. The Conqueror-Vamp will be a bit more brusque, but intoxicating and over-powering all the same. Another sign you're being drained is that you feel intimidated and destabilized emotionally after you've been in this person's presence.

Or perhaps you are the power stalker. You may not realize you are a drainer. All you know is that you feel needy and lost without other people's attention on you. Also, you don't like it when someone else shares the spotlight, concludes the deal or garners praise, so you make little remarks and do little things to cut him or her down. Unfortunately, you can't build a truly secure and powerful career out of stolen energy and apprecia-tion. Actually, you are taking from others what you need to develop for yourself. If you do build a career based on this, your success will feel hollow. One man with whom I worked was worth $600 million; however, he went home alone every night and drank himself to sleep. His superiority complex had squeezed the juice out of his life.

The key to success in the workplace is being your own source of energy, value, meaning and purpose. Whether we allow oth-ers to drain our energy or we focus energy on draining others, in the end we are the ones who become depleted. A strong foun-dation cannot be built on sand. It needs to be built on solid ground. Likewise, we need to establish a solid foundation at the core, so we can build strong professional careers, move toward our goals, create financial abundance and interact with people on the job in a healthy, mutually beneficial manner. Until we do, our survival fears will lead us into a constant series of seemingly uncontrollable energy hookups, and none of us has enough con-sistent life force then to successfully accomplish our goals.

For a handout on the care and tending of your energy, go to the Web site *www.thepassionprinciple.com.*

Are Your Defenses Blocking Your Success and Income?

Here are some of the fundamental ways that the different passion signatures get activated in regard to jobs and money. These few survival patterns are very common. Once you notice them in your recycling bin, you can start making better choices.

Lover/Vamp: If you have this passion signature within you, chances are that you hunger to be taken care of. This means you may be fairly passive about building your career and earning income for one twisted reason: If you were to stand on your own two feet, you wouldn't need to be taken care of anymore. Then how would you know you were loved and measure your worth? One of the Lover/Vamp's biggest fears is abandonment, so you probably pull emotionally on your coworkers, boss and even your assistant and feel pretty bad if you get shut out or cut off for any reason. A key for you is to acknowledge yourself daily and be proud of all your accomplishments.

Another big tool of your self-sabotage is the drama you can create about everything in your life. The most productive, successful people in the world don't waste much mental energy on intrigues between coworkers or competitors, nor do they worry endlessly about their own motivations and sad stories. Rather, they get clear about their intentions and function as best they can in the face of their present circumstances. If you need help, remember to ask for it or seek it out from available sources. If you catch yourself dramatizing—rehashing stories about work-related events and people—stop and change the subject or find something new to occupy your attention.

Retire your drama queen tendencies. Don't spend fifteen minutes at the coffee machine going on about how Jane offended you when she used "that tone of voice" with you or continually talk over the cubicle divider because you can't stand to be alone. These tendencies include going on and on in meetings, asking more questions but never seeming to get your fill of the answers. Vamps can be talkers. They can drain the life out of people that way. If you have that reputation on the job, you can be sure it will cost you in salary and promotions through the years.

Creator/Martyr: If this is your passion signature, you've been programmed to fight deprivation. Thus, if you have two job opportunities, you may sabotage both offers or projects in order not to feel deprived of one at the other's expense. That's no way to get ahead. Success and careers are generally built one step at a time. Being able to say yes or no—to choose—and being able to stick to your plans is crucial to your growth.

Another pitfall for the Creator/Martyr is the inability to choose. Typically, you say, "If I commit to this now, what will I be deprived of later?" So you don't commit. Later when you realize there wasn't another great opportunity of its kind coming down the pike, it's too late. I speak from personal experience. Many years ago I sabotaged an enormous television opportunity this way. I was offered to be the on-camera therapist for a major talk show. But I immediately felt trapped and said to myself, "If I do this, what other offers will I be deprived of later?" Needless to say, I sabotaged the offer.

Creator/Martyrs are also afraid of being engulfed. Therefore, the quantity of your work, as well as the importance you attach to it, can easily overwhelm you. "Saving the world" may be a heavy burden, after all. Creators are afraid of taking their power in the world because they see giving as giving themselves up. So there is a natural conflict between the feeling of having a great deal of creativity to share with the world and the fear of the burden associated with giving. For this reason, you may be afraid of making commitments. Everything is processed through the fear of losing.

A Martyr friend of mine could rarely close a deal because she always felt paranoid that she was being "scammed" when she negotiated her contracts. All she could think of was what she might be losing in the deal. In another case a Martyr nearly drove the realtor she was dealing with nuts as she had herself escorted to over one hundred homes in an attempt to purchase. Each home, however, had some element or advantage that made it impossible to choose among them.

If you're afraid to commit to a project, job or deal, it can be helpful to get down on paper the nature of your true needs. For example, consider the deadline, your time requirements, your abilities, the support structure, built-in communication lines, possible best-case and worst-case outcomes, your acknowledgment, your earnings and so on. Review that piece of paper for pros and cons, then weigh them against each other, and bring any concerns to the table. Check for signs of emotional activation. If you're in your center, you will feel calm, unpressured and reasonable. If you're activated, you'll feel tense, constricted, reactive and anxious. Do your energy work, and then move forward.

It's also a good idea to check with a Visionary friend, if you have one. They are great at cutting through pros and cons, and can let you know if you are lost in a trap of your own making. Creators thrive with collaborators, so find one to help your project move ahead. Be sure this person has strong Visionary or Warrior tendencies.

Warrior/Conqueror: One Warrior/Conqueror worth $1 billion was an insatiable venture capitalist. He told me, "I've got to work hard to keep building the business."

"Stop!" I answered. "You have high blood pressure and a hot temper. You fight 24-7 with your wife. You're only forty-five, but you look sixty. At this pace, you'll be dead by sixty-five or sooner. You are on the downward slope of your life. Furthermore, you've already got more money in the bank than you can spend. So what business exactly are you 'trying to build'? You're not happy anywhere in your life. Although you have a great penthouse, your wife thinks of you only as her provider. Is that the life you want?"

If this is your passion signature, your tendency is to exert brute force in an attempt to win at any cost and prove you are right. Making deals probably also gives you such an incredible high that you never willingly rest. Being able to slow down long enough to feel your life—without adrenaline—is critical to your continued health and productivity.

A Warrior/Conqueror who had a spiritual awakening said, "Money has been my god. I have conquered many people, and making deals was the only thing that mattered. Then I found myself alone in my mansion, retired at forty-nine years old and emotionally empty. I had divorced my wife, I didn't know my kids, and I had everything but nothing. I was in a big crisis."

Visionary/Perfectionist: Of all the passion signatures, Visionary/Perfectionists, like Warrior/Conquerors, are most likely to succumb to workaholism. A true addiction, over-working is often rewarded by the corporate culture, which confuses it with working hard—a respectable behavior. Bryan Robinson, Ph.D., author of *Chained to the Desk* (New York University Press, 1998), writes that workaholism often origi-nates in childhood from attempting to control an environment that is not controllable. Some kids decide that they must work harder to get approval. Other kids decide that nothing is ever good enough. In adulthood, they seek out high-stress jobs in order to feed their addiction to the struggle.

Another underlying motivation of the Visionary/ Perfectionist is looking for value. If you were raised in a home where everyone focused on how you looked to give you value, then you will become a slave to achievement, always raising the bar in a never-ending race to find yourself. Deep inside, you feel empty. You believe that if you would only achieve this or that, then you will be "somebody" or worthy of love.

If you are a Visionary/Perfectionist, keep an eye open for signs of workaholism, including missing deadlines because your work is "not perfect yet," routinely juggling too many tasks at one time because you have taken on too much, and an unwillingness to delegate tasks to coworkers or employees because you fear they won't do them "right." If you hear yourself saying, "If I don't do it myself, it won't get done," stop and get some help. I had one of these nondelegating types as a business partner. He never trusted anyone to handle anything and micromanaged our employees unmercifully. I, on the other hand, trusted our employees implicitly. Incredibly, the same three employees were competent and skilled when handling my affairs and inept, forgetful and unsure when handling his. He came back from vacation with stacks of work piled on his desk. I came back to organization—everything having been handled.

Your mask of positivity also may make you unapproachable, and even annoying, to your colleagues. The phrase, "It's all good," is a sure sign of this defense. Get real. Life is many different things, feelings and sensations. You're not truly alive if you can't feel the highs and lows of life. Perfectionists often miss life because they manufacture and control feelings. One Perfectionist said, "I feel numb on the inside. I truly don't know how to have an authentic feeling." Your unwillingness to be a beginner can mean you limit your options. Beginners get to learn new skills and branch out, and fusion often leads to interesting career trajectories.

That you are a sucker for praise means you're easier to manipulate than most people. So watch that you don't surround yourself with "yes-men." Looking deeper and revealing your authentic self are keys to your ultimate success. You are the most likely of all passion signatures to be fooled by the looks or mask another is wearing. It is the Perfectionists who have never found their own cores who give raises and promotions and show favoritism to Perfectionist-Vamps. They are sitting ducks for the corporate brownnosers, only to discover much later that they have had the wool pulled over their eyes because they never looked beneath the surface.

The Warrior-Creator you never appreciated, because he didn't schmooze you or kiss your behind, was probably your hardest- working, most loyal employee. You repaid him by giving the vice president position to the apple-polishing Perfectionist-Vamp. Having listened to angry executives for twenty-two years, I have come to one undeniable realization: People who feel slighted, cheated or overlooked tend to get even. There is no other way to account for the millions of dollars, perhaps billions, that have been squandered by angry employees who play golf while they're on the clock, run other businesses out of their offices and play video games on the Internet during working hours. On and on it goes.

Prophet/Escapist: Let me be direct: Tend to the details. Speak your truth. Stand up straight, and look people in the eye when you converse. Hide, and your world will be small. Participate, and you'll make a great contribution. You have immense gifts to offer. When you take the risk to trust one other person and build that connection, it will help you to feel safe in the world. The world needs your gift of prophecy, your intellect and your spiritual teaching.

Face it, you have great visions for yourself as well as others. But taking your power into the world is your greatest challenge. From a soul-purpose point of view, you didn't come to Earth to hide out. You came here because you have gifts to share. Therefore, you will have to push your way out into the world. Self-employment may encourage isolation, so make sure to get involved. Many a Prophet has made a living as a psychic. If you can share your spiritual insights, musical or other artistic gifts, or whatever you see fit, you will benefit the world.

Since you tend to be ungrounded, time limitations, deadlines, groupthink and group activities are going to be tough for you. If you don't accept the fact that your boss means 8 A.M. when she says it, it can cause you to lose your job. I know you think you are above it all, but hey, play with the rest of us. Pretend you are a mere mortal. You might be surprised that you come to enjoy this journey called life. You could live in fantasy and create castles in your mind, but you could also make lots of money if you put those castles down on paper.

Management Traps of the Passion Signatures

Good managers are in service to their businesses and their bosses (including the board of directors, stockholders and so on) and also to their employees. Although they must keep an eye on the bottom line and also meet, or exceed, organizational objectives, successful managers know that productivity cannot be achieved without everyone on the team working up to their potential. For potential to be realized, there needs to be minimal conflict and resistance and maximal communication, teamwork and innovation. For people to show up on time in the morning full of enthusiasm, and persevere until their tasks are done, they need to be happy and feel adequately rewarded for their efforts.

Business success flows from the top down, as the managers in any organization set the tone for the culture at large. People subordinate to you adapt to the way you use your energy and wield authority. If you are activated, chances are you'll activate them. Here are a few management traps that are the different passion signatures' Achilles' heels.

Lover/Vamp: In a business setting, the Lover/Vamp signature usually arrives in a Combo Platter with the Visionary/ Perfectionist, which adds the assertive spine to this person's normally receptive energy style. Pure Lover/Vamp signatures are generally too focused on relationships to rise to management status, as they are not as focused on outcomes. But if they do, look out. When activated, Vamp managers can lack assertion and become like overgrown children. To avoid the dramatic meltdowns and temper tantrums of a dependent baby, staff members will erect mental, emotional and social barriers around this individual to buffer themselves and keep business on track. Unfortunately, this robs the team of its authentic leader. Watch out. Adults are not babies, and they shouldn't act like them, as it shifts the group's focus and energy from practical enterprises. If they have a dash of the Perfectionist in them, coworkers may feel picked apart and sucked dry—that nasty combination we explored at the beginning of the chapter.

Creator/Martyr: Years ago, like so many Creator/Martyrs do, Molly got caught up in overworking and in doing what she believed was expected of her. She was a somber person who rarely laughed or made time to play. As a human resources administrator, she spent her days listening to other staff members' problems and offering them advice, even though she felt at a loss to address her own needs and desires. At night she numbed her pain and attempted to recharge her batteries by stuffing herself with food and sitting hour after hour in front of the television. In those days her friendships and romances were marked by protection. They only reached a shallow depth because she didn't want to risk having more people in her life sapping her vital energy away from her.

It is nearly impossible to succeed in creative enterprises when you're hooked up to people who are draining you. This is true even for managers who you might expect to have people pulling on them. Sometimes the problem is one energy drainer. Other times it's that there are too many hooked up to you. As long as you're unconscious about these hookups, your colleagues will have the ability to turn on your energy tap whenever they create a new workplace drama. Then your life force leaks out without warning. If you are depleted of energy, the tempo and tone of your workplace will be reduced.

If you're going to be a powerful Creator working to achieve a variety of goals, you're going to need as much of your energy available to you as possible at all times. Being such a person doesn't mean that your goals must be lofty. It can be as simple as finishing your to-do list, so you can get into bed at night feeling that you accomplished what you set out to achieve instead of getting derailed. But as long as there are invisible forces throwing you off course, you will never seem to do what you really want done.

Discipline, discipline, discipline. As a manager, that must be your key word. To enhance this skill, first pick one area, like keeping your desk clean, making deadlines or saying no to draining employees and clients, and commit to small things first. Then commit to larger, more significant tasks. It is through a commitment process that you will believe you aren't going to suffocate. You can learn more about your identity as a leader and what you have to share if you maintain your discipline.

Warrior/Conqueror: The trouble with many Warrior/ Conquerors is that they think they're right and everyone else is stupid. Well, lots of times they are very smart with an overdose of common sense that they use as a garbage detector. As one

Conqueror was berating another employee with yet another item from his laundry list of reasons he was so unhappy and felt betrayed at the job, I stopped him midmonologue. Using as delicate a tone of voice as I could, because I reminded myself of the softy inside him, I said, "You have got a superiority complex. When there isn't one person with whom you work who you feel has any competency, something has to be going on with you."

In fact, other people often seem so idiotic to them that the Conquerors feel they must reiterate their statements and push their opinions on others without any regard for how the "medicine" is going down. Like quarterbacks, they can focus so much attention on getting the ball across the line that they dispense with human approachability. They put large contracts and sales figures ahead of office politics. It is exhausting to subordinates to have their decisions laid bare at every turn and for efforts to be examined in black and white—there are no gray shades in these managers' palettes. The pressure to bend to their will is extraordinary. As one person put it nicely, "Staff meetings with my Conqueror boss were like being fried with a blowtorch."

Everybody pretends that money is the bottom line in companies. But it is not. Politics is the real bottom line. Whose turf is it? How do you look, and to whom? Who is the boss listening to? How are you jockeying for place, and who is winning? These are the real office concerns that can make or break a career. The Conqueror quarterback is likely to run over his own team in the misguided belief that the company is the bottom line; therefore, he is the most likely to get plowed under one day by his team.

As Warrior/Conquerors are not subtle, are determined to win and can so easily view everyone—even the people on their own team—as their adversaries, conversations can feel like

confrontations. Because their delivery is blunt, they activate
the fighting spirit of those who work for them and in partnership with them. Simply put, people resent them and look for
ways to even the score. They create conflicted, agitated
workplaces.

Visionary/Perfectionist: A friend recently told me about a
boss she had, a jeweler who described herself as a "dog with a
bone." She was on a mission. In a single year, the Perfectionist
boss had succeeded in placing her pieces in a major department
store and got them featured in several women's magazines. She
attracted a celebrity clientele. As her business rapidly
expanded, she found herself in profound need of assistance.
She'd hired my friend both for her years of experience as an
office manager and because she is a creative, insightful individual. Nonetheless, my friend's Perfectionist boss scrutinized
every move she made, even telling her how to speak on the
telephone. It wasn't long before my friend stopped
caring. In the office, she transformed from being a cheerful and
enthusiastic contributor to a seemingly lifeless automaton.
"Since my boss didn't trust me to do anything right, I just did
what she told me to do, took my wages and went home."

Then the inevitable happened. The boss began breaking
down under the pressure and developed physical ailments. She
wanted a baby, but her doctor told her she had to reduce her
stress or she would be unlikely to conceive. Her relatively new
marriage was in trouble because her husband felt neglected
when she worked long hours. These private matters were leaking into the workplace atmosphere as the boss became more
irritable. At last my friend confronted her with, "As soon as I
get a better job, I'm leaving. You are a total witch." The
Perfectionist ended up crying and pleading, "Please don't do
this. I need you." She could finally see the gold mine standing
in front of her, but as she'd shut down every avenue until then

that could bring out the best in my friend, it was too late.

I've seen this pattern repeated by too many Perfectionists to count. They start a business, madly chasing success and micro-managing their staffs, but the business cannot grow that way because all the good talent soon leaves—going elsewhere to seek greener pastures. Perfectionists may get what they want, but if they're isolated, they'll be miserable. They have one-dimensional employees who contribute zero extra effort to their enterprises.

Prophet/Escapist: Honestly, I haven't met many pure Prophet/Escapist managers. In general, typical Escapists have too much trouble staying grounded in earthly requirements of business to make much headway up the corporate ladder. However, Prophet qualities are present in many successful managers who are Combo Platters. These folks can make highly intuitive employers and supervisors.

The Prophet/Escapist management trap is disconnection. If they relinquish their grasp on the tangible details of the work-place, Prophet/Escapists become targets for theft, and laziness can emerge among their staff members. Confusion, fragmenta-tion, anxiety and flakiness don't instill workers with a sense that the manager values what they're doing, so they lose inter-est in their responsibilities as well. It's draining to work for someone disconnected. There is an underlying sense that, "It doesn't matter anyway." That can tank any business or endeavor. The Escapist can lose a fortune or allow tasks like paying taxes to pile up so high that there is no return. Light bills, regulations, licenses, rules and regulations can fall by the wayside and get this type in big trouble. So tie your helium bal-loon to a strong anchor—a trusted assistant, perhaps? You are here on Earth, and it does matter. Try embracing this fact; oth-erwise, your life could be fairly miserable.

Bringing Out the Best
in Your Employees and Coworkers

In the workplace, we look forward to professionalism from our employees and coworkers. We hope the most evolved and competent aspect of them shows up on the job every morning. But we also must recognize the human factors, such as stress, loss and disagreement, which can rob them of feeling carefree and productive. Everyone has a passion signature, and everyone has trigger points of activation. So how can we bring out the best, most innovative and most reliable qualities in our employees and coworkers?

Motivating the Lover/Vamp: Lovers are enthusiastic and charismatic. They shine in relationships and thrive on being the center of attention. At their best, they are generous and love to show love to everybody. Thus, if you need to hire an emcee for the annual banquet, a restaurant host, a public relations expert, an entertainer, a healer or a recruiter, the Lover may be just the type of staff member you are seeking.

Lover/Vamps want to please you, and they'll work hard to do so in return for generous amounts of genuine verbal appreciation and gratitude. Since they are motivated by connection, spending a few minutes hanging out can regenerate their energy. Languish praise upon them, and you will watch them working harder and blossoming before your eyes. Lovers want you to love them. It is the relationship between the two of you that will motivate their gifts to thrive.

As a supervisor, don't reinforce game playing in a Vampish employee. Make sure their social acumen is backed by actual work. You must never tolerate empty flattery or mere people pleasing from them. And don't allow drama. To be successful, Lover/Vamps must become grounded in their creativity. They must learn to feel internally rewarded by their efforts. You can support such employees to become self-sufficient by teaching them how to handle tasks on their own. Team them up with more assertive passion signatures. Whenever it's appropriate, include them in your work processes. Shutting them out of the loop makes them feel lonely. Simply asking about their lives can do the trick of opening them up to their more expansive core essence. Also, look them in the eyes. You may need to put up cubicles to cut down on the chitchat. They are social creatures, and chitchat will always be their tendency.

If your hires are healed Visionary-Lover Combo Platters, you will be very pleased. They give attention to detail, are naturally optimistic on the job, can multitask and never burden you with unnecessary dramas. They carry the ball with aplomb, and you rarely feel drained in their presence. In fact, their energy naturally gives you energy. Since they take good care of their bodies, they rarely have sick days. They dress for success, are well mannered, on time and organized—what more could you ask for?

Motivating the Creator/Martyr: A Visionary/Perfectionist client of mine was supervising ten subordinates in his workplace and wanted to become a more effective manager. So I suggested that he go deeper in his employee evaluation process and take a closer look at the actual work that was being produced, both by the people who were smooth talkers and said the things he liked to hear, and by those who weren't playing the social game so well. In particular, he had complained to me about one Creator/Martyr on his staff because the guy's desk was incredibly messy. But when he examined the workload the man was tasked with, he was impressed.

I reassured him, "You can help that passion signature to blossom. Just answer a few of my questions. Is the employee self-motivated? Can he delay gratifying his own needs? Will he watch your back inside and outside the company? Do the people he works with like him?" Yes, my client thought so. "Then you can motivate him by acknowledging his efforts in public, teaming him up on projects with well-organized employees, teaching him to meet a disciplined timetable, letting him know you're always there to back him up—but that he has space to do his job in his own way because you trust him—and making sure he has enough time off." My client began to pay more attention to this Creator/Martyr. As he changed the way he related to the guy, it was like harvesting a genius.

Creators are friendly folks who can make excellent negotiators, communicators, problem solvers and mentors. They are industrious, reliable and adaptable. If there are any positions in your workplace that require these skills, talents and qualities, you may find a good fit in a Creator/Martyr or a Combo Platter with a strong Creator aspect. One Creator was promoted out of his skill set when he was transferred from problem solving in communications between managers to project management. He lost all motivation as he became overwhelmed with twenty different project details that took him away from interacting with people and into the world of technology.

Motivating the Warrior: Warrior/Conquerors might not say things the right way. Their mouths are a problem, and they can come across as a tad hostile at times or even cut to the quick. As they can get stuck in polarized thinking, they must be coached to find the gray areas in decisions and see the benefits of win-win strategies. They are driven competitors and committed to any enterprise they join, thus it's to your advantage to provide enough challenges for Warriors to overcome so that they'll stay occupied and thrive until they can rise to the top of your heap. You have a diamond in the rough here.

Your role as supervisor is to coach the Warrior/Conquerors about their impact on coworkers. Address their demeanor, for instance. Let them know they need to use softer voices and gazes. One Warrior began practicing speaking more softly, sitting back, crossing his legs and generally being much less intense. He nailed a promotion after being passed over repeatedly in earlier attempts. I encouraged another Warrior/ Conqueror to imagine how he would feel if one of his fellow vice presidents became restless in a meeting while he was speaking. "Imagine Joe tapping his pen, getting up and pacing, and periodically rolling his eyes in disagreement," I said. "I would feel completely undermined, pissed and would find the day when I would give it back to him," he answered. I pointed out that this was why guys stabbed him in the back at every job he went to, no matter how hard he worked.

Warrior/Conquerors absolutely must be helped to learn social grace. It's their blind spot. Natural leaders, they must develop humility to come into their own. So teach them they're not the only ones who matter. Insist they be courteous when others are speaking. Never, ever tolerate them bullying other team members. They also must restrain from bellowing, "No," at their coworkers' ideas and otherwise restrain themselves from berating people with why some answer won't work. If they tend to be curt, they must learn civility. Send them to anger-management courses, and train them in meditation practices, if necessary. Above all else, make sure they regularly take time off and tend to their physical health.

You can be blunt with these individuals. In fact, it's advisable, as they don't read subtleties too well. But remember they have marshmallow centers. Make sure when you are speaking with them that you don't make them seem wrong. Be gentler than you think you need to be when giving them feedback. There is a real softy inside, and this person must be able to save face while receiving criticism, or he or she will fight you. Warriors will be intensely loyal to you so long as you do not lie, cheat or manipulate them. Remember to honor Warrior/

Conquerors even when they are your underlings. Do not tease them in public. Let them know the value you see in them. There is a Lover/Vamp inside who wants connection, but a barrier has been put up to protect vulnerable feelings. Care about them, let them know you understand their positions, and they'll appreciate you for it. Consistency from you makes them feel safe. Use humor.

Warriors make great team leaders, protectors, role models and entrepreneurs. They lead with humility, because they are in service to those they lead, and teach others to have courage by demonstrating courage on a daily basis. If they can learn essential social skills, they make good executives. They can also manage a loading dock where toughness is required, be a cop or soldier, or an adventurer. Integrity is their hallmark, and so high-security jobs can be entrusted to them.

Motivating the Visionary/Perfectionist: Visionaries are fantastic at establishing structures and organizing human and material resources. Harness their nitpickiness for your corporate benefit. Jobs that require scheduling, details, punctuality and design are right up their alley. Cities are built on the insight of Visionaries. They can see how each part should be put together to make it all work, and they have the discipline to follow through on goals. As a Creator, I always make sure those who work with me have a lot of this trait. They are self-motivated and naturally linear in task completion. That's just what the Creator, as well as most other passion signatures, need. Visionaries make incredible managers, as long as they show respect for their teammates and don't micromanage. They are great at assimilating and synthesizing massive amounts of information, then finding the inherent themes and structures within it. These people are often leading trendsetters and innovators with laser-sharp imaginations.

Where the Visionary/Perfectionists may need some

guidance is in being in touch with their emotions. Emotions keep them from becoming lifeless automatons. They also should be encouraged to stretch to do things they may not be good at initially, as this cultivates flexibility in them. As a supervisor, you must never humiliate them by pointing out their failings. They need to be right. So let them be right if at all possible. Appreciate them, for they love praise, and don't oppose them needlessly, because they will get easily frustrated. You cannot win an argument with them, so don't bother trying. Instead, carefully choose your words to set up a win-win conversation. You're the boss, but these people are self-motivated individuals in need of autonomy. Treat them with respect and they will achieve far beyond your expectations. Remember, these are the students who bring apples to the teacher every day. They thrive on approval.

Visionary/Perfectionists will respect you if you let them know the rules, so they don't *have to* make up their own (they will anyway). Usually a Creator or a Lover is living underneath the Visionary mask, so you would benefit from addressing their subliminal desires as well as their surface desires—specifically for love and acknowledgment. Get them involved in charitable projects, so they think less about looking good and more about what they are contributing.

Motivating the Prophet/Escapist: People with this passion signature as their primary energy style need the understanding of their bosses and coworkers to stay grounded. Don't raise your voice to Prophets or they may suddenly leave their bodies. At those times you can see the light going out in their eyes and their gaze getting blurry. Move gingerly, and try not to stimulate their energy. Give them safety. In general, even when they're not activated, they require periods of time to be on their own and renew their sense of self. So give them opportunities—and space—for that. Large teams are not their preferred gigs. One-on-one

interactions and partnerships are. Prophet/Escapists are powerful beings, and they know it, so encourage them to express their
voices and share their most precious truths with you. In the
meantime, support them to develop discipline.

Prophet/Escapist insights can be enormously valuable. If you
need someone on your staff who can read between the lines of
what others are saying, or who can give you an intuitive sense
of what to do in a pinch, this may be the person you need. He
or she could be a creative genius in the back of your animation
studio or writing code for your computer program or a mad scientist tucked away in a corner coming up with the next great
scientific breakthrough. Don't expect more than they can give.
These folks are often socially inept in staff meetings, but sit
them in front of a computer where they can be away from others and let their imaginations run free, and you will be very
happy with the results. There's no use hoping they'll notice they
haven't changed clothes in a week or that they need to clean up
the row of Starbucks' empties littering their cubicle.

Ironically, as I was editing a draft of this chapter in a coffee
shop, I sat for several hours next to someone of this type who was
a writer. He was a skinny man, completely unaware of his environment, and he had buried himself in his computer. His eyes
were bloodshot and intently fixed on his creation. He seemed to
be taking in no one around him but instead was lost inside the
world of his creativity. I thought nothing of it until he received a
phone call, and a waiter personally carried a phone to him and
called him by name. Recognizing his name, and recalling the cal-
iber of his work, I realized I was sitting beside a genius.

Getting Along with Your Boss

When you accept a job of any kind, you step into a world
populated by people who are caught up in their own routines

and agendas. To get ahead, you need, of course, to contribute what you're assigned to contribute. But you become truly impressive to a boss when you contribute what he didn't even know he needed. You can target your contributions to the gaps in the skill sets of your boss's passion signature.

Impressing the Lover: This person is feeling-based and relationship-oriented, so you need to tend to the boss's emotional well-being as much as business. However, your abilities to be linear, punctual, organized and persevering are golden to your supervisor, as these are not his or her strong suits. With your assertive aspect matching the boss's seemingly magical receptive aspect, you will make a valuable member of the team.

Relationships matter and everyone's feelings count to the Lover boss, so you will be nurtured and supported by them, as they bring the best out of you. If you've never had a boss like this one, you won't believe how much more productive you'll be with one of them in your corner.

Impressing the Creator: Creators admire people who can get things done without complaining. They admire follow-through. As willing as they are to help, by virtue of their nature they've got lots of people seeking their guidance and energy, so they can get scattered and depleted. Therefore, if you can shield your boss from needless energy grabbers by becoming a screener — and handle some issues on his or her behalf — not only will you learn much about business affairs, your boss will also gladly come to rely on you. As with the Lover and Prophet, your ability to assert can make a valuable counterbalance to your employer's primarily receptive nature.

Impressing the Warrior: Be direct. Get to the point. Don't waste your boss's time with idle chitchat and socializing, and you'll get along great. Sometimes a new employee will be tested by the Warrior to determine his or her ability to handle pressure. You must have gumption. If you can stand up to a measured confrontation with your boss without losing your temper or abandoning your deference for his or her authority, the Warrior will admire you. Also you'll be indispensable if you can make the Warrior belly laugh.

Don't take your boss's barking tones and orders personally. This type doesn't respond well to high-strung, sentimental or "too sensitive" people who need to "process" feelings all the time. They like it when you can stand up to them and not be intimidated by their authority. Of all the passion signatures, Warriors are the most likely to respect you when you stand up to them—as long as you don't try to conquer them or make them wrong. Try that, and you are going down. Be loyal, dedicated and hardworking, and you will have a boss who will fight for you to the death. In today's corporate culture of layoffs and instability, a Warrior ally will go the extra mile whenever possible.

Impressing the Visionary: This person is going to have high standards. Follow his or her rules as much as possible. Let your boss know you want to develop your skills and ask if he or she would be willing to help you plan a course of action. The Visionary will notice details, so dot every *i*. Correct grammar and spelling and having an overall well-presented look to everything you do will win big kudos with this signature. Like a benevolent drill sergeant, the Visionary will cause you to reach for your highest ideals of who you are and toward your most advanced capabilities.

Stand on your own two feet, and do not expect micromanagement. Dress for success, even if it's casual Friday. The Visionary doesn't like disorder, slovenly dress, unkempt hair or that earring you put through your upper ear. As I asked one Creator working for a Visionary boss, "Do you ever wonder how much that diamond stud is costing you per year in terms of salary?" Figure out what is expected in the corporate culture you work in, and provide exactly that—and more. Make your personal preference and fashion statements outside of work.

Let your supervisor know you're loyal and that you are seeking to make *him* or *her* shine in the eyes of the boss and the public, and the Visionary will be pleased. Remember that the Visionary has a natural desire for perfection and beauty in the universe. That means beautiful presentations, clean office spaces and organized meetings. If you can't comply with this, you may need to work for someone who is a bit more lax than a Visionary. The Visionary responds well to positive thinking and attitudes and an optimistic presentation of even the most difficult facts.

Impressing the Prophet: It is immensely valuable to the Prophet/Escapist if you can function for him or her as an anchor and safety net. These creative, prophetic geniuses need connection and safety to thrive in the physical world and share their gifts. Perhaps helping someone like this is your calling. There is a lot of room here for you to step in and accomplish. You will find that the Prophet boss adds mystery, imagination, expansiveness and illumination to your life in whatever you share. On the other hand, you may find that being the one who has to take care of all the details is a bit more than you can comfortably handle. Don't expect the Prophet ever to be as focused on the details you present to him or her as you'd like. Prophet/Escapists' lofty sight comes from flying high. They would have to give this up to become masters of the mundane. You can learn something very important about integrity from a healed Prophet. This person has a golden gut instinct for what's going on behind the scenes. Never disregard the Prophet's high level of intuition.

CHAPTER 11

THE MAGIC OF FRIENDSHIPS

Of all the different sorts of relationships, a love affair is perhaps the most similar to an intimate friendship, because friendships have a special, delicious quality. But because we choose our friends and they choose us, a friendship is a different sort of relationship than any other. Unlike with our blood relatives, we rarely feel obliged to stay connected to friends who bother or mistreat us or with whom we share few interests. We can walk away from friends with comparatively little fuss. Unlike the people in our business networks and at our job sites, usually we aren't dependent on friends for our livelihood. If we disagree with a friend or feel violated, we know we have the right to say so freely, whereas with a boss or client, we might hold our tongues. There is an equality of being we have with our friends that can be liberating—unless we deliberately or habitually hold back for some reason.

Of course, walking away from friends is the reason we often miss the opportunities for growth that lie dormant in our friendships. Remember, the subconscious mind doesn't care whether you're at work, with family or with a friend. Anybody you relate to over a long period of time turns on your internal projector. When we abandon friendships, we miss a lot of chances to nurture old wounds. Friendships can be safe places to heal childhood trauma or mirrors in which you may come to know your dimensions. In this chapter, we'll explore the magical growth potential in friendship.

Our Friends Are Our Mirrors

A friend is an invaluable mirror of both our positive and negative attributes. By "mirror," I mean someone who helps us see ourselves more clearly. Friends can do so on purpose by providing us with feedback, as well as incidentally, stirring us up inside by activating long-standing family imprints and survival mechanisms.

After spending a three-day weekend at a conference awhile ago, I was exhausted. Because of excitement, I hadn't been able to sleep enough, and the shortage was catching up with me. There was a final six o'clock seminar on Sunday, but I decided not to go. I called a good friend at four and told him my decision. An hour after we got off the phone, he called me back and said, "Donna, I've been giving this some thought. You are writing a book on relationships, and so you need to be in the seminar that's coming up."

Because I am aware of my Creator/Martyr defense patterns,

I knew that my friend was probably right. Besides being tired, I was slightly overwhelmed by the commitment of having to show up. Therefore, I was letting my survival mechanisms make decisions for me. Luckily, my trusted friend intervened and told me the truth about myself, and in doing so guided me to reconsider. I surrendered to his vision. Once I got to the seminar and saw what it was, I was glad to be there, and it was absolutely right for me.

Being humble and having the ability to say, "I don't know what's going on; I need to check in with a wise friend," is a fundamental aspect of integrating the gifts of your passion signature. In Zen Buddhism, this attitude of humility is called "beginner mind." Intimate friendships can be our greatest teachers if we give up trying to look smart.

Some of us need relationship mirrors more than others. Why? Because we are so heavily programmed that we cannot see our own programs clearly. Our thoughts, feelings and beliefs are held in place by our family imprints. We imagine we are in charge of our lives and taking steps to attain our goals, while the subconscious mind runs us straight into a series of brick walls. Relationship mirrors, like the friend I just mentioned, serve to snap us out of our illusion of being in control when really we're blocking expansion.

One of the greatest gifts we ever give other people is seeing them and valuing them just as they are and just where they are. Our direct acknowledgment of what we see helps them experience our perceptions, for themselves, as real. We can reassure friends that they're normal—or at least the same as us—and not isolated in their experience of life, love, work or an emotion. They're acceptable. We can affirm what we find fabulous and delicious about them and acknowledge the transformations and steady progress they've made. We can gently and considerately inform them of where we feel they could improve. We can also help them to lighten up and stop being so hard on themselves.

When the gift of friendship and acknowledgment is given, it has a surprisingly powerful impact. Sometimes the only thing we need in order to shift from a stuck place is a new perspective or acceptance of the place we're stuck in. A friend can provide that perspective or acceptance. We tend to get stuck in our resistance to feelings frozen in the past. We tend to project those negative feelings and the things about ourselves we do not like onto the people around us—and then fight against them. A friend's acknowledgment has a simple power to stop that fighting. In an instant, merely by having a friend tolerate or embrace us, we can reclaim a lost fragment that previously we have not made peace with internally. This is soul retrieval and soul expansion at its best.

One woman's mother and father often told her she was "too noisy and boisterous" when she was a kid. They shushed her and penalized her for her enthusiasm. Subsequently, as an adult she often felt guilty when she would become elated by her experiences and laugh loudly. She was embarrassed when people commented on her behavior. She didn't trust her judgment about whether or not it was appropriate to the situation she was in. She felt "too big and loud" for her surroundings, so she tried to "make herself smaller and quieter." For some reason, she just couldn't shake these feelings even though she did many years of therapy and made tremendous progress in healing other wounds. One time she was particularly euphoric and babbling excitedly on the phone with a new friend. Catching herself going on and on, she apologized and said, "I really need to ground myself and stop this; it's too much. I'm so sorry."

Her friend said, "Why? I think it's great that you're happy. You're not hurting anyone. I wish I could be as free and happy as you are right now."

In a flash she realized that she loved the way she was being. She was at peace, she was connected to her friend and her happiness was "contagious." Maybe as a kid she hadn't always been able to grasp the needs of the people around her and so her high-spiritedness was occasionally disruptive. But as an adult, she was capable of discernment. If anyone was "hurt" by her presence, she knew exactly how to quiet her energy. Most of all, it was safe to be happy—happy-quiet or happy-noisy. Both were fine. By her friend's simple acceptance of her joyful exuberance, she reclaimed a lost fragment of her soul.

If I am connected to myself as the source of love and grace, and everything else that my soul is thirsty for, I know that anything is possible. When I walk down the street, it doesn't matter if it's the same street I walk down every day. I am going to see new things on that street. I am going to take in the people I pass in new ways. I am going to be touched and moved by the simple presence of the trees, dogs and birds. The world will mirror me, and I will mirror the world. The environment and I are in communion.

During the writing of this book, a new facade was being put on the building next door to mine. I saw one workman there every day, carving intricate artwork above the entrance. A true artist, he'd probably been doing masonry for forty years, but I don't know if he'd ever received much acknowledgment. Every morning I would stop and comment to him on his work, and I could see that my admiration and interest impacted him. To him this was just a job, but to me his skill was amazing. As I appreciated the actual moments of his creation, he could feel his own value. After a while, whenever I would come down the street, all the workers there would be smiling. The men stopped and invited me to see what they were doing. We had a beautiful, easy exchange of friendship. It made my day.

In an "unconscious" life, I would have stepped out the front door and gone for coffee at the corner, either not truly seeing anyone or saying hello only to people I already knew. I'd come home or sit and read the newspaper in the coffee shop, but every day it would have been the same day over and over. I would have missed the masonry, the original moment of the new structure being built on top of the one-hundred-year-old structure. I'd have missed the friendly connection with the workmen. I'd have missed seeing how much I mattered to them. We helped each other feel special.

Our Friends Can Accelerate Our Growth and Expansion

If we befriend people who have issues similar to ours, then we can learn through sharing each other's life experiences and role modeling. Friends are people for whom we feel such an affinity that we might say, "We're so alike," "I feel just the same way" or "We have so many interests in common." But their personal skills and perspectives on every aspect of existence may be hugely dissimilar to ours. Which is fantastic, because it makes a broader range of options available to us whenever we have a problem to solve or are seeking a new understanding of anything in our lives.

Mirroring aside, when we are attracted to like-minded and like-hearted people, on a subconscious level we perceive them not only as akin to us, but—literally—as being us. When I look into your eyes I see ME. When you look into my eyes, you see YOU. And not because of a reflection! There's a jubilant feeling of recognition, "No way! I do the exact same thing! I feel the exact same way! It's incredible that we're so alike. We must have been separated at birth!" Hearing reports of a close friend's trial-and-error learning in romance, business and family affairs is like buying a two-for-the-price-of-one ticket to the stadium of life. A part of the magic of friendships is that they accelerate our personal growth because the "at-onement" affords us extra information about "doing" life. If I see you finding a solution, and I feel you're ME, that solution is now a part of my resources. If you see me make a mistake, and you feel I'm YOU, you'll now sidestep that error.

If we purposefully only pick people for friendship whom we view as "opposite" to us, or who seem remarkably different on the surface from our previous friends, it may be a sign that we are in an avoidance pattern. Essentially, we've had an experience in the past that made us feel bad, and we want to protect ourselves from having it again in the future. But restriction is not the same thing as freedom—it's not even relief from pain. It means we are enslaved to the issues we are striving to avoid. In friendships and other relationships, whenever we narrow our range of options we shut down possibilities for connection and soul expansion. Being in a survival-based mode is how we rob ourselves of fresh and original moments. It removes the element of surprise—favorable surprises as much as unfavorable ones.

Friendships are arenas where we can feel safe while exploring new dimensions of character. One friend may be a fabulous dancer, the next a successful businessperson, yet another a terrific parent, and still another a tireless advocate for a political cause. With the first we laugh and play, we go to the second for tax advice, we trade babysitting with the third, and the fourth friend motivates us to form new opinions and participate more in the world beyond our doorsill. We do not expect each of our friends to embody all the traits we value, and we know that having several friends allows us to pursue a variety of interests. In the company of friends, we are sustained as we elevate our abilities.

Being taught by a friend doesn't make the friend higher in status than us. We give back to our friends through an exchange of talents and gifts. They teach us, and we teach them. It's mutual. A wise man once said that if we can even perceive a quality in another, we must have a seed of it in ourselves. We couldn't see it otherwise.

A friendship typically has fewer agendas than a family relationship or romance. It is an ill-defined relationship, because we basically make up the rules as we go along. But we are usually willing to let our friends be as they are, without seeking changes, even though we do form deep attachments. Research has shown that male bonding is different from female bonding—men are activity oriented, women are talkers—but companionship, time spent in good company, is the main point of friendship for both genders.

We also admire our friends and want to be more like them in some capacity. In fact, when we're around them they strengthen those desirable qualities in us. Remember, a friend can be anyone of any age, ethnicity and gender. I've had younger friends, older friends, male friends, female friends, and friends of many races and orientations. Each has stimulated me in some fashion and opened up my world. Unfortunately, friendships can also do the opposite.

Warning! Friendships Can Be Places Where We Hide or Get Lost

My brother Chuck died of a drug overdose. I believe this wouldn't have happened if he had been able to talk about the pain he hid from other people under his nice-guy facade and caretaking of the world. He died on the anniversary of my father's death, which was four years earlier. Even though he had reached out to get help for his addiction in the months before his death, I believe it was his unexpressed grief over the loss of our father and some of his friends that ultimately took him under.

He associated with a group of guys who seemed to have no internal compasses, and no sense of hope or purpose larger than themselves to live for. His friends "partied," which included taking recreational drugs. Ten have died, like him, in drug-related accidents, such as car crashes and overdoses. They were working-class guys, trapped in their worlds, numbed with beer and drugs. Not one ever acknowledged that this pattern was more than having a "good time," but one after another they started dying. And no one who knew them ever acknowledged that these guys were killing themselves. Each was a nice guy. They were not bad men. They held paying jobs. Some had families. But as one friend after another died, the remaining friends became more self-destructive.

Chuck was a classic wounded Warrior-Creator who did many wonderful things for other people and yet was a poor self-nurturer. At Chuck's funeral, a woman stood up and told a story about being in a bike race with my brother. She said he had hung back with her at the very end so that she would not be alone when she finished. This was typical of him. He worked in our family's carpet business. Another story shared was that once when he was sewing trim around some of the smaller carpets, one of his friends asked him, "Why are you doing this?" He said, "We spend so much time focused on the big guys. But you can't forget the little guys; they're important, too."

He fell victim to one of the biggest downfalls of the Conqueror-Martyr. He felt he had to be strong and have the answers, and so was unable to ask for help. At his core he had self-hatred. His low self-esteem kept him hanging out with other guys with similar issues. Even when he joined AA, he fell back into his familiar social world.

The additional tragedy of this story is that four years later my sister Diedre also overdosed on drugs. She was also a Conqueror-Martyr who would never take advantage of outlets that were offered to help her release her pain. Like Chuck, she went to AA but fell back into friendships with people who weren't making the effort to heal.

The stories of my brother and sister are extreme examples of how we can get lost in friendships. If we're not associating with people who are trying to lift themselves up, we may fail to grow. Some people find their friendships a place to hide. However, there are many ways people hide out that do not involve addiction. Groups of friends who gossip behind people's backs and criticize one another's efforts to expand their lives are also hiding places, and places where people typically get lost. Social and religious organizations where people are not really allowed by their peers to drop their masks and be authentic with one another are also hiding places.

Anytime we hold emotional energy inside ourselves without expressing it or working through it, it is like being a teakettle on a slow burner. After a while the steam builds up and blows the whistle.

Friends Are Our Catalysts for Transformation

Eventually every friendship that's working activates the old, reliable movie projector in the brain that perceives anyone with whom we interact as Mom, Dad or a sibling. The closer friends become, the more we seem to resemble each other's family members and the more we also serve as an extended family for one another. In one of my friendships, a girlfriend and I both reacted to each other as if we were dealing with the unhealed qualities of our mothers. We had a classic Lover-Creator dynamic: She wanted my nurturing, and I was fighting engulfment. It took us awhile to cope with the mutual activation. The boxing match was on! We would clash for a round, go back to separate corners and come back. But our mutual awareness of the passion signatures enabled us to work through our projections. We finally agreed we were not each other's mommies.

As our earliest imprints begin to frame our thoughts about our friends, the subconscious mind takes control of our emotional responses to what they do and don't do and to their personal revelations. Sooner or later we begin reenacting past scenarios with these individuals. But that's actually okay. If we're aware, the freedom of choice about interacting with our friends, coupled with the sense of familiarity between us, gives us an opportunity we wouldn't have otherwise to work through our survival patterns surprisingly quickly and most often with minimal effort.

Of course, we have to be alert to the reality that we're dealing with another person's nervous system. We must accept responsibility for coping with that reality, as much as for coping with our own nervous systems. Then friendships can accelerate our healing processes. As we replay the childhood scenes that traumatized us in our family of origin—perhaps as a neglected child, perhaps as a child who had to grow up too soon—this time we can correct them by talking openly about what is going on.

We may struggle in our enmeshments with biological family members, they resisting us and we resisting them, whereas a friend can move us quickly out of the stuckness by serving as a healing proxy. Think, for example, of one of your own friends. Does this friend seem like a parent to you? I would lay odds that there is a sense of recognition of how this person "fits" into the matrix of your life. What is this friend's role or place? On an emotional level, you know the answer to this. Perhaps you call one friend in times of trouble, another for games and another for romantic advice. You do not expect to have your entire set of needs met by a single friend, so there is greater freedom between you than with your real parent. That freedom and release allows growth to happen quickly.

Sue and Barbara frequently travel together with touring groups. Often they share the same hotel rooms. Sue finally realizes that every time they go away, she freezes Barbara out. She doesn't want to sit with her friend in the dining room, walk around tourist sites beside her or hang out with her in the evenings. For years Sue had been playing out an aspect of her maternal model with Barbara, a mental imprint that dictated: The closer you get, the icier you must behave. Sue's mother had been nurturing to the world at large but cold to the people with whom she was intimate because, "Close people are irritating." On their trips Barbara felt "irritating" to Sue.

Barbara had noticed the distancing happening, and from time to time she'd responsibly ask, "Have I done something to hurt you or make you mad?"

Sue had always lied in response, "Don't worry, I'm just tired/hungry/distracted." For years she'd been getting away with making excuses, "It's me, not you." But it was also Barbara. It was how Sue's imprint "read" her friend. On the last trip, however, Sue took a risk and admitted to Barbara what was happening inside her. The two had a long talk about their history: the bad and the good, their mutual admiration and their wounds. It made them even closer than before. And Sue's irritation completely evaporated.

When our nurturing wounds with our parents get activated, triggering a tiny internal time bomb, the brain switches control of us to our deepest emotional centers. According to research, this primitive place within us cannot be accessed by talk therapy because it is preverbal and doesn't listen to what you say to yourself. It only learns through direct experiences, such as through interactions with friends.

Your friends will be your catalysts for transformation, as they'll stimulate your oldest survival patterns while simultaneously offering you some of your most expansive experiences. They'll literally be your initiators. You have a baby inside you who wants to fuse with someone, but you know you may lose the one you love and to whom you attach. And this triggers your deepest fear: Who will take care of me? So friendships bring you back into your family relationship patterns, but they're also the containers within which you may heal these archaic patterns. If you and your friends consciously take on the healing process together, a friendship can be an essential support system so both your lives can reach their highest potential. It can be the security base and the foundation you need. But your commitment to your friend could make you feel several things you would prefer not to feel in the process: trapped, exposed, stagnant and so on. Our defenses get activated, and we begin behaving in extreme ways. Here is how the shadow side of each passion signature can affect your friendships.

Vamps in Friendships: Vamps tend to ask too much of their friends. They can become like stalkers. "What are you doing right now?" Every move the friend makes, the Vamp wants to make. The Vamp wants to fuse entirely with the friend's experience of life. Everything the friend has seems valuable to the Vamp. "I want your grass because you value it—it is greener than mine." The kicker is that the stalking Vamp not only wants to attach to the friend like a parasite, but the Vamp is also the friend's fiercest competitor. Because of feeling unworthy, the Vamp will not value anything he or she has or does as much as what the friend has or is doing. Thus it can become maddening when the Vamp wants to know where you got your shirt or envies you for having a love connection (especially if the Vamp is coy and flirtatious).

By the way, it's not always an unconscious pattern; it's just out-of-control behavior. The Vamp is addicted to the feeling of validation and so needs to suck up all the energy and life that's around. Vamps can also burn you out talking about the dramas in their lives. They will have a litany of troubles, from the people who aren't treating them as well as they should, to the unhappy jobs where they are the victims of circumstance.

Martyrs in Friendships: Martyrs tend to do too much for their friends, and then they retreat in anger. When the emotional ice wall slams between them, the friend doesn't know why, and the Martyr doesn't offer explanations. As well meaning as the Martyr is, the friend seems too needy, so the Martyr is activated. "Go away, I feel claustrophobic." Every gesture of connection makes matters worse. "You wear me out, but I'll go the extra mile for you because I want you to depend on me." The martyred and overburdened Martyr gives so that the friend will find the Martyr worthy of love. The Martyr often seeks out friendships with the Vamp. It works great in the beginning because Martyrs feel secure when they seek out the neediness of others. But the day will come when Martyrs feel like they will drown in the onslaught of needs directed at them by Vamps. Suddenly and seemingly without provocation, the Martyr will withdraw and become short tempered and unavailable.

Because the Martyr was typically a peacekeeper in the family growing up, he or she is always trying to defend everyone's position. But sometimes you just need the Martyr to be on your side. Where this breaks down is when you say something to your Martyr friend wanting them to understand your point of view, but instead of listening and leaving it there the Martyr explains the other person's point of view. That's not what you want to hear unless you ask for it. Now you may feel betrayed and upset, like your feelings are not valid.

Conquerors in Friendships: Unless they are Combo Platters, Conquerors won't have many close friends. Generally, Conquerors will show devotion to your friendship by doing things for you, such as helping you move, being there when you need an ally and offering a strong arm when you need a place to lean. But what comes out of their mouths can piss you off, because they bark orders. So you will have to read between the lines with your Conqueror. His or her voice may be overbearing, too loud or too commanding, but you can tell that underneath all that roughness is a buttercup. Conquerors are the guys who haze one another in the sports bar or men's club. Above all else they want to win. Their humor and camaraderie are likely to be a bit rough, but if you can take it, they will respect you and a bond of loyalty will be established.

Perfectionists in Friendships: Perfectionists tend to criticize their friends and also to pretend they know everything even when they know they don't. Forget about seeing your Perfectionist girlfriend with a hair out of place. The rest of the girls feel like toads in comparison because of her ability to look beautiful all the time. You haven't been able to get your extra weight off in fifteen years? She weighs a perfect 125 pounds. She's the friend you "hate" because she never shows her humanity or flaws. You can't get close to her. She says all the right things and does all the right things, but her Teflon exterior makes her impossible to feel really close to.

If you're having a glass of wine with a Perfectionist, the conversation can drive you a bit numb as he or she one-ups you with the last word about everything that comes out of your mouth. You feel somehow pushed away by the Perfectionist's big, beaming smile, which projects someone who is on top of the world, perfect over and above everyone else. You may not want to spend too much time with your Perfectionist friend unless you are a Perfectionist yourself, because you see your own flaws so vividly after being in his or her presence.

Escapists in Friendships: Escapists tend to flake out. By the way, a lot of folks have some Escapist lurking under the surface, but you are going to have to have a special interest in

unusual people to befriend a pure-blooded person of this signature type. If you do, you are someone who doesn't go for
superficial connections and instead enjoys deep intellectual or
philosophical conversations. You will have to meet at the
Escapist's house, probably in the basement, because the
Escapist lives in a world away from worlds. Once you've tack-
led that hurdle, your Escapist friend may drive you nuts
because he refuses to go anywhere else with you. On top of
that, once you get deep into the relationship, if you run into
any troubles or things get too tough, the Escapist can vanish
from your life as if your connection had no meaning at all.

The anger of an Escapist can be a bit scary, as well. Because
Escapists go out of body when they feel threatened, they can
be dangerous when provoked to rage. One Escapist reported a
flash rage where he found himself out of body, and even
though he was frail, he tore into a group of young men in his
neighborhood that had been harassing him. When he was done
beating the largest bully to a pulp, nobody messed with him
ever again.

**On the Web site *www.thepassionprinciple.com*, you'll find a
free handout on the wounded aspects of the passion signatures, as well as their strengths.**

Sharing Our Strengths

Although the least evolved parts of us can show up in our
relationships with each other, we all have parts of our lives in
which we're very advanced. We can choose to loan our most
evolved parts to each other, making us more strongly united.

Lover Friends: Lovers nurture you like crazy. They are
incredible playmates because they love just being with you,
experiencing both you and your world. Last February, a Lover
friend and I took an exhilarating walk through Central Park

late one night. It was a winter wonderland lit up by the moon, quiet and windy. Snow flurried around us and lay ten inches deep, like a carpet beneath our feet. Arm in arm, we were two playful trekkers in a foreign land, completely oblivious to the urban environment of Manhattan outside its borders. In the stillness of the tundra, we paused. We prayed and did a blessing ceremony for one another and the world. Our connection was exquisite in that moment.

Lovers are so diligent, loyal and encouraging that you feel you can go an extra mile when they're around. From their point of view, they see the good in you and are eager to help your special qualities emerge and blossom. I have been fortunate to have had two assistants, whom I also count as friends, who have strong Lover tendencies underneath their Visionary aspects. This created a beautiful situation in which I felt nurtured, supported and cared for by dear and beloved friends who were in my corner.

Creator Friends: Creators give you the verbal support to break through any block you have on any subject. They are quintessential problem solvers. If you're scared to talk to your boss, you've got a problem with a family member or you're in the midst of existential angst, your Creator friend can help you work out the kinks. You feel "understood" by your Creator friend in a way that is unique to this type. The Creator is eager to help you think through your troubles. You will feel better after you've been with a Creator because they are great people to talk to.

Since Creators have many creative impulses, they can mentor you in your creative endeavors. These could be anything from building a new business to baking cookies. As a hobby, I've been writing songs and learning to play guitar. When I decided to record a few of my songs in a sound studio, the producer I hired was a Creator. This wonderful man, whom I now consider a friend, spent hours with me layering

tracks and mixing and tweaking musical phrases. He talked me
through my insecurities and reassured me about my composi-
tions. He never got tired, and his enthusiasm for my composi-
tions never flagged. After each take, he articulated praise for
my work along with suggestions for improvements. I felt honored by his tender supervision and took my abilities more seriously. You can depend on Creator friends to take care of you
and care about you.

Warrior Friends: Warriors stand up for you. They've got
your back. If I thought I would have to confront an adversary,
I'd want a friend like this to come along with me. I spoke to a
fireman who had been at the 9/11 disaster site. He was the captain of a firehouse but had been off work for the day. Although
he was across the river in New Jersey, when he saw the first
tower being hit, he immediately made his way back into the
city to be with his team.

When the first tower went down, the men reporting to
him—all dear friends after so many years working side by
side—begged him to take them to the site. But a gut feeling
told him that he would be putting his men in danger. So he
stalled, telling them they needed to get more equipment from
the basement. He felt the need to protect them. On their way
downtown they heard the news over the radio: the second
tower had gone down.

As a friend to these men and a boss, this Warrior thought
beyond what was expected of him as a fireman, which was to
run to the scene of a disaster. In addition to doing his sworn
duty, he wanted to protect his friends' lives. As their captain he
was responsible for their lives. Two years later, his main regret
was that he couldn't protect more of his men. Six from his firehouse died that day.

Your Warrior friend may be a man or woman of few words
or a bit rough around the edges, but this individual will protect

you and watch out for your being to the full extent of his or her capability. A Warrior's friendship gives new meaning to the word "loyalty."

Visionary Friends: Visionaries are great at understanding structure, form and organizing principles. If they're in charge of a project, it's in pretty good hands. When I moved from Texas many years ago, I surrendered to a friend's Visionary abilities. He arrived at my two-bedroom condo, where I was walking around in a fog of confusion and overwhelmed by disarray, and he started throwing things away. Then with my help, he somehow packed the rest of my belongings into a twenty-two-foot truck, and we drove to New York.

Your Visionary friend can open your mind to greater possibilities and then help you come up with the strategy to carry it through. For instance, my cowriter, Stephanie Gunning, was brilliant in her ability to take the comprehensive body of information that makes up this book and give it an accessible structure. Previously I had worked with other writers who were not able to capture the essence of my work in as precise a format. What made her different were her Visionary abilities. In retrospect, I believe Visionaries have a broader understanding of their fields of interest than other people do. When you sit with a Visionary that person will open your mind to the broadest possibility of whatever you're endeavoring. They help you dream in a concrete way that includes action steps. They give you hope and inspiration. And they pump energy into your projects.

Prophet Friends: Prophets reveal you to yourself. I am lucky to count so many people of this ilk as my intimates. If I've lost faith in my path through life and need help reconnecting to my higher spirit, a Prophet can set me straight by saying what he or she sees ahead. There's a different quality to this telling. It's matter-of-fact, like something so evident that I might have tripped over it. If I'm going through a life transition or making an important decision, a Prophet can affirm one course or another. "I don't see any red flags ahead." "It's going to be a tough conversation, but there won't be any permanent damage." Prophet friends have told me where I am blocking my expansion, and they've also told me I'm on the right track. The best part of a Prophet's revelation is that it can be checked against one's internal compass.

It was a Prophet who helped me understand what was going wrong with the man I thought I would marry. We had been getting therapy, and it wasn't getting us anywhere. Then I went to speak to a Prophet, or "seer," out of pure frustration. She closed her eyes and described in detail what was going on in the connection between us. It was as though she were in the room with us, looking at our interaction from a bird's-eye view. Her insight helped me understand what was broken that would make moving toward marriage a bad idea. In later years, looking back, I have always been grateful to this woman for her assistance. If it seems true, it is true. If it seems false, it can be disregarded. Truth helps me feel calm and centered and to know any outcome is okay, so I don't have worry or struggle.

One woman phoned a Prophet friend on her birthday because her new boyfriend was taking her out for a celebratory dinner, and she had a hunch that the plan was activating him. She wanted to know if there were any hidden land mines, so she asked the Prophet to tune in to her date from afar and see if she also felt a sense of imminent threat. Her friend got an image that the man was resistant to having expectations put upon him. He had strong unrealized Creator tendencies. It appeared he was anxious about disappointing her, and that made him angry. Because the woman really liked the man and didn't care to argue with him, she decided to let go of any expectations about her gift, the restaurant and the tone of the evening—to treat it as another, regular day. She was glad she'd been prepared. She used the opening formula of giving him freedom to do what he needed to do. The man was a tad snappy until the middle of the meal, when he suddenly took her in and his whole energy shifted. Later he admitted that his former wife had always demanded high-priced gifts from him. He'd been afraid that she would be the same way, and he'd thrown up a wall to avoid this.

Of course, revelation is not always communicated through words. A Prophet can guide a friend through healing touch or by sitting close by. In such instances, a sense of transcendence arises around them both—and the world seems clearer. A Prophet is a conduit for higher energy. When you feel spirit come through a Prophet, it gives you a directly felt, undeniable, in-the-body experience of something greater than one person. Particularly if you've just begun to follow a spiritual path, this can strengthen your faith.

Interview Your Friends

We all have our blind spots. Often we see ourselves one way while the world sees us in another, totally different way. Unfortunately, our biggest problems arise when we don't summon the nerve to ask others how we are coming across, much less to change something we're doing. A man had a painful awakening when no one other than his best friend showed up for his birthday party. Many people got invitations, but as one woman put it, "That guy never does anything for anybody else. Because I would've had to put myself out, I just decided not to go. He's too self-serving." After his disappointment, the man dedicated himself to transforming his unrelenting Conqueror-Vamp tendencies and became the Warrior-Lover. A few years later, another party was thrown for him. This time a natural gathering of attendees came who wanted to celebrate with him.

Summon your nerve and ask the folks in your world how they see you. Literally sit down and interview them on this matter. Otherwise, you'll be the only one who is not clued in to what's happening. One man spoke to me of a friend. "She drives me crazy. She is an unbelievable penny-pincher. But the other day she commented, 'Some people are very selfish.' I stood there aghast, not knowing what to say to her and also not feeling it was my position to say anything." She didn't know that she herself is perceived as selfish! But she would have if she had taken the time to request her friend's feedback.

This sort of thing happens all the time. The most difficult person to see is oneself, which is why feedback can ultimately help us transform our lives. Our friends' feedback can let us know how we are using our energy in relationships.

Hold Safe Space for Your Friends

A well-meaning man lost an opportunity to acknowledge a friend and remain connected with her. As soon as she started sharing her sadness about running into a former boyfriend, he inadvertently shut her down by saying, "Don't feel bad! He should feel bad for what he did to you!" This man was not being malicious in the slightest. He was naive, however. He didn't know that when we deny someone else's experiences and tell them how to feel, it's a closing formula. To go to a deeper level of intimacy, people need to feel safe to reveal their feelings. They need to get emotional and, in that moment, see that they are accepted and openly received by another being in that state. Otherwise, they cannot remain open or open even further. Research has shown that clients in counseling get better if a therapist listens to them actively without giving any solutions. The same is true of a friend listening to another friend.

We can be containers that hold space for other people to express the truth of their humanity in a given moment and show them that they are not alone. When we show them that we are with them, and not afraid of what they are feeling, this helps them to not be afraid of themselves. Or if we are afraid, we can show them that truth but also that we aren't trying to change them or make them conform to what we need them to be.

A powerful neutralizer of emotional charges is to express it to a good friend and be heard. If your friend is upset, it's a good idea to validate his or her emotions, rather than trying to stifle them. The number one place to begin in any interaction with friends is to leave the focus on them when they speak about something. If a friend says, "I am upset because this happened," you would say, "How did that make you feel?" "I can see how that would make you feel that way," or "Tell me what happened." Ask any question that keeps the focus with your friend until your friend comes to a natural ending. These are profound opening formulas.

Most of the world offers (maybe) one statement of support before jumping in and telling a story about their own lives and how they've had that experience, too—or telling you how you should feel. These are closing formulas. Your friend will be your friend even if you jump in and cut her off, but she won't walk away feeling like you are someone she can "really talk to."

If a friend needs to cry or rage, you give that person a valuable gift by being still. Don't jump up and offer a Kleenex. Even though you are trying to nurture your friend, you are sending a message to your friend's subconscious to stop crying. I learned the power of not offering Kleenex from a brilliant therapist with whom I had worked many years ago. I had seen many therapists to no avail. This was number seven. I had almost given up on the idea of therapy, but this woman was different. She asked penetrating questions that seemed to carry me into very emotional places within. Her name was Romelyn Woodruff. I began to cry and cried throughout every session for six months. She never offered me a tissue. This gave me the message that it was good to cry.

Most people think crying makes you feel bad and that they should make you feel better by helping you to stop. I learned this lesson firsthand when my brother Chuck died. At his funeral, two well-meaning people came up to me as I was swept by waves of grief. One took me by both arms, looked me square in the eyes and said, "Don't cry. Things could be worse." I walked away from her stunned. The next well-meaning family friend took me in his arms and said, "Donna, you have got to be strong." These people were trying to help. But they did not realize that the best thing for me to do to heal from my great tragedy was to cry until the tears themselves subsided.

The entire church was filled with people fighting back tears. Finally, during the closing blessing, when the priest was doing an impersonal blessing over the man we loved so much, my brother, it was as though the hand of God reached into my chest and pulled me out of my chair. I stood up, and with my voice quivering with tears I said, "Excuse me, Father. I would like to lead a blessing and send-off for my brother." Stunned, he had no choice but to acquiesce, probably hoping I was not a crazy woman. I asked everyone to gather around my brother's coffin at the front of the church and lay a hand on it. Then I asked each to give a blessing, if they wished, and together, in a symbolic gesture, we raised our hands and lifted his spirit up into the hands of God. This acknowledgment seemed to lance the pent-up grief in everyone in the room. They wept unabashedly then. It was a beautiful moment of release for all of us as one.

Later I wrote a song about my brother and his friends. Singing that song in the privacy of my own home has allowed me to release the profound levels of grief over this loss. A very wise therapist once said to me, "Donna, you need to cry—even if it's every day—until there are no more tears." Chemicals are released in tears that bring the body back into balance. Remember that whatever is happening is your friend's lesson, not yours. Your friend will learn by figuring out a way to tap into his or her resources. If your friend is ready for your advice, let your friend ask for it. Do not psychoanalyze or preach. Just let your friend be. Hold and touch your friend. If your friend needs to vent verbally, listen compassionately, offering only simple expressions of empathy, such as the following:

- "I'm sorry you're going through this."
- "I'm sorry this happened."
- "I can't imagine what this must truly feel like for you."
- "I'm here for you."
- "If you need something from me, tell me what it is."
- "I don't know what to say. This must be so painful."

Feelings are valuable. To have feeling is to be alive. If we were to shut down sorrow or anger, we could not feel joy or ecstasy. Without feeling, we are automatons. We don't learn or have a true experience of life. People with big soul purposes have to go through substantial challenges because that's how they learn what they share with others. If everything were only "positive," they would not master their special gifts.

Suggestions for Sustaining Friendships

The minute an intimate relationship begins, both of the people who are involved are vulnerable to being hurt. Friendships are no exception to this rule, since everyone on Earth has baggage and rough edges. It is a fact of life that people make mental projections and get activated. That's why we should not cut potentially viable friendships out of our lives too soon. Personally, as an unrealized Warrior-Creator for many years, I had several friendships that drifted apart or ended badly because we got stuck somewhere along the line. This was before I knew about taking care of myself and my own needs, so I was the most enduring martyr in the world. Part of cleaning up my own unfinished business was to go back to as many of these friends as possible and clean up our old business.

Some of these cleanups were natural endings for two people whose lives were truly taking off in different directions. One of them had been a beloved best friend with whom I had not spoken for seven years. We had gone into business together, and it had taken a toll on both of us. One day, in the seventh year, I realized that if she died, and I had left things like they were, it would devastate me. So I faced my fear and called her. It took many conversations, tears, expressions of anger, revisiting old wounds and taking responsibility on both parts, as well as God's grace and forgiveness, for us ultimately to heal all the wounds we had given each other. Recently we celebrated the twenty-seventh anniversary of our friendship. My relationship with my friend sustains me through the ups and downs of life. I am deeply grateful that I swallowed my pride and went back.

An unfortunate by-product of having the freedom of choice to leave a friendship fairly easily is that frequently we mentally scan back through our lives and find we have created a veritable boneyard of terminated relationships. Too many friends in my own life have been cut off due to bad blood as well as other, less volatile reasons. Once I started awakening, however, I realized that reconciliation with these folks would be responsible soul work. When our friendships don't survive, we can suffer from regrets about what was said or left unsaid and from missing the now-absent people who were formerly so special to us. As spiritual beings, for better or for worse, we maintain our hookups to anyone with whom we've ever been close. Therefore, we need to clean up old connections and, if necessary, make amends for our wrongdoings, so everyone can move on. It can be good for us, and it can be good for them, but only if they're open to it.

Friendships have no rules, even though we may believe they do, and we may expect certain defined behavior from our friends. Everyone's lofty ego sits back and judges other people, deciding what they are and whether or not they are worth getting to know. For instance, we might say: All women are this. All men are that. All jobs are like this or that. Dogs suck. Cats suck. People can't be trusted. And so forth. You know you're finally awakening when you stop using platitudes, assigning labels and blindly making rules. The longer we know anyone, the more our defense patterns lock. Your friend becomes your mother, so you have the same opportunity to heal with your mother through your friendship as you do if this were a love relationship.

Throw the rule book away, and don't judge people's behavior. Be friends with people who do things differently than you do. Life is about facing challenges and having new experiences. If your friends weren't diverse, your life would be dull indeed.

If one friend says, "No, no, no," to another friend all the time, then these two pals are on a collision course of obstinacy. Denying another person's individuality and enthusiasm is dangerous because it creates resentment. You are better off getting outside the box you live in and challenging your beliefs rather than saying no to a good friend.

Let's say there's a human being in front of you doing what he or she is doing—that's not your responsibility. However, your reaction to what your friend is doing or saying is completely your own responsibility. If it upsets you, ask, "Why is this action pissing me off so badly?" Perhaps because it reminds you of old feelings you would rather not feel. Maybe it feels like the same-old-same-old again. Your friend is not responsible for your past or for your feelings. Do not try to make it so.

If a friend activates you, then go and discharge your feelings. When you feel anger, your energy comes across as agitated. Do something physical to get rid of aggressive energy that is eating you up. Take a run. Do some jumping jacks. Imagine your friend's face in a pillow, and pound on it. At first many folks recoil from this idea because, especially if they have been raised with religious beliefs about loving everyone, it makes them feel guilty. But ultimately, we are all human. To love is to want to clobber people sometimes. The problem comes when we don't find healthy outlets, and so we take those feelings out on the people we love.

Everybody has an inner saboteur that feels they are not good enough, a part of self that beats up on self, is too critical, too demanding and wants to steal our thunder. A profoundly effective way you can be a friend to yourself when you hear that voice in your head is to give it a real voice and act it out. If you find that saboteur talking to you, imagine seeing your face in the pillow and pound on it. I call this activity "beating yourself up." You can also do this while standing and facing a mirror. I did so once before a very intimidating meeting with a TV agent in which I felt completely inadequate. Before the meeting started, I went to the bathroom and checked the stalls to make sure they were empty. Seeing that the coast was clear, I stood in front of the mirror and let out all the self-loathing that was inside. I spoke into the mirror, "Donna, you can't do this. You don't deserve this. . . ." After I let out every sabotaging thought in my head, I went in and the interview went great. In the process of allowing your feelings to come out, you may become grateful for the opportunity to heal.

If you cope with your own feelings, you won't need to pull on other people so hungrily, feel so angry or so frustrated, and you'll be calm. Your expectations will drop away, and you'll be able to be with the person in front of you. Friends are wounded creatures, too. They are not our parents. We don't win by resisting them or controlling them.

When you're dealing with someone who's activated and you're also activated, don't try to talk about being activated or about the issue between you. If you do, you will both get locked into your activation and fight to hold your positions.

Learn when you cannot trust your own thinking processes, or else you will get into trouble. If someone significant, a friend I trust and honor, offers me a piece of advice, I always take it into consideration. My job in that moment is to listen. When I spend too much time defending myself from hearing or taking the advice, I know something is wrong. If I am defensive, I am probably on autopilot. I am acting in ways that are counter to what my forward-moving, conscious, higher self would like to be doing.

Expectations in friendships are often murky, but people need to know what you and they are hoping to get from a relationship. So be clear about your expectations. Even though as we get closer the brain switches over to our imprints, friends often can develop a language of intimacy and a way of understanding themselves and each other that can circumvent a lot of the negative stuff that goes on between other people. With honesty you can move to a level of communication that opens each other up.

Understanding your survival mechanisms is a process. If you approach it from the perspective that you are actually a being of power with a soul purpose, then you need to understand why you adhere to your limiting patterns. You must come to terms with whatever flips you into the survival side, so you can spend more time over in the freedom side, doing what you came to do. If you can learn how to shift from the wounded to the evolved embodiment of your passion signature, you can begin to hold the frequency for every other human being you meet to tap into their passion and be happy.

During a friendship, if both participants don't keep growing inside themselves, the relationship becomes like still water. In that stillness, passion is blocked and stagnant, and the connection soon dies. Healing our defense patterns makes us more available to have original moments with the people in our lives. It makes room for spontaneity, expansion and surprise. These qualities make friendships interesting.

One research study about the significance of female friendships revealed that these relationships help women get through the ups and downs in their lives. There's so much at risk with husbands, family members and romantic partners that women don't always feel they can be completely honest in these relationships. It's when women come together over a cup of coffee or a glass of wine that they have a chance to step back, review their lives, talk about their relationships and help each other manifest new ideas. Friends often provide a port during the storms of life.

In recent years, with the advent of the men's movement, men have been forming men's groups and also gathering to talk about their lives and share camaraderie beyond competition or watching sports. Many men have shared the deep meaning these connections have in their lives—for instance, that they don't feel so alone in the world and can now step outside their roles as husbands, fathers and sons. They find common experiences among these men they call intimate friends. It is the inner world of men that often remains a mystery to those who love them. Yet as a therapist for over twenty years, I see that men are hungry for friendships, and when they find these friendships they blossom.

Ultimately, my belief is that friends are God's gift to us. They come in all shapes, sizes, ages and lifestyles. We can be friends with either sex. When these relationships have clearly understood boundaries, they can be enormous and healthy additions to our lives. Sometimes our friends become our spiritual families. They can fill holes left by broken homes or chaotic families. Friends much younger than I keep me connected to the vital force of eternal life. My life experience is shared as wisdom; the wisdom they share has taught me that the soul is ageless. It is my belief that we are born at different soul levels. A teenager can be a sage; an elder can be a child.

My elderly friends have been the surrogate grandparents I never knew. These relationships are some of my most precious jewels. I believe that everyone should have at least one older friend. These friends help me see beyond the moment of my current age. They help me appreciate my life where it is in time. They also make me aware that time is passing. Most of all, these friendships have taught me that the spirit is truly immortal. Although our bodies may age and fall away, the spirit lives and is eternally young and vital. Girl talk is girl talk at any age.

I was raised in a small world in Houston, Texas. I was not connected to foreigners, gays, or religions or races other than my own. Early in my life, I was entrenched with prejudice and judgments I thought were reality. Befriending my high school teacher, a woman who was dying of breast cancer, cracked open my consciousness and was the beginning of my awakening. In the process, I learned to value life in a vivid way that only death could have taught me. The gift my teacher gave me through her friendship and mentoring was the seed of who I am today. She saw what was within me. She told me I had gifts to bring to the world beyond what anyone knew. She set me on my life path.

It wasn't until I began traveling the world, moved from Texas to New York and began befriending people from all over the world that I was forced out of my comfort zones. It is my beloved Egyptian surrogate father, Mohammed Shata, who taught me about the openhearted ability of the Egyptians to love. My German girlfriend taught me how similar we are no matter where we are from in the world. My gay friends have taken care of me, held me while I grieved my brother, taught me to allow others the grace to follow their own paths and that God is with all of us. Friends I made in countries like Tibet and India have taught me that living in obscurity with little in the outer world of form can be bliss. My Peruvian friends taught me that life is about passion and living in the moment.

Some friends are meant only to touch our lives for a moment, others for months, years or perhaps a lifetime. When we are open to our passion signatures, we are open to the original moment that is available in those we touch on a daily basis. We are alive. We are connected to our passion, the vital force that flows through us all the days of our lives. We are free to fuse with all of life around us as we share our gifts and talents with others and celebrate them as they share their gifts and talents with us. Our purpose on this planet is to learn to love. Our friends ultimately play a vital role in our soul's evolution.

As one Zen master said, "Friends are like potatoes in a pot. When you turn up the heat of life, they bump against each other until all the rough spots are cleared away." Cherish your friends, and your life will be rich in dimension and new experiences.

For Men and Women
THE WEEKEND
with Donna LeBlanc, M.Ed.

Are You the Visionary, Warrior, Creator, Lover or Prophet?
The answer to this question determines the outcome of everything
you do!

Each soul signature has a survival style, built into the nervous system, which can make you feel stuck and unable to move fully toward what you want in your life. In this workshop we will unblock your energy so you can truly feel your **Passion, Power and Purpose.** Once aligned with your soul signature, you can become **who you were born to be.**
Join me for a LIFE-ALTERING weekend, in a transformative-sacred space with the support of others.

I am passionate about and committed to creating an environment in which you feel in charge of your process and are supported in going where you feel ready to go. Step out of your history, stand in your radiance and become available to all new possibilities.

Donna LeBlanc

Testimonials:
Truly deep, inspirational and earth-shattering work. Donna brings her gifts in powerfully in helping us access our core issues, which would otherwise cripple our ability to give these gifts to the world. One of the best seminars I've done.

Mark Thornton
Author *Meditation in a New York Minute*

Donna is truly gifted. During the weekend workshop I participated in, she gave herself over wholeheartedly to the task of releasing me from the blocks that had been running my life. The Weekend was, without a doubt, a turning point in my life. I am happier and more buoyant than I've ever been, and I have Donna to thank.

Mario Diaz
Filmmaker

Donna has a rare gift, allowing her to go far beyond the generalities of typical workshop material. Because of her broad experience and remarkable intuition, she is able to quickly zero in on YOUR core issues, and knows how to efficiently crack them open.

David Kinney

For more information e-mail *www.donnaleblanc.com*

Learning Materials

Introduction to the Passion Signatures 1-CD 60-minute lecture

Exploring the Passion Signatures 2-CD 2-hour lecture or 2-DVD 2-hour live lecture

Raising Passionate Children e-book

You Can't Quit 'til You Know What's Eating You: Overcome Overeating by Donna LeBlanc (HCI, 1990)

Emergency Binge Busting Kit 1-CD lecture

Compulsive Eating: You Can't Quit 'til You Know What's Eating You 6-CD set with workbook (includes affirmations and visualizations)

Free Yourself, Free Your Mother 1-CD discussion and meditation

Free Yourself, Free Your Father 1-CD discussion and meditation

Donna has ongoing tele-seminars to support your process and learning.

For training in using the Passion Signatures in your personal or professional life,

Please call Donna at 877-63-DONNA or

e-mail her at *www.thepassionprinciple.com.*

Additional products and information on live appearances can be found at

www.thepassionprinciple.com

ABOUT THE AUTHOR

Donna LeBlanc has devoted her career to helping people live more fulfilled lives. She is passionate about bringing harmony to the foundation of our society; individuals and families. Donna's gift is helping people remember who they were born to be and creating an environment that empowers them with the insight and tools for self- and relationship-mastery.

Donna is a spiritual psychotherapist with over twenty years' experience coaching and training others in "breakthrough thinking"™. She maintains a private practice with a global clientele for individual and group programs. Donna is also highly sought out by executives seeking new leadership strategies to enhance business communication and increase team productivity and motivation.

As part of her focus on planetary healing, Donna has traveled to sacred sites in Bali, Egypt, Tibet, Peru, England and Mexico studying ancient paths of human transformation.

Insights and wisdom gathered from these journeys have impacted not only her own personal growth, but have assisted her in lifting others into completely new thought in relationship to everyday challenges.

As a television broadcaster Donna has made regular appearances and provided commentary on a variety of relationship issues for *Donny Deutch, MSNBC, The Bill O'Reilly Factor, Inside Edition, The Montel Williams Show, The John Walsh Show, Sally Jessy Raphael* and *The Queen Latifah Show*.

Donna has a master's degree in education and is a Texas Licensed Professional Counselor, Certified Relationship Specialist, Certified Eating Disorder Specialist and a Diplomat of the American Psychotherapy Association. She is a faculty member at the Omega Institute and provides training around the country. She is also the author of the bestseller, *You Can't Quit 'til You Know What's Eating You: Overcoming Overeating* (HCI, 1990).

More from our author

You Can't Quit 'til You Know

What's
★Eating
You

Overcome
Overeating

Donna LeBlanc
M.Ed.

Code #1038 • $7.95

If you have a problem with food
and eating, then *You Can't Quit 'til You Know What's*
Eating You can help you to help yourself.
